IOWA SKY

In Iowa, 1986

Iowa Sky

A Memoir by
Donald D. Gibson

COMPILED AND ANNOTATED BY

Dai Sil Kim-Gibson

SHOULDER FRIENDS PRESS

FIRST EDITION, FIRST PRINTING

Iowa Sky: A Memoir

Copyright © 2013 Dai Sil Kim-Gibson

Published by Shoulder Friends Press

Cover image: *Iowa Field in Winter*, oil on canvas by Dai Sil Kim-Gibson
Book design by Janice Olson
Printed by Lightning Source

Library of Congress Control Number: 2012924262
International Standard Book Number: 978-0-692-01904-7

For
Norma and Donald L. Gibson,
my parents.

Who is entitled to write his reminiscences?
Everyone.
Because no one is obliged to read them.

In order to write one's reminiscences it is not at all necessary to be a great man, nor a notorious criminal, nor a celebrated artist, nor a statesman—it is quite enough to be simply a human being, to have something to tell, and not merely the desire to tell it but at least to have some little ability to do so.

Every life is interesting; if not the personality, then the environment, the country are interesting, the life itself is interesting. Man likes to enter into another existence, he likes to touch the subtlest fibres of another's heart, and to listen to its beating . . . he compares, he checks it by his own, he seeks for himself confirmation, sympathy, justification. . . .

~ from *My Past and Thoughts* by Alexander Herzen

FOREWORD

I INVITE YOU TO MEET DON GIBSON.

One recent morning, I was cleaning Don's study. While dusting the bookcase, I brushed against a cane hanging on a shelf. It was Don's, the black one he was given during one of many hospitalizations, his cherished third leg.

Don is gone, but he is everywhere and in everything. It is this living Don—my life, my soul mate, my husband—whom I want you to meet. I invite you to meet him not through my memories, but through his writings.

On his last day on earth, I promised Don that I would finish our joint memoir, which we'd been working on for several years. Within a year, I had a manuscript to circulate to agents and publishers, but to little avail. What I heard back was: these are well-written, interesting, and sometimes fascinating stories, but not commercially viable because you two are not famous enough; furthermore, making two voices work in one book is enormously challenging.

While I continued to pursue the goal of publishing a joint memoir, I wrote a small book about Don and myself, *Looking for Don: A Meditation* (Forest Woods Media Productions, 2012). Readers' responses to this personal reflection have been far more moving than I'd ever expected.

Then, one sleepless night, an idea bolted me upright, as if I'd been struck by lightening from one of those Iowa storms about which Don had told me so often: You must let others meet Don in his own voice without interruptions! You must let Don be the author of a solo memoir.

Don and I were an unlikely couple. We were born a month and two days apart, in the summer of 1938. The son of tenant farmers, Don was born and grew up on an Iowa farm. The child of a wealthy North Korean landowner/industrialist family, I escaped with my family to South Korea in 1945 and in 1962 came to America to pursue graduate studies at Boston University.

We were married in 1979 in Washington, DC and lived there until 1997, the year of Don's retirement from a distinguished 20-year career at the National Endowment for the Humanities where he ultimately served as acting chairman under President Clinton. During this time, I was a senior program officer at NEH, where Don and I met, and subsequently became a freelance documentary filmmaker.

Late in 1997, we moved to the small college town of New Paltz, New York, in the foothills of the Shawangunk Mountains about 90 miles north of Manhattan. Here, away from the big city, we pursued our freelance work. We started writing tales of our lives together and alone. As we wrote, we became increasingly convinced that our life stories might be worth broader exposure and we thought that telling them together in a joint memoir would be a good way to go about it.

In late 2001, a catastrophic fire destroyed our house. We moved to the city—Manhattan—and continued working on and off on the memoir. But Don passed away on January 18, 2009 at New York's Columbia Presbyterian Hospital.

Don left me, but his life is not finished.

Don is alive as long as I'm alive. I am happy that you'll meet him in his words.

~ *Dai Sil Kim-Gibson*

CONTENTS

PART **IV**   Into the World

PART **V**   Into the Unknown

PART **VI**   National Endowment for the Humanities

Honeymoon, 1979

PART I

Coming Together

Crossing over the Bridge

DAI SIL AND I MET AT WORK. It was at a federal agency, the National Endowment for the Humanities (NEH). Two white guys, a former professor at the University of Iowa and a senior official at NEH, soon to be my boss, found me a job there. I think Dai Sil should add those two to her not-very-long list of "some white folks who are okay."

I spent the early part of my life in Iowa, raised and schooled there. I first went to DC as legislative director for an Iowa Democratic congressman, Edward Mezvinsky, whose campaign I had managed in 1974 and won. But two years later, we were defeated, leaving his campaign debt looming and me in a mess, with no prospects for a job.

Then, as luck would have it, one of my professors, Ralph Giesey, volunteered to help me find work. He said, "Don, I know you must be looking for a job. A former student of mine, John Barcroft, is a senior official at the National Endowment for the Humanities. I think you'd be a perfect fit there. I'll give him a call."

Huh? What's the National Endowment for the Humanities?

My thoughts were much more focused on the political world, and I didn't know anything about this place. But this, I thought, should be given a shot just in case nothing else materialized.

Then, in the middle of a particularly challenging chess game with my colleagues in our soon-to-be-closed congressional office, the phone rang and I was summoned.

"Hello, this is John Barcroft. Ralph Giesey called a few days ago and I think we should have lunch."

"Well," I fumbled, "Fine."

"Let's meet on Friday at the Madison Hotel coffee shop."

We met. He drank two Old Grand-dads and I had two martinis. The conversation was pretty engaging. I got the job.

One day during 1978, as I was going through my usual morning routine at NEH, I noticed a woman sitting at a desk, most definitely not the same woman who had been there just a few days before. This was an Asian woman with jet black hair, simply but elegantly dressed, her nose buried in a piece of paper, deeply absorbed in whatever it was she was wading through. I felt my heart beat a bit stronger than usual but walked on, ignoring it.

I had been working at NEH for about a year and, at that point in time, was far more concerned about professional than personal matters. Or so I told myself. At forty years of age, I had largely abandoned thoughts of marriage and family. I'd had a number of affairs, which led me nowhere. Compounding that, I had long held the conviction, and had practiced it assiduously, that one should never get involved with a coworker. So I told myself quickly to get rid of any thought of pursuing this Asian woman who made my heart sit up and take notice at a glance.

Not long after I'd spotted her, we had meetings of the National Council on the Humanities, an advisory board, in the elegant chambers on the first floor. During those days, Council members, appointed by the president of the United States, came and reviewed what the staff called committee books. These were carefully prepared reports about all the applications we received for NEH grants, with recommendations from the staff about which ones were to be funded or rejected, with elaborate reasons. Then, the Council members would vote.

The staff was scattered in chairs arranged around the edges of the chamber. I was sitting, somewhat bored, doodling on a yellow legal pad with my Montblanc fountain pen. A few seats away from me was that Asian woman. Unlike some of the others who were chitchatting with their colleagues, she pulled out a booklet with Chinese characters and began writing something. I was fascinated. What could she possibly be doing? Then something else drew my attention. She wasn't writing with one of those government ballpoint pens. No, she wielded a Montblanc fountain pen remarkably similar to mine. I was intrigued, fascinated. *I must find out more about this woman,* I told myself, my workplace dictum notwithstanding.

Shortly after that, on a Saturday morning, I was startled but delighted to find her burning the weekend oil at the office, just like me. I couldn't help it: my feet just stopped at her door, we exchanged a few pleasantries, and I went to my office, pleased at this small encounter. The next thing I knew, I heard her voice and saw her extended hand, offering me some tangerines. I knew right then and there that something was developing between us. Of course, by that time, I had learned her name but was not quite sure how to pronounce it, since it looked so unlike other names: Dai Sil. (She later told me that it is pronounced very close to Dashiell, as in Hammett's first name.) After that Saturday, we regularly traded small talk in the hallway.

Our first drink in late December led to dozens of after-work liaisons at the Hay Adams Hotel, a fashionable place on Lafayette Park in DC, immediately across from the White House. The hotel was so named because it stood on the site where both John Hay, Abraham Lincoln's assistant, and Henry Adams had once lived, but that historical tidbit was of minimal interest to us. We just liked the place.

Finally, a day of our first "formal" date—an evening at a play, *On Golden Pond*, at the Kennedy Center. I drove to Dai Sil's apartment in Arlington, VA and picked her up. I took a wrong exit three times on the 14th Street Bridge before I reached the Kennedy Center. I could not navigate correctly en route to the center—an embarrassment. Oh well, the play was delightful, and our relationship not only survived, but flourished thereafter, giving Dai Sil a chance to repeat the experience with different flair each time.

I need to explain why I was so nervous.

It was a joy to be with her, pure and simple fun, though complexities mounted soon enough. Dai Sil and I didn't make any overt attempt to converse about "significant" or "serious" things. Much of our chatting was intellectual banter, it is true, but neither of us had any compulsion to display our knowledge or expertise. We just talked, as she sometimes put it, like playing ping pong. It was spontaneous. We often exchanged stories about our separate pasts on different continents. Occasionally, we'd giggle about our colleagues. Yet somehow we always ended up discussing ideas.

I had dated quite a few women with PhDs, highly learned and well informed. For my taste, most of them were too eager to display their knowledge, not so much in the sharing of ideas as in polemic assertions. More than that, what bugged me was the way they did it, with so much arrogant certitude. When Dai Sil talked about ideas and social issues, her passion was palpable. But that passion did not come across as aggression so much as a strong commitment to what she believed. Her passion was not something I wanted to get away from, but rather something to savor and cherish. My eyes were riveted, drawn to her, a thirsty man drinking his fill.

Despite my early attraction, I approached her in a cautious, hesitant, and wary manner. I had not been successful with women for reasons I did not really understand, and at that point in my life I had determined that it was simply not going to happen. I wasn't the type, I told myself. I didn't have the skills or the natural instinct for relating to women. Perhaps it was too much focus on work. Perhaps I was simply too selfish. I would, I had concluded, dedicate myself to work, to professional life, to political activities and goals. As much as I enjoyed working at NEH, I still felt compelled to view it as a temporary berth until I could find my way back into politics and progressive causes.

Alas, despite that determination, I could not resist Dai Sil. When she invited me to dinner at her Arlington apartment, I wanted to say no but instead I found myself sitting across from her, wolfing down chicken legs cooked in a delicate sauce of ginger and soy. If she could not obtain my heart with her mind, I felt she clinched the deal with her cooking. What to do? What to do with this woman, so intelligent, so strong, so compassionate, so beautiful, so resourceful?

One day around 7:00 p.m., I stopped by her office. She was on the phone. I heard her say, "Oh, so sorry. Me just a cleaning lady here. Everybody home. Ya, ya, she gone." She hung up to find me at the door, looking bemused.

"What was that all about?" I asked.

"One of my applicants from California. Complaining is her way of life. If I let her talk, I wouldn't get off the phone for at least an hour. I was in no way obligated to spend an hour with her after closing time. How about some food? I am hungry."

I was simultaneously elated and terrified with ever mounting feelings that were different from any I had known in the presence of other women. My relationship with her was moving faster than I was prepared for, though it seemed I could do little to slow the pace, and truthfully, I didn't have much desire to.

Yes, I remember our first meeting very well. Every morning I rode the subway from Pentagon City to McPherson Square in DC. Each time I pushed open the door of the grey building at NEH my heart felt grey. One day I heard a husky voice saying, "Well, don't you have better things to do on a Saturday morning?"

That was the day we shared a bag of tangerines I had bought—ten for a dollar. That was the day all the lights in the world came on, and the building was no longer grey. For our first date in the evening, I wore a crushed cranberry velvet dress and an elegant purple Mexican shawl and Don wore a beat-up brown corduroy jacket he got from a garage sale. As we drove, he sang:

Cross over the bridge
Leave your fickle past behind you
And true love will find you..."

His breath was already in my lungs, and my soul was already in his.

~ *DAI SIL KIM-GIBSON*

Will You Marry Me?

THEN CAME JULY 25, 1979. The usual Hay Adams martinis with Bombay gin, extraordinarily dry, were in our hands, and the playful words crossed between us flying like a ping pong ball over the table with speed and ferocity. I heard myself saying, "Here I am trying to ask you if you can think of one good reason why we shouldn't get married and you're sitting there insulting me."

"What did you say? Can you rephrase the question in a normal way?" said Dai Sil.

"Will you marry me?" I said.

"Sure," she said.

That evening, I had to be off to a DC Humanities Council meeting. We both went to the Metro and stood on the opposite sides. As we watched each other from across the platform, we waved good-bye. I knew, then, that no speeding train or anything else life put in our path would ever separate us. We would be together for the rest of our lives. I was so intoxicated with love that I was almost shouting when I told the news of my engagement to Delano Lewis, then Mayor-elect Marion Barry's principal aide. I was probably so loud it disrupted the entire meeting, but nobody chastised me, perhaps because I was the only federal official in the room.

We had informed no one of our courtship (if that is still an acceptable term), even after we got engaged, at least no one at NEH, and I had intended to keep it that way. But my excitement about marrying Dai Sil was so high, so palpable, that one day I walked into Carole Huxley's office—she was my immediate supervisor—and asked her if there was any rule forbidding one federal employee from marrying another. Carole's face lit up with an impish smile and she said, "I'll call personnel and find out," and she grabbed the telephone. I'm certain Carole knew what was up, because she turned from the phone to face me with an even broader grin and said, "Absolutely none."

We had never directly discussed any kind of formal announce-ment, but it came out one evening at the Kennedy Center, not too long after our engagement. The occasion was a memorial celebra-tion for Charles Frankel, philosopher, founder of the National Hu-manities Center in North Carolina, and tireless promoter of the disciplines in the humanities—philosophy, history, and literature. He was best known for promoting a term he had personified: public intellectual.

Frankel had been brutally murdered in his Long Island home by an unknown intruder. The crime was never solved. In his honor, NEH sponsored a major Kennedy Center gala, complete with som-ber speeches and a lavish reception. Though I was a fan of Frankel and frequently quoted him in speeches, Dai Sil dominated all my thoughts that evening. I walked from the speeches to the recep-tion with Geoffrey Marshall, then deputy chair of NEH. Suddenly, without planning to, I blurted out, "Geoff, I'm getting married."

"To whom?"

"Dai Sil Kim."

Geoff expressed great pleasure, and word proceeded to spread through the reception like wildfire. I recall seeing clutches of people chatting idly and sipping away as they do at receptions, and then someone would join them and share the news, and Dai Sil and I would find ourselves surrounded with a bevy of well-wishers.

In the months that followed, our after-work-drinks ritual con-tinued. These evenings were delightful, amusing, insightful, and always fun. The more we spent time together, the more aware we became of our commonalties—our shared sense of humor as well as values, including a robust work ethic, and a commitment to civic and political engagement. Above all, I related to Dai Sil's passionate devotion to causes of social justice. Sometimes I was almost startled by her dedication to her ideals. It was fierce. In the end, though, I could only admire it, especially as I came to appreciate her deep compassion for others—friends, family, children, as well as the dis-advantaged. That was what made her gentle (well, most of the time) rather than rigid. We discovered that we were both good at crying. Watching a movie, I often felt tears streaming down my cheeks. I wanted to wipe them before she could notice, but she'd generally be crying even harder than I was, though she would try to deny that and tease me instead.

Easter morning, 1979, I found myself in a room with Don in a town called Chincoteague overlooking dazzling white water waiting to be warmed by the sun. Ever since I had crossed the 38th parallel on foot, holding my grandmother's hand, fleeing from our hometown in the winter of 1945, I was adrift and lost in this world. Now I had found a home in Don. An Iowa farm boy with hazel-green eyes was to be my heart's anchor for the remaining days of my life. What we could not know then, but soon found out, was that our "relationship" was the way we'd learn more about ourselves.

~ D S K-G

Troubles?

DAI SIL ALSO IMPRESSED ME WITH HER RESOURCEFULNESS. She had an uncanny ability to assess situations and identify alternative solutions. This also meant that she could be relentless—once she put her mind to something, she never, and I mean never, gave up on it. I admired that.

None of this meant that there was no dissonance between us. If our values and principles were virtually identical, our approach to *means* differed significantly. She was comfortable being the dissenter, the protestor—whereas I believed one must work within to reform institutions, to make systematic change through organized action, through diplomacy. That was the lesson I adopted during

the anti–Vietnam War years. I recognized that the protest demonstrations played an important role, but I thought the ideals that
informed those protests had to be translated into durable public
policy. And occasionally that means not always asserting loudly
what it is that I believe on a particular issue and insisting on winning. So Dai Sil and I had arguments between us, sometimes quite
heated, but never hostile.

Prior to our marriage, those arguments actually made our encounters even more fun. We rarely got mad at each other, but there
was one time that stands out in my memory, precisely because it
was so unusual and unexpected. I had decided to give a party at my
Capitol Hill apartment for the people from several state humanities
councils throughout the country. They were in town for a meeting
at NEH and to attend the endowment's annual Jefferson Lecture.
There were probably about fifty guests at the party.

Naturally, Dai Sil was invited. She'd even volunteered to prepare
some of her delicious food, which delighted me, even though I had
hired a caterer. The party was a raucous event. Tom Roberts, head
of the Rhode Island Committee and an irrepressible actor/come-
dian, organized a mock Academy Awards ceremony complete with
hilarious, outlandish awards to various pompous personalities both
at NEH and the state councils. It was a big hit. I was frantically
busy, rushing about to see that food and drink were available and
accessible to all.

Dai Sil left early. She was clearly upset. All these years later, I recall with anguish catching her on the staircase just as she was headed
out the door. I don't recall precisely what I said or how she responded,
but it filled me with misery. I had trouble getting through the evening after that. I was clueless. What could be wrong? What had I
done wrong?

The next day, I asked her why she didn't stick around longer.

"If you have to ask that question, I was right to be pissed and
take off."

"What do you mean? I don't get it."

"You mean you didn't notice anything about your friends?" she
exploded. "How they were with me? I felt so out of place. The worst

part was that you seemed to have no inkling about how I felt."

"Can you explain that, please?"

"Your friends either ignored or patronized me."

"I still don't get it. They seemed okay."

"Well, maybe you don't understand how I felt because you are a racist too!"

When she blurted out the word racist, the anger and despair I felt was something I still have trouble describing. I was furious, but at the same time, I was also deeply despondent. If she really meant what she said, that was the end of our relationship. I could tolerate lots of things, but not an accusation about something so crucially important to me. Racial equality and racial justice were among my core values. They had, in fact, been the origin of my political awakening, the basis of my revolt from my family and my roots. Dai Sil's charge may have been true, but I could not, would not, accept it.

If Dai Sil believed I was a racist, I could not be with her, and yet I was desperate not to lose her. After a while I quieted down, and pleaded with her to explain.

"Well, none of those people uttered explicit derogatory remarks to me. Sometimes the racism I feel is not so much in what people say or do overtly, but rather in what they do *not* do, in their attitudes, their unspoken expressions, their body language. They were all jolly and having a good time, but they made sure that I was not one of them, that I remained an outsider. If you need me to give you examples in detail, I could do that, but generally speaking, I can only repeat—they either ignored or patronized me. And you were with the crowd, not once checking in with me to see how I was doing."

I thought of the previous evening at my apartment, putting myself in her shoes. Well, she made some sense. I should have paid a little more attention to her. She was among strangers. Yet, I wasn't convinced that her feelings were totally justified. Perhaps she was too sensitive. That incident, however, made me resolve that I would pay closer attention to her in any similar setting. It also made me wonder whether one can grow up in this country as a white American and *not* be a racist to some degree. My entire political philosophy, my very being, had been predicated on the assumption that one can.

With that crisis behind us, I once again looked forward eagerly to our daily rendezvous. But my long-held fear that I wasn't up to being a good husband to anybody worried me. Am I going to be a good husband to Dai Sil? What if I fail with this very special woman, a woman like none other before?

I had read a fair number of books on Far Eastern history, culture, and religion. I had even taught some of that stuff in high school. Perhaps because of that, I had never shared the stereotypical images of Asian women as so often portrayed in America. When I was with Dai Sil, I did not relate her to the Far East and Asia. Much of the time, it never occurred to me that she was an Asian or a woman. To me, she was just her own person acting with strength and quiet confidence. (I was soon to learn that she was not always quiet.) As long as I could remember, the thought of being married to a dependent, subservient woman had turned me off. I wanted a fully equal intellectual partner. And wow, was she, is she, that.

Even her physique did not fit the stereotypes of Asian women. This was not a tiny woman, her head bowed, with a shy smile. She was tall, taller than many American women I knew, well proportioned throughout her body, her skin smooth and fair, not white as most Caucasians, but beautifully fair to me. At almost five-foot-five, I guessed she weighed about 125 pounds. She refused to tell me her weight. To me she was always a beautiful woman, regal and elegant.

Shortly after our engagement, we were at Nieman Marcus one day. Dai Sil was trying to find something or other. As we were wandering the aisles, who should we bump into but my psychiatrist, Dr. Fred Hilkert. He was a decent, sober, quiet man. I'd seen him once a week for a little over a year to deal with a depression that started in Bremen, Germany in 1973, when I was engaged in archival research and feeling utterly alone. (I know I had been depressed before Germany, but this episode was severe enough to warrant a therapist.) Dr. Hilkert concluded that the source of my suffering was not having anything at the center, the core, of my life. In Nieman Marcus that day, I told him that I was getting married and introduced Dai Sil. He beamed calmly and said, "Well, at last you found the core of your life. You don't have to come see me anymore. The depression won't automatically vanish, but you will be able to deal with it without my help." So I had my last therapy session at the department store with Dai Sil by my side.

Don and I shared one nationality through arguments, exhilaration, and sanctuaries of peace-filled moments. I had forgotten that Don was Caucasian. On the autumn day in 1962 when I left Korea, my second brother said, "I trust you will study hard, come back in one piece, and never show up with an American husband. Is that clear?" Now, at age forty, when I had to tell my father of my marriage, the message came back, "You can marry, but not with my blessing."

I said to Don, "Maybe my brother would think it best, after all, for his sister to marry a white man than wither away as a spinster." Don bristled, "So I'm simply better than having no man at all?"

"Ha!" I said—and I took him in my arms. Don thought maybe that my brother would have liked him. Don remembered he was the one hit by shrapnel trying to save my family when the bomb dropped on our house in Seoul in 1950.

In our personal union, for all we knew, Don could be my Korean husband and I could be his white wife. It didn't matter. Or maybe there would be only one nation, and it would be ours.

~ *D S K-G*

Iowa, Summer of 1979

DURING MOST OF THE TIME WE DATED, I never really focused that much on Dai Sil as a Korean American, even though we talked a great deal about her early life. But it certainly made a big impression when she told me how scared she was to inform her father that we were getting married. I thought to myself: Dai Sil, the fearless rebel, afraid to tell her father about her engagement at age forty-one to a white guy? Well, yeah, *white guy* could be a challenge. It gave me a whole new perspective about our relationship. It meant I needed to prepare myself to get to know her folks who I now knew must be different from mine, not just in terms of ethnicity and race, but also class. Because by that time, I had learned that she came from a wealthy family of landlords who ran a flourishing business in northern Korea, at least until August 1945. That's not the background I came from, not by a long shot. For my part, I had told my family via phone, and as far as I was concerned, that took care of it, but Dai Sil thought we needed to go to Iowa to introduce her to my parents.

When Dai Sil suggested that we drive rather than fly to Iowa, I readily agreed because I too wanted to test out how we'd manage for an extended period in a confined space. To my pleasant surprise, we did not have a single argument. It was a smooth trip, without incidents. Chatter and laughter filled the car. Dai Sil wanted to drive for a while to relieve me. Shortly after she took the driver's seat, in a little town in Illinois, we heard the siren from an approaching police car. Dai Sil, unaware of what was happening, just continued to drive.

I said, "Dai Sil, you must stop. The policeman is signaling you to pull over to the side of the road."

Her face darkened and I could see that she was literally shaking with fear. She didn't know what to do.

"Dai Sil, just slowly pull over to the side of the road and stop."

Instead, she drove with haste, that is to say, without slowing down at all, heading for the graveled shoulder which made the car wheels swerve. That frightened me more than the cop. I thought we were headed for the ditch. A chubby, sweaty policeman emerged from a car marked SHERIFF. Typical of many small towns, his uniform resembled that of a potentate in a banana republic.

"May I see your license, please?" She took out her license. "Do you know why I stopped you?"

She shook her head without a word.

"You just passed through a town where the speed limit is twenty-five miles per hour. You were driving over forty-five."

"Oh, I am so sorry. I had no idea. I, I was so eager to meet my future in-laws."

She talked slowly and quietly, conveying a sense of helplessness. Her voice was tinged with deep regret and that got across to this local sheriff.

With just the hint of a smile, he said, "Where are you going?"

At that point, I intervened and told him that we were on our way to Iowa to meet my parents and announce our engagement. The sheriff hesitated a moment.

"Please be careful for the rest of the way," he said, and extended his hand to shake Dai Sil's hand. She thanked him with a series of polite little bows of her head and carefully steered us off the shoulder and back onto the highway. That was a perfect example of her resourcefulness, the same kind I was to witness time and again over the years. She, who had an exceptional ability to communicate in English and who could forcefully speak truth, could also make herself sound like a shy, submissive Asian woman, quite nervous and confused. She was none of the above, of course. None of what the sheriff thought he perceived.

Finally we reached the Iowa border, and as we rolled past the endless cornfields, coming ever closer to my parents' home, my bonhomie/good humor receded and I became extremely nervous. I started remembering heated arguments with my family over the years, especially with my older brother David and his wife Jill, about African Americans, whom they referred to as Negroes or colored people. I could still hear myself one day at a long-ago Iowa dinner (which means lunch) with David and Jill, in the presence of my little niece and nephew, Julia and Jim, screaming that they simply could not raise the children with that kind of racist attitude. I recalled storming out of the house, dinner unfinished. Oh God, what would Dai Sil do if any one of them expressed even a tinge of that racism toward her? For that matter, what would I do? I would storm out of the house yet again.

Actually, I don't think my father was a racist. He never expressed any such inclination and always remained quiet during these family disputes. Perhaps he should have spoken up, but that was not his way.

I recall vividly pulling the car into a gas station a few miles from our destination on the pretext of filling up the tank. I shared my misgivings with Dai Sil and tried to caution her not to take it personally. Her response is etched in my memory: "Who do they think they are? They are tenant farmers. My father used to own hundreds of them!" I was momentarily taken aback. My wife-to-be was expressing class discrimination against my family! I closed my eyes for a long minute trying to ensure that my reason would prevail over anger. Silently, I pulled out of the gas station and drove the few remaining miles to my parents' house. During that time, neither of us uttered any words.

When we arrived, my father and mother were standing outside to greet us in the fading end-of-the-day light. All my childhood affection surged. I pushed my wary body toward them and shared a big bear hug with these two decent people who had given me life and raised me to meet Dai Sil.

The few days we spent there went remarkably well. Falling flat on my ass trying to open a champagne bottle was definitely a good beginning. Dai Sil met several of my aunts and, most importantly, my maternal grandfather. He was in his late eighties at that point but, alone among my family members, he seemed to recognize and appreciate the strength and character in Dai Sil. He saw her as a woman of intelligence, education, and power. He noticed, for example, how the other women relegated her to an inferior seat at the dining table. My take on this was that they considered her a nice oriental woman whom Donald wants to marry. I think that's what the men of the family felt as well. Grandfather took me aside to point that out, which made me proud of both him and myself. I had done well. Though, in truth, it was not familial approval I sought on this trip. I had never been so certain of anything in my life. This was the woman with whom I wanted to share the rest of my time on earth.

After Dai Sil and I returned to Washington, my mother sent a letter expressing her fervent hope "that we country hicks didn't ruin your chances." It was clear that she didn't reject a woman from the Far East as a newcomer to the family. Indeed, to her *eastern* meant the East Coast of the United States, and she feared that a highly educated woman like Dai Sil from that "sophisticated" milieu might reject them. What a curious world.

Many years later, after the catastrophic fire that destroyed our home, we were sitting in our temporary rented space when Dai Sil brought out that letter. I hadn't seen or even thought about it in a very long time. She read part of the letter out loud to me:

> I wish you were closer so we could have more time together
> and get better acquainted with Dai Sil. I just wonder what
> impression she got of us hillbillies. I hope we didn't spoil
> your chances. We are plain old farmers, but we have love in
> our hearts.

I was amazed that it had somehow survived the fire. Dai Sil explained that it was among a pile of papers in a trunk we had stashed in the basement, which escaped the flames.

≈

At last, I saw Don in his own territory. The Iowa skies were indeed as beautiful as Don had described them. I was entranced with Don's world as we rolled past the fields of deeply planted corn, row after row, its leaves swaying. We were riding into a summer splendor and I was captivated by the pulse of life around us—the place that had given Don life.

When the car pulled into the front yard of a brown house, much like a California bungalow, his parents were waiting in the last light of dusk. For the next three days, I concentrated on washing dishes to hide my nervousness. This task took me away from the family and relatives' curiosity, and left me with the peace and pleasures of running water and Don standing by me with a dish towel.

Of the plentiful food, the most memorable was corn. Growing up in North Korea, our tenant farmers harvested corn and I adored it, but Iowa sweet corn was something else entirely. My education was to be complete with chicken-fried steak, a favorite dish in the prairie states. Of course I expected chicken, but it turned out to be beef. Both of Don's parents are gone now and I will always miss them and their kindness. And I will especially miss his loving grandfather, whose eyes brimmed with tears when we left.

My first visit to Iowa with Don was to remain with me all through our years together and beyond. To this day, I can see Don's Iowa skies—the wide expanse of colors and warmth that first protected me during my journey toward marriage.

~ D S K-G

Stunned to Be Married

Upon returning to DC from our trip to Iowa, it was time to set the date for our wedding. I suggested October 1, but Dai Sil hesitated.

"Well, we have a panel meeting that day."

"Come on, Dai Sil, a panel meeting can go on without you!" I had thought I was a hopeless workaholic, but even for me that was too much. To worry about a panel meeting!

So the date was set. OK, what next? Right away Dai Sil and I agreed that neither of us wanted the usual routine—fancy wedding, lots of guests, tons of gifts, rehearsals, bachelor parties, receptions, etc. At age forty-one, there seemed no need to follow conventions that were really devised for young couples just starting out in life. Happily, our parents didn't impose any formalities on us either. They were simply relieved that their children were finally acting like normal people and getting married. Primarily, we didn't want to burden our family, friends, and colleagues with the expense of airline flights, lodging, costly gifts, and such.

So, we invited nobody, not even our parents. It was Dai Sil's idea that we travel to Boston—actually Newton Centre—and be married by her mentor, the Reverend Walter G. Muelder, retired dean of the School of Theology at Boston University (where Dai Sil received her PhD) and a distinguished scholar. Muelder was also, not so incidentally, a teacher of Martin Luther King Jr., who has credited Muelder with introducing him to the philosophy of nonviolence.

And so it was that on October 1, 1979, we stood in front of the fireplace in the Muelder's living room and took our vows, with the reverend presiding, and his wife, Martha, as our required legal witness. Martha also played the piano as Dai Sil descended the stairs in a simple white suit.

I shed bountiful tears during the ceremony. And I was embarrassed, although everyone else was polite enough (or embarrassed as well) not to comment on it. Martha, in addition to providing the music, also served a tuna casserole for lunch. I thought Boston might offer finer cuisine, but then I learned that Martha grew up in Iowa!

That night we drove to the Wayside Inn in Sudbury, Massachusetts, where Longfellow is said to have stayed. The room was small, but we both liked its ambience, cozy and old. The next morning, I watched Dai Sil wake up and look at her left hand. No wedding ring. She jumped out of bed. I knew what was going on. I said nothing for a minute, enjoying her frantic search.

"Dai Sil, look on top of the dresser. I saw you take it off last night and put it there."

"Why didn't you tell me right away?"

"Well, I wanted to have my fun watching you. By the way, why did you take it off?"

At last, a hint of laughter relaxed her face, and she said, "I am sure I was simply doing what I had always done. Taking off my jewelry before bed. If it is any consolation to you, it is the first time I was ever married!"

The next day, we strolled over to the quaint white Mary Had a Little Lamb Church, right next to the Wayside Inn, and took pictures. I still remember setting up the camera for the two of us and composing the shot, with us putting our arms around each other's shoulders, wearing identical gray sweaters. That's when I was first introduced to one of Dai Sil's favorite Korean expressions—shoulder friends—referring to friends who grew up together, with arms on each other's shoulder. Much later in life, when we decided to write a joint memoir, Dai Sil repeatedly said that the Mary Had a Little Lamb Church photo should be on the cover, since we felt as if we were shoulder friends.

From the Wayside Inn, we drove on to Cape Cod to the hamlet of Wellfleet, where the parents of our dear friend Richard Cohen owned a home.

Our honeymoon in that house was one of the intense moments of my life. I will never forget my days there with Dai Sil. I spent the entire time stunned, both at the fact that I was married and also that I was so happy. It was a gorgeous setting, right on the water, with the tide coming in and out like breathing—the first time I ever slept by the ocean. Far beyond that, of course, it marked the beginning of a radically different and far happier stage of my life.

Marrying Dai Sil was far and away the greatest decision I ever made. And I could tell that Dai Sil was equally happy.

In that Wellfleet dream house, Dai Sil claimed that she learned something new about me every day. She found out that I talked a lot in my sleep. So the secret was out, that I talk a lot in my sleep just like my father. I remember Dai Sil telling me, "One night, I sat bolt upright, awakened by your loud voice. You exclaimed, 'Let's not get all excited about it. First, let's have a long talk. Dai Sil, Dai Sil, Dai Sil.'"

Well, that dream became a sort of pattern of our married life. Whenever Dai Sil's emotions ran high, too high, I would say, "Let's not get all excited about it," and I'd try to calm her down and inject some rational sense into her passion-filled heart and head. Actually, I took on that job with pleasure and enjoyed it.

Oh, one more thing I want to tell about our honeymoon. From Wellfleet, we went on to Boston to spend a couple of days in the city where Dai Sil lived for the first seven years of her life in America, although she claimed she didn't so much live there as merely study there. We got a room at the Hyatt Hotel in Cambridge overlooking the Charles River and Boston University. As soon as we checked in, we went out for a walk. She carried the bundle of daisies that she had held at our wedding. The daisies, by then, were withering. She wanted to throw them into the Charles River. I didn't ask her what meaning that had, but I felt she was coming home to me, as the flowers flowed down the river, the river that befriended her for seven years in a foreign land.

Watching the daisies in my beloved Charles River, I felt them move toward an unknown destination.

~ *D S K-G*

You Are a Good Man

Now onto our receptions. Consistent with our idea of not wanting friends and relatives to spend their money to attend our wedding, we opted for a moveable feast of receptions, and we were the ones to do the moving around. That meant we hosted gatherings in four different cities: Washington (principally for friends and colleagues, since that's where we lived and worked); Iowa City (because that is where I attended graduate school and, more important, did most of my political work); Indianola, Iowa (where I went to college and taught high school); and Toronto (ah, the most important, for Dai Sil's family).

Toronto was quite an experience. I confess that I was more than mildly nervous. Dai Sil had explained that her father had not taken kindly to the thought of his daughter marrying a non-Korean, "a round eye."

I didn't meet the Kim contingent until after we were already married. We flew to Toronto and attended a lavish banquet at the home of one of the brothers. It was certainly festive, with enthusiastic drinking starting early and continuing late. At a certain point, copious amounts of food were brought out and quiet was called. Before we feasted, Dai Sil's father delivered a homily directed at me. He welcomed us all and then admonished me, saying that I should reject American culture and embrace the superior Korean traditions and mores. He added that I should not, under any circumstances, make his beautiful daughter into a common American wife. He did all of this in English. (Dai Sil later told me that he had gotten up at five in the morning for several days to prepare the homily all by himself.) I smiled.

Then, Dai Sil's mother stood up and offered prayers of thanks to God for the abundant food and joyful occasion. The prayer was long and delivered in Korean. I understood not a word, but could tell that it was heartfelt. Finally, a relief from prayer came with the amen, and vigorous eating ensued. The mood seemed festive but I sensed an underlying tension building.

Finally, at one point, Dai Sil's four brothers stood up and went outside. I followed. One of them said something in Korean to his younger sibling, who responded in an angry tone, stretching his arm with a dramatic flair. The next thing I knew, Older Brother's fist slammed into Younger Brother, knocking him down. Dai Sil later told me that Older believed that Younger's outstretched arm meant he was about to strike. A weak defense for his actions, as even I knew that a younger brother would never hit the first son at a wedding celebration. (Alas, Dai Sil and I never found out the real cause of the fight).

In any event, the fight was broken up by their father, who appeared outside and shouted something that stopped them cold. I guessed it was something like, "Look at you. How shameful that you would fight on this occasion with a new brother-in-law present. You bring disgrace to our family. Stop this nonsense immediately!" (Dai Sil confirmed that my guess came very close to his actual words.)

The rest of that evening was a blur. At least the fight dissolved my own nervousness. Afterwards, I went back in the house and made a wise decision to hang around with the little kids who were running all over, having the time of their life, all chattering away in perfect English. I was more than welcome in their midst and it mattered not a bit that I was a round eye. I especially remember Stella, the eight-year-old daughter of Dai Sil's sister, who anointed herself a sort of group leader and made sure that I was included. There among the children, I gained firsthand insight into the immigrant experience—an appreciation for how the first generation of family members born and raised in the adopted homeland intuitively claim their independence from some of the strictures of the past.

Far and away, the most memorable moment for me of that entire trip took place at the Toronto airport, as Dai Sil and I were about to head back home to Washington. Just before we said good-bye, her father rested his hand gently on my shoulder and said, "You are a good man." That meant the world to me. He had accepted me into his family.

⚬⚬⚬

"Cross over the bridge
Leave your fickle past behind you
And true love will find you...," I whispered in his ear.

~ D S K-G

Shoulder friends forever

Visit to Iowa, summer of 1979

Visit to Korea, fall of 1987

*Our wedding,
October 1, 1979
and scenes from
the early years of
our marriage*

On a trip to the Virgin Islands

Visit to Korea, fall of 1987

Another summer visit to Iowa

Don working on his college fund

PART II

Growing Up on Iowa Farms

How Did You Get to Be Ninety-Seven?

MY DAD KEPT HIS RAZOR-SHARP MIND and his earthy sense of humor until the last days of his life. In the spring of 2006, reduced to skin and bones, he lay in bed, waiting for the time when he would rejoin my mother who had been gone since December 1994. He had a visitor who was just trying to make idle conversation.

"How did you get to live to be ninety-six, almost ninety-seven?"

Without missing a beat, Dad responded, "That's easy. You just had to be born in 1909!"

The only trouble was that he never really knew how smart and how funny he was. Or, if he knew, he never wanted to acknowledge it. He refused to think of himself as anything but an entirely ordinary person, of average intelligence, and average talent. Sometimes, not even that.

I am getting ahead of my story, but I feel compelled to tell this now. I was thirty-three years old and studying for my PhD in Germany when my parents, after months of urging on my part, visited me so I could show them a bit of Europe. It being their first ever trip outside the United States, they felt self-conscious and out of place. Our roles had reversed. I became the guide and mentor.

Our first encounter on that European holiday was in Luxembourg. I had arranged for them to fly on Icelandic Airways and booked them a hotel room in Luxembourg. At that time, I was teaching a course at the U.S. military base in Mannheim and couldn't shift my schedule to meet their plane. As early as I could, I boarded a train and was fortunate enough to arrive in Luxembourg sooner than expected.

I detrained and walked briskly across the square to their hotel. As I entered, they were standing at the front desk with their luggage piled in front of them, in a hopeless attempt at conversation with the front-desk staff. I quickly surmised the situation, hugged each of them, then turned to the young man and asked if he spoke

German. *"Ja."* I asked if we could leave the luggage there while we had a cup of coffee and walked around a while. *"Natürlich."* As I turned around, my father said, "Goddamn it, you sound just like all the rest of them here." I smiled and we went off for a cup of coffee which, of course, was far too strong for both of them.

Later in that trip Dad commented that he had always thought it was silly to use symbols rather than language on traffic signs, but now, after being in a place where they spoke a foreign language, he approved. I am sure he wasn't aware of it and I didn't think about it then, but in retrospect, I realize what had occurred to Dad. It had dawned on him that there was a way to communicate with people who spoke different languages—the Tower of Babel could not and cannot prevent universal elements in different human beings.

During that trip, my father told me about a long-ago talk between him and the superintendent of my high school. He took my dad aside during the halftime of a basketball game and said that I, his son, had scored significantly above average on an IQ test. As if it wasn't a shock enough for him to wait all those years to tell me this, he added, "I never told you that, because I couldn't believe that any son of mine could be above average." Sitting in a German restaurant, I almost cried and would have, had it not been for my parents watching me.

My father and mother were both Iowa natives. Iowa is deep in my blood. Long after I left for the East Coast, I often still see in my imagination the Iowa night sky brilliantly strewn with stars. I still feel that pure, bracing, frosty air of the winter nights when I'd sit outside of our farmhouse, dreaming of the world beyond our door. If the glorious Great Plains sunrise gave hope for the day and for my unknown, unbound future, sunset gave me the promise of that magical night sky.

In Iowa, the sky is so huge that you can see a thunderstorm coming from miles away, always from the west. The clouds would build, getting darker and darker, and soon you would see streaks of lightning. It would take half an hour or more to cover the sky and the rain and lightning would be devastatingly beautiful. I do not know how many times I made Dai Sil listen to stories about Iowa storms as we sat on the porch of our DC house.

If the Iowa sky at night is what I best remember, Iowa is generally better known for its land—26 million acres of grade A earth, one-fourth of all the premium soil in America. It was to this fertile land that migrants flocked from northern Europe, Ireland, Germany, Holland, Norway, Denmark, and Sweden. Most settled with their own kind. Elk Horn, for example, a few miles from where I grew up, was exclusively Danish and retains that flavor today. Pella, just a few miles farther east, was and is entirely Dutch. Of the thirteen small farm towns in my home county, seven were pretty much exclusively Roman Catholic (principally Rhineland German), and the other six were predominantly Scandinavian Protestant.

Scots-Irish Roots

MY FATHER'S FAMILY DID NOT SEEK OUT IOWA, coveting its rich land. My Scottish forebears had been part of the 18th-century migration to Ireland when Scots were actively recruited by the English crown to settle in Ireland and help subdue the rebellious Irish peasants. Subsequently, they along with the native Irish were starved out by the Great Potato Famine of the 1840s and many fled to America, settling in the Appalachian Mountains.

My father's grandparents (both with the surname Gibson, curiously enough) met and married in Ireland and moved shortly thereafter to Wheeling, West Virginia, where they gave birth to a single son named Harry. The boy's father died almost immediately and his mother went to work as a domestic servant in Wheeling to cousins of Samuel Clemens, A.K.A Mark Twain. This story was repeated often in our family as our one connection to any kind of fame—my great-grandmother being a maid in Mark Twain's family! She died when Harry, my father's father, was just seven years old and he was raised until early adolescence by the Clemens cousins.

A restless Harry left West Virginia for Birmingham, Alabama, hoping to find work in the iron mills. He did but, according to tales he told later, he often ended up in fights on the job, once being rescued by a couple of Negro youths. Undeterred, he traveled on to Colorado in search of gold. As luck would have it, he arrived much too late. The Gold Rush was over. Sick of standing waist-deep in frigid mountain streams with nothing to show for it at day's end, he decided to head back to West Virginia. But, with just 25 cents in his pocket, he stopped along the way in Portsmouth, Iowa, to drop in on two sons of the Clemens family, who in a surprising turn of fate had left West Virginia and became farmers in Iowa. They gave my grandfather Harry a job.

Harry never moved more than six miles from Portsmouth again in his life. Really a plumber and somewhat hot tempered, Grandpa was not interested in farming. He just couldn't abide putting seeds in the ground and then waiting months for anything to happen. He wanted immediate results. My grandfather was also the township assessor. He would walk miles, driving once in a great while, to appraise the value of properties. He only put up with farming for his kids. I guess all the other work combined could not support his family with enough to eat and a roof over their heads.

Grandma Gibson's maiden name was White and she came from a large family that lived just east of Logan. Her father fought in the Civil War. One of her brothers farmed in the Nebraska Sandhills and my dad recalled going there to visit when he was about eleven years old. The uncle hitched up a four-horse carriage and gave them a tour. Not much to see out there, Dad noted.

I wonder why I didn't know my paternal grandmother better. For some reason, we didn't visit her often. She sounded like a feisty character but also very kind. She passed away in 1952. My Dad once told me that he remembers hearing her recite the following, although he could not recall in what context:

> Here's to good old whiskey
> It makes you feel so frisky
> Drink it down
> Drink it down

Of his many stories, whatever the context was, I warmed to my grandmother, often reciting that verse myself.

When my dad was about five years old, one day during threshing season, his brother Harry Jr. was riding a pony out to the oats field. While Dad was begging to go along, Harry fell from his pony on Dad and broke his arm. A neighbor who had the only automobile for miles around took Dad to the hospital, charging $5 for the favor, a huge amount in 1914. The man's name was Bob Ellison and Dad never forgave him. The only event Dad could recall as an adventure was his trip to Johnstown, Nebraska, in around 1920. He went with his parents to visit an uncle there. They traveled by horse and buggy and took the ferry at Blair, Nebraska to cross over the Missouri River, the "Big Muddy."

Dad attended a one-room school for eight years. In those days, Iowa had one schoolhouse on every section (a 640-acre, one-square-mile tract of land). Sometime in the 19th century, the state had set aside a parcel in each of its ninety-nine counties for a county school. The schoolhouse, along with a woodshed and two outhouses, stood on an acre of land. It was heated by a wood stove about five feet high. Each desk had a bottle of ink and the kids would place them on the stove so they didn't freeze. Dad recalled the day one exploded, spreading ink all over the ceiling and also over several children.

Transportation being what it was in those days, for the first two years my father boarded with a Mrs. Mary Schreves, a widow, and her mother, Mrs. Houghton, who was a Mormon. He paid $4 a week for room and board. To come up with the money, he worked at Gilbert's Cafe, waiting tables from 7:30 p.m. until midnight and sometimes until 2:30 in the morning. That notwithstanding, his high school years were apparently pleasant. He took commercial courses, meaning typing and shorthand (this struck me to be odd, but that's what he did), played football, and dreamed of not returning to the farm. Dad wanted something different from what his own father had done.

My Father, a Reluctant Farmer

MY FATHER, AFTER GRADUATING FROM WOODBINE HIGH SCHOOL IN 1928, landed a job with the telephone company as a lineman, basically stringing wire. He worked for Northwestern Bell in South Dakota and Iowa, then transferred to Omaha. He liked the work and liked as well living in the city, but then the depression hit and, in 1932, he was laid off.

His only recourse was the farm. He returned to Harrison County and lived with his parents for a few years and farmed the home place until he, Donald L. Gibson, married Norma Mikesell, my mother.

I do not know much about my mother's family other than her father. Reared on a farm, my grandpa, Jonathan Lloyd Mikesell, worked for the local telephone company for decades, became the mayor of Glidden, Iowa, and finally retired to the tiny town of Logan. My grandpa was far and away my favorite nonparental relative. To me, he was special, unlike anyone else in the family. He was kind, decent, and insightful. I learned from my brother David that Grandma Mikesell came from a large family, the Conrad family in Pennsylvania. She came to Iowa as a young woman to keep house for her brother who had moved to Iowa. Apparently, she was very strict and religious and just loved Bing Crosby.

Based on her father's work experience, my mother insisted that she was a town girl as opposed to a farm girl. I fear it was her way of insisting that she was smart. Early on, my mother had aspirations beyond marriage and actually enrolled in courses that certified her to teach elementary school. She did in fact teach in one-room schools until she married my father in December 1933, and then she quit at the end of the school year. By law, at that time, married women couldn't be employed as teachers in Iowa.

My parents were old-fashioned high school sweethearts and had their first date when they were both freshmen. Dad loved to tell the story about that infamous date. It was a costume party and he dressed up as an American Indian, a costume that included a pair of fake, flimsy moccasins. After the party, he walked my mother home and then had to keep walking all the way across town and his feet were killing him. But courting my mother was worth the pain. He was still relating that tale, and still chuckling over it, on his ninetieth birthday.

My parents got married on December 23, 1933, in Harlan, Iowa, in the minister's house with only two witnesses, Dad's brother Harry and his wife Alice. Dad drove to Woodbine to pick up Mom, and then off they went to Harlan to get hitched. And that was that. I asked my dad why they didn't have a church wedding. "That was all I could afford," he said simply. "It cost $5, a lot of money in those days." Then they drove south to Oklahoma to visit with Mom's grandmother, Flora Wolf, and returned home less than a week later. What a wedding. What a way to start a married life. But then again, that was the Great Depression.

Dad started farming in 1934, but didn't harvest a crop that year due to a drought. That happened again in 1936. Many times, my dad told the story of July 4, 1936. It was 100 degrees at midday and my mother washed the bed sheets and hung them over the windows to dry in the hot summer sun. Then they took my three-week-old brother for a ride in the car, hoping to find a bit of breeze. Later in the afternoon, my father walked the cornfields and declared the crop dead.

With the loss of his job and a rough start in farming, it is no wonder that my father forever remained in the grip of the depression mentality, the relentless fear of debt and unemployment. He remained a tenant farmer until he was well past fifty, even though he managed to share in the general agricultural prosperity of the post–World War II years. He simply couldn't abide the idea of holding a mortgage. He had to pay *cash* for the farm, for anything. He never had a credit card in his entire life. Years later, in the early 1980s, when my parents visited Dai Sil and me in DC, we always ordered their meals for them in restaurants, lest they should see the prices.

My parents were a loving and loyal couple, but they did have their differences. Mom felt we should all be religious, or at least observant, which meant going to church on a regular basis. Dad did not oppose her, but he didn't want to be a churchgoing, conventional Christian. He never said the word to me, but on the basis of my own observation, he was really a pantheist. Once he became a farmer, he took delight in seeing all those growing things and he felt awe in everything around him. Dad also once told me that he had never attended church or Sunday school as a child, which was pretty amazing at that time. His family didn't shun the church, but was open enough to let the children explore their own way of being religious. The more I think about this, the more amazed I feel.

I have often wondered if my mother was truly religious. I don't think so. Her real concern was social acceptance and I believe that going to church was primarily an act of propriety, a gesture of conformity and social correctness. She certainly didn't know much about any denominations within the Christian church other than her own, Methodist. I still remember the day Mom cooked for our Catholic farm workers. It was Friday and she had broiled steak. They couldn't eat it, of course—remember fish on Friday?—so they were stuck with Velveeta cheese.

We rarely said grace before meals or any other time. Both my mother and father did teach me bedtime prayers. My mother's version was: "Now I lay me down to sleep. If I should die before I wake, I pray to God my soul to take." Dad's version was: "Now I lay me down to sleep, while the bedbugs around me creep, if one should bite me before I wake, I hope to God his jaw will break." I preferred my father's.

My parents were both twenty-nine years old when I was born at 4:30 in the afternoon on August 15, 1938, in a farmhouse in Douglas Township, Harrison County, Iowa, about five miles from the town of Portsmouth, population about 200. My mother was attended by a midwife. Later in life, after I was an adult, I learned that they had wanted and expected a girl and her name was to be Carolyn. They hadn't even selected a name for a boy. They must have thought that not choosing a boy's name would enhance their chance of having a girl. This was my birth crime—I was a boy, not a girl. Moreover, I also learned later that it was a day mixed with a deeper sadness—my mother was informed that she would be unable to bear any more children. A precious daughter would never be hers. They hired a local woman to take care of Mom and me for $2 a day. Dad had to borrow $20 from the bank to pay her.

The way it was told to me, each time my mother gave birth, a lineup of other women who had also just delivered—prospective wet nurses—would be brought before my grandmother and she would interview each of them, carefully checking out their health and family background, sometimes consulting a doctor and making inquiries of their neighbors and friends. For the duration of the grandchild's breast feeding period, my grandmother went as far as supporting the entire family of the wet nurse. I wonder what the Iowa farmers would have thought of such a practice.

~ D S K-G

My Mother and Oreo Cookies

THE WHOLE TIME I WAS GROWING UP, WE MOVED FROM ONE HOUSE TO ANOTHER. From birth to college—1938 to 1956—I lived in five different farm houses, all on rented farms, none more than ten miles apart. We were tenant farmers, though I never thought of that status at that time as particularly distinctive and certainly not inferior.

All those houses had a certain commonality. They were all wood-frame structures, all two stories. None had central heating. There were two to three bedrooms, a kitchen which normally also served as the dining room, and a living room. Heat was provided by a single oil burner in the living room and our cooking was done on a woodburning stove. The upstairs rooms were unheated and Iowa winters could feature temperatures well below zero. So we'd burrow beneath piles of blankets at night. The frosty air combined with cold, hard linoleum floors tended to inhibit any quick leaps out of the bed, even in response to my mother's bacon sizzling downstairs.

The house into which we moved in 1952 also had a parlor, a nicely furnished room that no member of the family was allowed to enter unless important guests were present. I do not once recall any guests important enough to merit that honor. The parlor was used for opening presents on Christmas Eve. The only other time I remember its being used was for my high school graduation party. That was it. Perhaps it was a remnant of Victorian sensibilities but maybe it was also a statement that we, although tenant farmers, were not poverty-stricken peasants.

Of all the farms of my childhood years, my favorite was the Kay farm (the owner's name), a 240-acre spread one mile north of Tennant. It was a comfortable house with a small yard and a large farmyard with a big barn where we kept the mules, a grain shed, a horse tank, and other outbuildings. I loved the hollyhocks and morning glories growing just beyond the garden fence.

The Kay farm was the third one my father had worked. The first one was his home place (his parents' property) before my birth. I was born in the second farmhouse, a few miles from Portsmouth in Harrison County. We lived there until 1942. I was too little to remember much about that place. The only clear memory of that time comes from a snapshot of me climbing the fence. Years later my mother relayed the history of that picture. When she saw me climbing the fence, she yelled and demanded to know what I was doing. I told her that I was running away. She chuckled, disappeared for a minute, and came back out with a camera. Only after she took the photo did she walk over, grab me, and place me safely down on the ground. I loved that picture because it reminded me of my mother's sense of humor. Come to think of it, perhaps it might also reflect, albeit unconsciously, an urge I had to escape from the rural isolation of my childhood. Dai Sil loved that picture even more than I did, not just for that little boy climbing the fence, but also for the story of my mother. Alas, it was destroyed, along with so much else, in our house fire.

I do remember quite well the day we moved to the Kay farm. I was four years old. The first morning I woke up in that house, I ran down the stairs and found my mother sitting in the kitchen with a neighbor drinking coffee. The kitchen was pleasant, filled with sunlight. Then in the evening I went with my parents to the chicken house, which they wanted to check out. Not too many years after that, my parents put me in charge of cleaning chicken houses, definitely not one of my favorite chores as a farm boy. On that evening, though, I was just happy that my parents took me there.

Every Saturday night my mother gave me a bath in a metal tub in front of the wood cookstove in the kitchen. Actually, we burned corn cobs, not wood, because they were much cheaper and more plentiful. I can still recall my mother in that kitchen stirring a stew on the stove and my father coming in wearing overalls, fresh from the day's labors, wiping his shoes, mumbling, "Something smells good."

My mother not only kept my growing body well fed, she also nourished my mind with a love of reading even though we didn't have many books in our home. (Neither my parents nor later my teachers had much to recommend beyond textbooks). I don't recall either of my parents actually buying or talking about a specific book, or even a magazine article. Well, there were a few magazines—*Reader's Digest* and *Wallaces' Farmer* (an Iowa essential). Later I honed my skills on the *Saturday Evening Post*, and particularly recall the tales of Tugboat Annie and the stories of Ernie Pyle, the famed World War II correspondent. But limited though her repertoire may have been, I still owe my lifelong love of the written word to my mother. She read extensively to us from an early age and, through that activity, I was actually able to teach myself to read even before I started school. I also began writing stories and plays, and I would insist my parents watch the plays while I acted out all the parts. No copies of those remain—probably a good thing.

While I loved my mother, even as a boy I started observing some traits in her that bothered me, although I didn't understand why and what they were. Only as an adult did I realize these traits indicated a certain pretentiousness, an excessive concern about what others would think of her. Now looking back, I fear I might have been too harsh in my judgment. For all I know, if she was anything like me, she could have had a sense of inferiority, rooted in our humble circumstances, and all she was doing was overcompensating for inadequate feelings and frustrations about her social status.

That said, I remember some childhood scenes that heavily influenced me to form not-so-kind feelings about my mother. My mother entertained lots of neighbors at the same table where she dressed me. One time she served Oreo cookies, which I believe were part of the dessert. I sat there too, opening the Oreos to look inside, pleased to be sitting at the table with the grownups. I was enjoying myself. Then I noticed my mother looking at me, clearly embarrassed. She asked what I was doing.

"Mom," I said with a clear, loud voice and even with some pride, "I once found a worm in one of these cookies."

I don't think my mother ever forgave me for embarrassing her that way in front of her company. Luckily, at least they were store-bought cookies and my mother could hold up her head because she wasn't the one who allowed a worm to crawl inside.

My father was a man of few words who didn't express his feelings very much, but I always knew he loved me and that I could rely on him for anything. However, he too had his share in breaking my little heart. I am thinking about the time he pulled my tooth by attaching a string to it and to a doorknob, and then slamming the door. I knew he had to do it and that he didn't enjoy it. So I wasn't mad at him exactly, but I swear, it was not a pleasant experience, to put it mildly.

Then there was his accidental destruction of one of my few precious toys. Toys were not a big part of my boyhood. Clearly my parents could not afford to buy them. All the more reason I treasured the few I had—the erector set, Lincoln logs, an electric toy train, and a plastic duck. One summer evening, I was playing with the plastic duck in a medium-sized puddle of water. I left the duck there when I went to bed. The next morning I woke up to discover that my father had destroyed my pond along with the duck by covering it with a pile of dirt. I still think of that poor little duck, one of my few cherished playthings, buried alive.

I am writing this in 2006 and my father has passed away. I feel grateful that I lived long enough to say goodbye to him, but I fear my turn to join him will come sooner than I wish, and much sooner than Dai Sil fears. My father witnessed his son's ill health, but he could not fix it. I was a boy with a positive outlook on life, but I guess I always had secrets that darkened my mood.

Well, enough speculation. Time to go back to my childhood stories. My brother David, two years older, was a constant presence in my life on our isolated farm. We played together of course, but not often enough, only once in a while. When we did play, there were some sparkling moments. We invented a game, bicycle polo, that we played with croquet mallets and balls while riding on our bikes. Quite fun, but I am afraid I broke a lot of the spokes in my cycle's front wheel.

A Boy in the Attic

As much as I yearned for friends to play with and enjoyed them, most of the time I played alone, mainly with imaginary playmates. Iowa farms were isolated in a way that city folks can hardly imagine. (I would recommend Hamlin Garland's *Son of the Middle Border* for those who would like to know more about this. Garland evokes this sense of isolation much more eloquently than I ever could.) We had a car, a rattletrap Ford, one generation removed from the famed Model A, but it wasn't reliable. I can only recall riding in it once or twice.

Essentially I was a loner, of necessity but also by temperament. I often created my own games and played them by myself. In truth, I relished it. I loved climbing trees, scaling the windmill, or hanging out the top of the barn. Most of all, I loved being alone in the attic of the Kay farm, my favorite of all time childhood places. I would climb up a narrow staircase from the second floor and disappear into that attic, my secret haven with nothing but me and a small potbellied iron stove. I'd play vocabulary games—for example, how many new words can I find in a newspaper? Or I'd read the funnies and comic books lying on the floor on my stomach, warmed by the red-hot stove. Or sometimes I'd draw. One time, I painstakingly glued a key chain in the shape of a heart onto a piece of wood and gave it to my mother on Mother's Day. Quite shabby work, when I reflect upon it, but my mother tried to express enthusiastic appreciation. When I got a little older, I'd write stories in that attic room, pouring out my thoughts safe in my private refuge.

One day I was reading a *Superman* comic book and came across something about the year 2000. I stopped reading and figured out how old I would be in 2000. I would be sixty-two. Gosh, I thought, it is unreal, sixty-two! Would I ever really live to be so old? It hardly seemed possible. Well, I am some years older than that now. I realize that sixty-two is not that old. More importantly, I realize how two forces in myself—a loner and a social being—carry equal power simultaneously. Prior to my retirement, I counted on my being a loner. I had believed that I would enjoy my solitude and write in isolation, but alas I am learning that I was mistaken. I need social settings more than I had ever imagined. I need to go to my office in the morning in order to enjoy my solitude in the evening.

Social life with other families was minimal and spontaneous. It consisted of occasional, unannounced drives over to a neighbor's farm. And once in a while, they would reciprocate. But those visits were few and far in between. We watched movies in a vacant lot in Tennant on summer evenings. The organizers would hoist a huge bed sheet (actually several bed sheets sewn together) between two poles and as soon as it got dark, they'd project some ancient film. We would all sit on the ground eating popcorn, candy, or whatever. I remember watching *Abbott and Costello, Tarzan, Roy Rogers, Gene Autry,* and *Song of the South.*

Of course, this being the rural Midwest, our big family outing was going to fairs. I especially remember one particular state fair in Des

Moines. I was probably about six years old. There we were, enjoying ourselves at the fair, when my brother David suddenly became quite ill. My parents located a doctor in Des Moines and we rushed over. He advised that the best remedy would be a little whiskey with sugar. I'll never forget, young as I was, the look on my mother's face as we all entered the liquor store. She was religiously opposed to the consumption of alcohol but also resolutely in support of anything she could do for her child. So needless to say, they bought the whiskey. I was bored and tired and a tad angry with my brother for being such a nuisance. My parents apparently sensed that and bought me, to my great delight, my first foot-long hot dog. Far better than whiskey.

Farm life didn't offer many adventures or surprises for an experience-starved boy. I found my escapades in whatever way I could. I tried to turn every experience into an adventure. Believe it not, I made going to the outhouse, especially at night, a form of adventure for me. We had no indoor plumbing and no electricity. I hated having to make my way to the outhouse on a cold winter night when nature called. As a child I was both frightened and fascinated by the dark, and dark it could be on a farm in Iowa in the 1940s. There were no yard lights, only kerosene lanterns in one room of the farmhouse. I don't ever recall carrying a candle, probably because my mother was frightened that I might burn myself or set something on fire. Even with all these obstacles, I still felt grabbed by the awesome mystery of the dark Iowa sky as I walked alone to the outhouse. Me and the dark night. Somehow I felt that was going to be part of my life still unfolding.

My first, shocking lesson about real life came from a dog. My brother and I had what was then called a rat terrier, which I later learned from a friend is actually a popular breed known as a Jack Russell. Our dog was a male named Spot. I raised Spot from a pup and loved his cuddly, friendly nature. When I was about six years old, and Spot more or less an adolescent, we walked down to the corn crib one day where Dad and some neighbors were shelling corn. I stood in utter shock as Spot noticed a bunch of rats running out from under the corn crib, immediately positioned himself perfectly about six feet away from the opening, and then systematically, caught rat after rat by the throat, flipped them over his shoulder, and grabbed for the next one. It was killing, pure killing, with no intent to eat, simply to kill. I was dumbfounded. My affectionate, cuddly pet was a cold-blooded killer; it was in his genes. It was my first (vague) awakening to the harsh fact that things are often not as they seem and that nature, whether of the human or animal variety, could be downright cruel.

Because we were a largely self-sufficient farm, we didn't run to the store to buy food. We pretty much grew or raised everything ourselves. But preserving food during the summer months was a constant challenge. Without electricity, there was, of course, no refrigeration. We did have a shed with a well (not the same well we used for drinking and washing water). My father would lower meat in sealed cans down into that well on a rope to keep it cold and fresh. One summer the rope broke and we lost all the meat.

I started having regular chores on the farm when I was six, mostly helping out my mother. I would gather eggs in the chicken house and as winter approached I'd chase the chickens from the yard to get them back into the chicken house. I liked digging potatoes in the fall with a pitchfork. I also took care of the pets—various dogs and cats we kept outdoors. The vegetable garden was my mother's exclusive territory. We raised potatoes, sweet corn, lettuce, radishes, horseradish, peas, string beans, carrots, onions, beets, watermelons, muskmelons, parsnips, and asparagus. In the fall, my mother would can all the vegetables and store them in the storm cellar. I would help her with the canning.

Whenever my mother tended her vegetable garden, I watched carefully. I was eager to be a good boy by helping her. One summer afternoon, some neighbor farm ladies were visiting and I was left alone. I felt neglected and unappreciated. So I went to the garden, took up the hoe, and started weeding industriously, chopping out three long rows of plants that I took to be weeds. A few days later, I overheard a conversation between my parents in the kitchen. Apparently, I had destroyed the entire tomato crop for the year. To my amazement, they didn't chastise me or even mention it. I doubt they ever knew I heard their conversation. After that, I gave up hoeing for a while. I didn't appreciate then as much as I do now the way they handled the situation—it was, in a word, magnificent.

My childhood aspirations were pretty modest. I dreamed of becoming what was known as a maintainer driver. Throughout my youth, we always lived on dirt roads, which became frightfully muddy and sometimes downright impassable if the rain was heavy enough. The maintainers came in with trucks to smooth out the ruts and maintain some semblance of a smooth ride. I thought those operators were masters of our universe.

I also admired mail carriers and could imagine myself in that role someday. Our rural postman arrived every day, placing mail in the box mounted on a post at the end of the front yard. I exulted at delivery time and would run to pick up the mail, though rarely if ever was anything addressed to me. The third and the loftiest ambition that occurred to me was to be a veterinarian. Vets frequently came to the farm to deal with sick animals. To me, they seemed so knowledgeable and self-confident. And, of course, I loved when they were able to cure our critters. So I thought I just might try to become a vet myself when I grew up.

I was sad when we left the Kay farm. I felt most at home there. We went on from there to the Best farm, owned by Art Best, where we lived for the three or four years before I was in high school. Our house was about a half mile off the road, and David and I walked that distance each morning to catch the school bus, which stopped at the big house where the Bests lived. On cold days, we would huddle inside their house to wait, trying to stay warm at the bottom of a short staircase that connected to their kitchen and the basement. But they never once invited us into the kitchen, never once offered us anything to eat or drink. I thought it was strange. But that's how they were, perhaps because they didn't much like children, as Mom had mentioned.

After we were married, as Dai Sil told me stories about her childhood and elementary school—and of being punished by a teacher for speaking in Korean and not in Japanese, as per instructions of the colonial government—my stories felt so mundane and ordinary. I did not think of any experiences that would be worth comparing with hers. But I now remember one incident. When David was sent to school and I wasn't, clearly due to my young age, I was terribly unhappy. Each morning when David disappeared onto the school bus that stopped on the country road in front of our farmhouse, I pleaded with my parents to send me too. One morning, when I was five, I ran away from the breakfast table before they could stop me, and ran all the way out to the bus and asked the driver if I could ride to school. He just grinned and told me to go back and talk to my parents. That was also my very first, serious attempt at negotiation, which failed. I felt lonely on that forlorn farmland.

Dai Sil also told me many moving tales about World War II coming to an end. I racked my brain to think of anything whatsoever I could recall related to that war. I do remember World War II, but only through games we boys used to play. Fallen pine cones became hand grenades and downed tree trunks were fighter planes that I piloted, tin cans metamorphosed into walkie-talkies and branches we found on the ground served as rifles. There were no television images yet, of course, or any relatives or neighbors in uniform whom I could remember. An uncle of mine did serve in the Army, but I only learned about that much later. We did have radio, but it was only used for the weather and livestock market reports.

Poignantly, in retrospect, I celebrated my seventh birthday on August 15, 1945, the day World War II ended in Asia and the day Korea was finally liberated from Japanese rule. But I don't remember any of that, of course. The end of the war didn't register. Nor do I recall my seventh birthday for that matter. Yet that day was of singular and profound importance to Dai Sil. She heard the emperor's voice and her father's voice in joy. That day was also important to the world, and it must have resonated with my parents. My father's best friend had been killed at the Battle of the Bulge just a year earlier. Years later, after Dai Sil and I were married, her father marveled that my birthday fell on Korean independence day. It used to piss off her brothers that their father couldn't remember their birthdays but he did mine!

Once Dai Sil came by with a book in her hand—*If He Hollers Let Him Go* by Chester Himes. Its main character is an African American named Bob Jones. There was a passage she wanted me to see. "Read this," she said, "it is painful, but I know he is telling it like it was." Then she showed me an underlined passage: "Now I was scared in a different way. Not of the violence. Not of the mob. Not of physical hurt. But of America, of American justice." Jones was pondering what would happen if he was tried in a court of law for the false charge of raping a white woman.

Then something I must not have wanted to remember popped in my head. It had to do with a counting rhyme my dad would say when I was a little kid, placing his fingers on my toes one by one:

> Eeny, meeny, miny, moe,
> Catch a nigger by the toe.
> If he hollers let him go.
> Eeny, meeny, miny, moe.

Would you believe that I thought it was delightful at the time? I also remembered that, among the candies and nuts that my mother brought out at Christmas time were Brazil nuts, which we called nigger toes. I sat still for a long while after that, quite sad. Finally I decided that I should be happy that times have changed, though we still have a long way to go.

One of the childhood memories that has remained with me is of a large vegetable garden. Its exact location escapes me, but I know it was near the house. It must have been the pulse of life from all those growing plants that drew me to the garden with magnetic power. I loved to see the buds of tender greens flourishing each day. I can still see the rows and rows of spring onions and garlic. I did not realize then how essential they were for Korean cuisine. The root vegetables fascinated me—carrots, turnips and potatoes. The most unforgettable time was when we'd dig potatoes. For me, it was like a treasure hunt, finding so many fruits from one root. I was mystified and moved by the wonders of nature emerging from the rich dark soil. By the end of the day, when a mountain of potatoes stood before us, joy sent me floating into the sky.

~ *D S K-G*

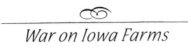

War on Iowa Farms

AFTER HEARING SO MUCH ABOUT THE KOREAN WAR FROM DAI
SIL, I began to think about my wars on Iowa farms. Certainly not
any actual wars. But the Korean War was the first international
event that crept into my consciousness in any cerebral way. I had a
cousin, Jerry, who served in Korea and I wrote him several letters. I
also recall President Truman's dismissal of General MacArthur. It
was outrageous, I thought—how could this boring little man fire a
military hero? The war was far away, yet it marked the beginning of
my political education.

For me personally, as a boy in Iowa, the threat of death did not
come from man-made events like war, but from nature itself. One
of the most exciting, albeit scary, experiences in my life was a natural event that occurred in 1947 or 1948, I'm not precisely sure
which, when I was nine or ten. A huge blizzard hit southwest Iowa.
We were in school at the time. Around noon we started hearing
vague warnings of something awry. Shortly after lunch, the principal came to tell us that he had ordered the school buses and we
would be taken home right away. We took off, and in less than
thirty minutes we couldn't see more than a foot ahead of us out the
windows. It was a total whiteout.

Seconds later or so it seemed, we felt the bus lurch and stop
with a bang. It had veered into a ditch and tipped on its side. There
we were. What seemed like many minutes later, the driver ush-
ered us out, demanding that we form a single line and hold hands
with the person in front and back of us. I could see nothing at
all, only white, but stumbled forward until I lost touch with the
hand in front of me. There was no one behind me either and I fell
face-down into the snow. Never in my life have I been so terrified.
Moments later, someone picked me up and we made our way to another bus, which eventually took us back to school. There we spent
the night, sleeping fitfully in the gymnasium. I vaguely recall the

teachers scurrying about trying to find something for us to eat and keep us entertained. They showed a movie, but I totally forget both the name and the content. It was perhaps my first revelation that adults didn't quite have everything figured out. They were certainly confused that evening.

Then a few years later, on the afternoon on June 23, 1950, a tornado struck a farm one-and-a-half miles northwest of us. Dad, my brother, and I were outside washing our hands in the basin and getting ready for supper, when Mom came running out, pointed to the sky and said, "That's what a tornado looks like." It was a tiny black spout, barely visible. Mom had experienced an Iowa tornado in 1913, when she was three years old. It struck their house, lifted it a few inches off the ground, and then dropped it on a diagonal. She was handed out the window by her father. She claimed to remember it.

I recall watching that tiny spout and dismissing my mother's claims. But it grew and grew, and kept getting closer to the earth. We scurried to the fruit cellar and waited a few minutes, emerging just in time to see it hit a farmstead dead on, flinging boards, pigs, whatever into the air as if it were a giant plow. We drove over to see the site, along with all of our neighbors, and stared in awe at the damage. Mercifully, nobody was hurt or killed. The family had retreated to the basement, and the tornado missed the house by about thirty feet. If the Korean War signified my political awakening, that twister birthed in me a healthy respect for the destructive power of the natural world.

The year 1946 stands out in my memory for the arrival of electricity. I was eight years old. I sat on a turned-over tin bucket in the front yard as workmen erected the poles and extended the wires into the house. That night the kerosene lanterns were put away and bare light bulbs, with no fixtures, illuminated the entire house. I thought those lights were magnificent, but I was also very confused. I could not fathom where the light came from. It seemed like magic.

We moved five times before I finished high school, but always to some farmstead near the town of Tennant where I went to school for all twelve years. Tennant had been established with high hopes in 1903 when the Chicago Great Western Railway built tracks connecting Omaha and Chicago. More than 1,000 people arrived early that year for an auction of lots. The town gained its name from Charles Tennant, an Englishman who was an officer with the railroad and, according to a letter from his son written in 1953, a major figure in British railroading. That letter is the only evidence. Despite the high hopes, Tennant reached its peak population in 1930 with 118 souls, declined to ninety-five by the time I graduated from high school in 1956, and at the turn of the 21st century stood at seventy-three.

At its height, Tennant had a drug store, a school (encompassing all twelve grades, no kindergarten), a Methodist church, a general store, a trucking company for hauling livestock to the slaughter-houses, a grain elevator, a hardware store, a blacksmith shop (for welding farm equipment), a post office, a tavern, and outdoor mov-ies. There had also been a bank, but it closed during the Great Depression. I especially enjoyed the post office—the entire space couldn't have been larger than ten-by-eight feet, and only three people could fit in the public area, but it still made room for the FBI's most wanted posters. By 1956, only the blacksmith, the grain elevator, and the general store remained. Today there is only the trucking company. Before I married Dai Sil in 1979—twenty-six years after I graduated from high school and left home—I gave her a tour of the town. It lasted ten minutes.

I don't remember a great deal about my elementary school years. I do recall an incident involving the superintendent when I was in first grade. He entered my classroom and apparently all the chil-dren were expected to stand to attention. I was happily, obliviously drawing some pictures at my desk and wasn't aware of his arrival. He snatched me up to his height and yelled at me for being disobe-dient. I don't remember his exact words. It was too traumatic for me to say anything or even cry. Though I could not articulate my feelings, I must have felt that the way the superintendent treated me was unfair and too authoritarian. After all, I was a mere first grader, enjoying my own world. No way for an adult to treat a child who made an innocent mistake, if it was a mistake at all. I believe those feelings stayed with me all my life and helped me to be fair to people, especially to those who worked for me.

I can only recall a few of my teachers. One whom I do remember was a young and unattractive female. I admired her because I felt she was a good teacher—strong, determined, and fair. Both elementary and middle school were monotonous and unexciting for me, driven by memorization and regurgitation. Spelling bees were popular, as was being asked to stand and name the U.S. presidents in order. One girl in the fourth grade failed because she referred to the 32nd president as FDR, not Franklin Delano Roosevelt. I considered that quite unfair at the time. I was always concerned about fairness. My parents must have instilled a strong sense of fairness and justice from the time I was little.

I wonder if trauma is what lodges in our brain most enduringly. In the seventh grade, we were assigned by our teacher to write an essay. I cannot recall the nature of the assignment or the topic of the essay, but I felt tormented by it. At that time, we were living on the Best farm. Sitting at the kitchen table on a Saturday afternoon, twirling my pencil and furrowing my brow, I was having trouble tackling the essay. Mom came from the living room, and I confessed my problem. She made some simple suggestions, which I've also forgotten. But for whatever reason, her words inspired me and I wrote feverishly—in longhand of course—for the next two hours, and proudly turned in my endeavor first thing Monday morning.

My teacher loved the essay and even read it aloud to her high school classes, chastising those older students because they didn't write as well. I heard about that from those abused high schoolers for several days, and I listened with horror as one even alleged, with others nodding in agreement, that someone else—an adult—must have written my essay. For weeks I felt hurt and saw a glimpse of what I needed to do to succeed in the future. Just doing good work would not be enough. I should learn to use whatever talents I had wisely if I wanted to go beyond the confines of Tennant.

Driving a Tractor

In those days, the importance of my schooling was easily matched by chores on the farms. My duties started as far back as preschool days, but my parents waited until I turned ten to assign me serious farm work. At that point, my father hauled a tractor and taught me to drive it. The task was harrowing a recently plowed field to level it, root up weeds, and to break up clods, and the like. He told me that I should drive in a straight line, pointing ahead.

"Just drive toward that post with the bird sitting on it. But if the bird flies, don't move with it."

I believe this instruction registered in my consciousness: once you set your goal, follow it in a straight line. Don't be swayed by any other movements, political expediencies, or any stuff that sounds tempting. My farmer father taught me lasting lessons in work, politics, and life.

Soon I was driving the battered International pickup, as well as the tractor. Farm boys were allowed, if only unofficially, to drive trucks underage and unlicensed, as long as they stuck to rural roads. I felt manly whenever I drove as a ten-year-old kid, and amazed that I could move the tractor and truck. I definitely felt a sense of power.

No matter what the season, I would get up at 5:00 a.m. First I milked the cows, then separated cream and milk. Only after those chores were we rewarded with breakfast. My mother would cook me five eggs over easy, with thick strips of crispy bacon. Sometimes she would make pancakes from scratch. During the school year, I would then change my clothes and wait for the bus. It was a short ride, the school was close, and there were only a few kids to pick up. School let out about 3:00 p.m., so I would be home by 4:00, grab lunch (hopefully Mom had baked bread that day), and then it was back to milking the cows at 5:30.

My livestock care included not only cows, but also pigs and beef cattle, not to mention the beheading and plucking of chickens. And then there were seasonal chores, like earmarking piglets or castrating slightly older pigs. A few farmers cut the tails off pigs at a young age, arguing that it took a bushel of corn to raise a tail. I am happy to report that we never did that.

I am also happy to say that not everything on the farm was a chore to me. Starting from about age twelve, I pursued hunting and trapping assiduously. My trapping started with ground squirrels (moles), which dug extensive underground tunnels, piling the dirt in the middle of the hayfield. The county offered a bounty: 10 cents a squirrel. All you had to do was deliver the severed front feet to the proper office. Then I moved on to muskrats, the hides of which would fetch a whole dollar. The wily devils build their homes underwater on creek banks, gather their food from the cornfields, and then slide back down the bank to their abode. The trick is to place the trap underwater right in front of the burrow. I got pretty good at it.

A creek called Keg ran through our farm. Around 6:00 a.m., after I had milked the cows, I would check the traps, club any caught muskrats and reset the trap. I would place the corpses in a little-used shed and change clothes for school. That evening, after milking the cows, I would skin the critters and stretch their hides on a flat piece of wood I had fashioned. They did have a distinctive unpleasant odor. After a few days of drying and stretching, I would take them to the county seat. One morning I found a trap that contained only one muskrat foot—the desperate creature had chewed off its own foot in order to escape. That day, I gave up trapping.

By the time I was old enough to tackle serious farm work, the job was made easier by the introduction of tractors and mechanical corn pickers. Before then, my parents had to pick and shuck the corn by hand, and then throw it into a wagon pulled alongside by two mules and featuring high sideboards so that their sideway tosses of the shucked ears would land in the wagon. The corn would then be hauled to a crib, a wooden building with open spaces between the sideboards, so the corn could dry. Later, the corn would be shelled with a hand-operated machine.

Winters on the farm were quiet. The fields couldn't be worked, but the chores continued. Cows still had to be milked, hogs and cattle fed. To the same early morning routine were added winter-time chores like breaking up the ice in the water tanks and moving snow so the cattle could reach their feed.

I loved rainy days when I'd be sent to the machine shed to repair tools, and I could hear the raindrops on the tin roof while I worked. I also spent a lot of time taking apart radios and putting them back together. We didn't buy a television until I was thirteen. Naturally, radio dominated my evening life. I memorized the entire schedule and faithfully listened to *The Lone Ranger, Fibber McGee and Molly, The Great Gildersleeve, Amos and Andy,* and *Dragnet.* I also avidly tuned in for baseball, basketball, and even occasionally football games. My father was not keen about tuning in for programs, but he used radio to learn about the weather and farm news.

We had a telephone, that was on a party line of five to ten households, and any calls beyond the party had to be placed through the operator, almost always a woman. We virtually never called long-distance, that is, beyond the rural county where we lived. Nebraska or Oklahoma was long distance. The thought of talking to someone in California or New York never even occurred to us.

That meant long-distance calls were a rare and even frightening phenomenon—expensive and generally placed only in case of a death in the family. I recall with intensity when, in 1949, the telephone rang and my father answered. It was from my uncle (Mom's brother) in Oklahoma. His son Harold, age sixteen, had been killed. He'd gotten off the school bus and was starting to cross the street when a car hurled into him. That may be part of the reason why James Agee's *A Death in the Family* resonated so deeply with me. I read it while in college, and at least one more time years later. Death and unexpected happenings are all part of life, but still their impact on us and family is deep, complex, and tragic.

When I reached the third grade, I had the daily privilege of being the one to command my class to bow good morning to Teacher Kim. By then I was class president. I excelled in

almost all of my subjects, but I was especially good at memorization. During the Silla period, there had been a famous artist by the name of Sol Gur. The trees he painted were so realistic that birds would try to sit on his canvases and fall to the ground, or so the story went. There was a long essay about him in our Korean language book and we were assigned to commit it to memory. Once again, I stayed up a good part of the night, impatient for morning to come, eager to go to school. More than anything else in life, what I craved was Teacher Kim's praise. Sure enough, she asked if anyone could recite Sol Gur's story by heart. Instantly, I raised my hand. No one else's hand was up. It was an exhilarating moment. I didn't make a mistake, not even one.

~ D S K-G

What Studies?—Sports, Sex, Politics, and Hunting

MY HIGH SCHOOL YEARS WERE 1952 TO 1956. Actually elementary, middle, and high school were all in the same place, a single two-story brick building that sufficed for twelve grades. A flagpole stood in the tiny front yard, a baseball field sat off to the left. The left-field line ended abruptly in a wire fence and a cornfield, and center field abutted the tiny house where the school janitor lived. There were swings in the front. I recall with equal measure of joy and fear once at age ten swinging high above the top bars, so far that the chains literally sagged. I made it back down with a thrill I've never forgotten.

During school days in Iowa, I was not exactly indifferent about my studies, but challenging they were not. In fact, I was downright bored most of the time. I was torn in high school: I liked reading and I loved learning, but that was not what dominated our lives. No one I knew was thinking about college. And I don't recall a single conversation in class or in the hallways or anywhere else about *ideas*, be they political, intellectual, literary, or religious.

I loved English and history, but they were so easy that I guess I'd have to say I loved them despite school rather than because of it. Sadly to me, history was by far the worst taught of our subjects. That was because the coaches had that assignment, and teaching history was not their primary concern and certainly not why they were paid. They taught strictly from the textbooks, which were badly written, with no sense of choices, no questions about why and how—just this fact, that fact. American history was made to seem largely heroic. And I do not recall a single world history course. We certainly never heard of Africans, Asians, or Latin Americans. Well, perhaps the Monroe Doctrine was mentioned. I normally polished off the entire assigned history textbook within the first month or two of the term.

Literature was somewhat more interesting because we read real writers, not dumbed-down facsimiles. That included Shakespeare. But the only actual classes I found somewhat stimulating were algebra and geometry. And even then, I considered them fun games, not serious pursuits.

I had read all the books in the high school library before I reached freshman year. That was hardly a major accomplishment, since it couldn't have held more than 100 volumes. Frequently, I spent class time either talking with another student about something irrelevant or trying to write poetry. Nobody was much interested in the poems, so I eventually quit trying.

My boredom in the absence of serious intellectual stimulation drove me to talk too much in class and caused me to receive a D in deportment. This created a slight problem, and led me to engage in my very first political action. The school had a rule that a student had to receive a B grade or better to be included on the honor roll. I qualified on all my grades except deportment. Like I said, I protested, but to my dismay discovered that other students with less than satisfactory grades in deportment couldn't care less about the honor roll. I failed to ignite any group action. It was an early, if unconscious, lesson in the importance of rallying the troops to a cause.

Student politics didn't exist. There was a school paper of utter triviality called the *Tennant Times*. I wrote some pieces and spent hours printing it out on an antiquated mimeograph machine. It dealt almost exclusively with sports and petty gossip. I was the sports editor during my junior and senior years. Not much of an exposure to the world of journalism.

For all four years, I attempted every sport offered. The school wasn't large enough to field a football team. Other small towns in the area played six-man football; we couldn't even manage that. Baseball had a special place in my heart (about which I write more in my final chapter on baseball on p. 261), but basketball was by far more popular. It was basketball—for both boys and girls—that held the town of Tennant together. We were mostly farm families. Of the thirty or so students in the high school, only two actually lived in town.

Tennant belonged to the Po-Ha-She athletic conference, named for the collection of eleven small schools in Pottawattamie, Harrison, and Shelby counties. The schools included Persia, Underwood, Elk Horn, Shelby, Kirkman, Walnut, Defiance, Portsmouth, Harlan, and Earling. Tennant was by far the smallest in the conference, with most of the other schools numbering over 100 students. And we all played markedly different games. No standard courts existed in those rural schools. The one in Kirkman, was the most astonishing: a room so small that the free-throw circles intersected with the center circle and a ceiling so low that the ball would frequently hit it on a free-throw shot. There was no ten-second rule in that gym. Our tallest player, the big guy, was all of five-foot-ten. But then the other teams didn't have any tall players either, and certainly none of our athletes was African American or Latino.

For two years—1953/54 and 1954/55—Tennant's boys' teams were quite good, winning both the conference and county tournaments and advancing toward the state playoffs. That success resulted principally from a new coach, Tony Sebben, who introduced man-to-man and full-court press defense, which were unknown in our area. As a result, our team was able to score numerous turnover points simply by grabbing the basketball when it was thrown into play under the opponent's basket. I have to confess that I personally never caught any of those inbound passes. My job was to sit on the bench near the coach, clipboard in hand, and record a sketch of all attempted and successful shots. Later I would tabulate the percentages for the team overall and for each player.

One of Tennant's historic highlights was in the early 1930s when the Harlem Globetrotters played in the local gymnasium. That is an incredibly sad commentary on the status of African Americans of that time, that this renowned team would have to play in a tiny gym in a town of ninety residents. But nowadays, the locals speak proudly of it. Back then, as local lore has it, the gym was equipped with wood-burning stoves at each end. Players had to hustle to avoid them.

Truth be told, I never started a single basketball game, but if we were ahead or behind by twenty or more points late in the last quarter, the coach would send me in. My single moment of glory came one year during the sectional tournament in the fourth quarter. We were leading by twenty points. The coach waited a few more minutes to be safe and then sent me in. The first time the ball was passed to me, I was so nervous I just threw it at the basket, some forty feet away, much too long a shot for even the team's star player. But, as luck would have it, the ball dropped straight through the hoop, touching nothing but net. I was more surprised than anyone else in the gymnasium. I never tried that shot again. Actually I never had the opportunity to try the shot again, but that counts as one of the happiest moments in my high school days.

In high school, it was important to be a fearless hunter, a sign of being a man. I hunted squirrels, pheasants, rabbits, and foxes, normally using the 22-caliber semiautomatic Remington rifle I had ordered through the mail from Montgomery Ward or else my father's 10-gauge shotgun. The wolves were pretty much gone by then. I did see a wolf out in the field one day and watched with amazement how gracefully it leaped over a high fence.

My brother David, two years older than I, played some childhood games with me, but by the time we were in high school, we had little in common. Neither of us was proficient athletically, but I took great pride when Dad pointed out that I was superior with a rifle and shotgun. We had some pleasant encounters in childhood. I recall defending him, as a brother should, in certain school quarrels, but we never really shared anything and have grown farther apart in values and thinking. Perhaps the feeling of disconnection between me and David had already begun then.

Even as young boys, I believe David and I had different goals in life. Of course, neither of us articulated what we wanted in life, but I know my greatest pleasure came from reading in an attic, under a tree, or underneath the blanket with a flashlight. I always enjoyed playing alone. I loved finding little nooks where I could be alone and fantasize my own world. Strange, I don't recall David ever doing anything like that, but he was always practical and made sure that he got what he wanted. Eventually I got away from the farm and lived in the world of ideas and David became one of the wealthiest farmers in Iowa.

Two pals of mine, Vernon and Leon, decided one fall that we should all go hunting ducks on the banks of the Missouri River, only twenty miles or so away. Up before dawn with our shotguns well oiled, we drove to a spot we'd been told about. It was the migratory season. Seeing no ducks flying above, we sat down on the river bank, our legs dangling. It was beautiful. Then we started hearing large splashes in the water and glanced at each other in some confusion. A few minutes later we saw, on the opposite shore, a large chunk of the bank fall right into the river. The water was eating it away. Without a word, but with a definite scream or two, we scrambled as fast as we could, covering dozens of yards in a matter of seconds. And we never shot a duck.

Living as we did on a largely self-sufficient farm, shopping didn't occupy a prominent place in our schedule. If there was an important purchase to be made, we'd generally go to nearby Harlan. Saturday evening was shopping time. In junior high and early high school, before we had our driver's licenses, a few friends and I would walk around the town square, again and again, while our parents spent their money. Once we reached sixteen, our stroll became a slow drive around that same town square, again and again. The purpose was to see friends and to be seen. Seems silly now and, in truth, it did a tad back then as well.

As a teenager I managed to take part in many of the activities of my peers, but largely without enthusiasm. Boys were supposed to be interested in cars, so I learned all I could about the zany automobiles of the period. One buddy, Leon Klindt, had his car blocked, that is, had the whole rear section lowered—or was it raised?—so the car looked more like a hot rod.

I approached dating with more gusto. Many a Sunday afternoon, Vernon, Leon, and I would hook up at whichever house it was more likely that the parents would be gone, and then we would try to give each other the courage, or the bullying, to pick up the phone and ask some pretty girl out for a date. In truth, it was a scary undertaking. Pre-sixteen dating basically meant flirting at sporting and church events. Real dating meant lots of necking and some petting. Petting, we were once told at church camp, meant "above the waist." That, of course, only served to wildly encourage our imaginations about the lower regions.

Sex was never, ever discussed with my father or mother. The closest we came to it was when, sometime in my early adolescence, my father discovered a book I was reading that was about sex, but extremely mild by today's standards. His only comment was, "You shouldn't read those kinds of books." In the seventh grade, the girls in my class attended lessons on sex, or so we thought. We boys were left in study hall. I felt wrongly excluded. Why were they the only ones to receive this tutelage? Why weren't we told anything? All I learned about sex came from ill-informed rumors and chats with other boys. And eventually, first-hand experience. But then it came naturally, I guess.

I remember a scandal one time that involved the girls' locker room. I believe it was my freshman year in high school when my brother, a junior, was accused, along with his classmate, Jim Boardman, of having drilled a hole through a concrete wall in a closet adjacent to the girls' locker room and, of course, watching the girls undress, or should I say, undressed. They were accused, but nothing was ever done, because it was widely assumed that Slim Kolterman, the school janitor—and the only person with access to the closet— was the likely culprit. It certainly made for a lot of jokes in the hallways. Many years later, I asked my dad, who was on the school board at the time, and he confirmed that the janitor had done it. Now I wonder why he wasn't fired.

Sex wasn't the only subject left unspoken. Although I was expected to do well in school and to behave myself, never did we discuss anything I had actually learned, or even what I was studying. We never attended any theatrical or musical events, and I wasn't introduced to classical music until I went to college. Intellectual and cultural life in my childhood were nonexistent. My father actually disliked music; my mother feigned interest and we faithfully watched *Your Hit Parade* every week. But we never went to concerts or plays, rarely even to movies. It wasn't overt hostility to intellectual thought or the arts; they were simply not within the range of the many hard daily tasks of survival on an Iowa farm.

We also never talked about *ideas*, strangely enough, not even religious or political ideas. My mother constantly cautioned me not to "talk about politics or religion with company." I wondered what things of importance were left to talk about. On the rare occasions when my father did discuss politics, he condemned anything radical. When I pressed him on that point, he could never provide a definition, but it was clear that he found radicalism on the right or the left equally offensive. Part of it was quite simple and unsophisticated. One day when I was ten or eleven, while we were sitting on the farm tractor out in the field, he told me that he just couldn't understand why the government couldn't manage to balance the budget. "A family has to balance their budget or they have nothing to eat. Why should it be any different with the government?"

My dad's parents were lifelong Republicans, but they believed that one should support the country, not the party. Dad always believed that, too. Actually, I don't think he ever quite understood the role of parties in American democracy. Or of partisanship. To his dying day, he frequently complained, "Why can't those politicians just do what is good for the country, and not for the party?"

I read True Compass *by Edward Kennedy in December 2012, almost four years after Don left me. One story it told is that President Kennedy, after he'd talked Bobby into accepting the attorney general post, asked, "Please Bobby, just comb your hair."*

This made me laugh and cry at the same time, tears for the two brothers whose lives were cut short, and laughter for JFK's wit. And it also brought Don back to me. Don had dirty brown hair, plenty of it. He loved and was proud of his abundant hair. Many times I stole looks at Don as he was intensely engaged before the bathroom mirror in combing his hair and rearranging it in a variety of ways. Usually though, his hair did not quite look as if it were properly combed.

These thoughts took me to his older brother David. David became a millionaire by buying Iowa land and farming it with savvy business sense, intelligence, and pure hard work. The two brothers applied their shared work ethic to different things—Don pursued ideas and David tilled land. Because their outlook and goals in life were so different, they grew apart as the years went by.

David may have won the earnings competition, but Don felt rich on account of his plentiful hair. He would giggle with child-like joy about David's baldness, the thinning of his hair that left a large, shiny spot on his head. This always made me smile. It still does four years after Don departed from this world. When he died, his hair was still abundant and beautiful. I loved his uncombed hair and felt rich.

~ D S K-G

Thank Goodness for 4-H

IN SEARCH OF SOMETHING MORE THAN I COULD GET FROM SCHOOL and farm work, I turned to a Middle America triumvirate: 4-H, the Methodist Youth Fellowship, and baseball. I learned far more about myself through those activities than I ever did in school. Perhaps, most importantly, although I didn't recognize this until much later, I discovered where my strengths were.

In each of these pursuits I displayed penchants that later became central to my functioning, especially in my professional sphere. I found that I craved knowledge of how things worked, and I would master the respective rules and procedures with hour upon hour of study and observation. Two of the books I devoured were *Robert's Rules of Order* and the official baseball rules.

Though a mediocre athlete at best on the ball field, I could attain a modicum of success because I knew the rules—what constitutes a balk, for example—better than the umpires. I would stand in the batter's box until the pitcher started his delivery and would then turn and walk away. The pitcher, stunned, would stop. The umpire normally did nothing. I would yell "BALK!" and, if the umpire resisted, pull the rule book from my hip pocket and show the rule to him. (For the uninitiated, a balk is one of the lesser-known rules in baseball. It restricts the actions of the pitcher when there are runners on base. In general, a balk is called whenever a pitcher interrupts the pitching motion). Generally, I trotted to first base, pleased with myself. Unfortunately, this earned the disapproval of my coach, but that didn't blunt my satisfaction.

The sole church in town was Methodist. Many of us belonged to it. The Scandinavians, who were Lutherans, and the Germans, who were mostly Roman Catholics, attended churches in other towns. The Methodists were of no particular ethnic derivation or nationality, as we called it back then.

The 4-H program was established for farm kids in the first decade of the 20th century. The four H's were Head–Heart–Hands–Health, the group's symbol was a four-leaf clover, and its motto was "to make the best better." The program was based upon progressive, John Dewey–like educational principles, which emphasized learning by doing. It was aimed at rural youth and meant not only to instruct them in practical matters about plants and animals, but also, in cooperation with the U.S. Department of Agriculture and the Cooperative Extension Service, to bring progressive agricultural methods to isolated areas. All of that was fine by me, and over the years, I raised beef and dairy cattle as well as pigs to show at the county fairs. I didn't do badly, though only my pigs did well enough to win a purple ribbon.

The 4-H program was of immense value to me, but probably not primarily in the ways the organization intended. For me, it was more about human relationships, organizational skills, speaking ability, and aptitude for writing. It was also about self-esteem and self confidence: I found areas—not related to sports—where I could truly excel.

So I threw myself into the organizational aspects of 4-H and was elected president of the Tennant Future Feeders and also served as an officer at the county level. In my work with 4-H, *Robert's Rules* became handy. In meetings, I would simply say, "according to *Robert's Rules of Order*" and that would silence everyone. Most people had heard of the book, but none had actually read it. I could be obnoxious at times.

Through 4-H, I learned that I was good at dealing with people and that I could run a meeting with purpose and efficiency. All meetings of our local club were held in the homes of individual members. The very first meeting I chaired as president of the Tennant Future Feeders was at George Buman's house. His dad was a prominent and respected member of the community. Afterwards, Mrs. Buman took my father aside and said she had never seen a boy so young do such a magnificent and self-confident job. I did not hear that statement directly, nor, tellingly, did my father relate it to me. Rather, I accidentally overheard him telling my mother, with great pride, later that evening, when I was supposed out of earshot. Bless his heart, the old man never did want any son of his to get a swelled head.

My most memorable meeting occurred in the spring of 1956. There was interest among the girls in joining the boys' 4-H. They had their own club, the Lincoln Bluebells, but girls' 4-H focused strictly upon homemaking, and some of its members were beginning to think that they'd like to try their hand at raising livestock and other undertakings. The hot topic was scheduled for debate at what was to be my last meeting as president, at the home of Willard McLaughlin, a neighboring farmer. As the discussion on the motion to permit girls to join proceeded, sentiment was running decidedly against.

I had mastered *Robert's Rules* sufficiently to know that I could not participate in a debate from the chair. So in a clever feint (if I do say so myself), I announced: "I surrender the chair temporarily to the vice president." That came as some surprise to most members since they were unaware of any such rules. The vice president, who had already spoken against the motion, was equally astounded. I then spoke strongly in favor of admitting girls on the principle of equality and fairness. I returned to the table, resumed my chairship, and called for a vote. Gratifyingly for me, the measure narrowly passed.

I also managed to win the Shelby County crop-judging contest and demonstration project, which entitled me to compete and win a blue ribbon at the state fair in Des Moines. Demonstrations were, to me, a particularly rewarding part of the 4-H experience. The idea was that a team of two 4-H'ers would select a topic, research it thoroughly, write a script, practice extensively, and then present it to a public audience, ordinarily the other members of their local club. The winners at that level would go on to compete at the county level, and if victorious proceed to the state. (There was no national level.)

I was teamed up with Lynn Sorensen and we developed a demonstration project called How to Prevent Farm Fires. I must assert, with no apologies, that I did all of the research, collected the materials, and wrote the script. But I had to have a partner and selected Lynn, as he seemed the most amenable to direction. It wasn't so much about fire prevention as it was about extinguishing, but I guess we—or I—didn't know any better. We would actually light fires and then demonstrate how to put them out. It was a thrill to win in the county seat and especially exhilarating when the lead judge took me aside afterwards and said, "Your demonstration was by far the best presentation today." I do not recall that man's name, I am afraid, but his words are burned into my brain. It was that important to us.

After that, the state fair was a tad anticlimactic, but exciting enough nonetheless. We were well received. The judges were complimentary. Strangely, I do not remember if my parents were there, but they must have been. It was an absolute thrill to perform on the very fairgrounds that I had wandered as a child—at which point in my life, they represented the height of sophistication.

As a result of my efforts, I was appointed to serve as what we called a leader, or counselor, at the county's 4-H summer retreat. I also received the county Leadership Award in 1956. But by that time, I was a freshman in college and so frightened that I wouldn't do well there that I didn't return home to accept my medal in person. I've always regretted it.

Rural life is exalted in so much literature as a paradise, a place of innocent pleasures and unrestricted joy, where the inhabitants are honest, sober, and moral and live free of all the ambiguities, complexities, and corruption of so-called modern life while enjoying an ecstatic and continuing communion with nature. This is romantic rubbish, originating in European romanticism, especially in Germany, and taken up by various strains in America and other cultures.

Hamlin Garland in *Son of the Middle Border*, Emile Zola in *Earth*, and Thomas Hardy in *Far From the Madding Crowd* and *Jude the Obscure* provide far more realistic accounts of rural life. It is, or at least it can be, to steal from Thomas Hobbes, nasty, short, and brutish. Perhaps an even better fictional depiction of rural life in America is Ole Edvart Rolvaag's *Giants in the Earth: A Saga of the Prairie*, the tale of a Norwegian family struggling with the land in the Dakotas in the 19th century. This Norwegian American writer

(1876–1931) was a realistic chronicler of the lives of Norwegian immigrants on the farms. Granted his work is pessimistic, but nonetheless powerful due to its realism.

Life on an Iowa farm, as I experienced it in the 1940s and 1950s, was not impoverished. We had all the food we could eat. Dai Sil never tired of telling me that our food was a king's food in Korea. "All that meat, to begin with!" Though we tilled other people's land, we were never hungry, never threatened by man-made evil, and able to live in relative peace. By no means did rural life in America equate with peasant life in Europe, Asia, Africa, and elsewhere where much great poverty, despair, and cultural isolation were the norm. We had adequate clothing, furniture, household supplies—and generally good enough education, for farmers.

Despite the fact that I fled at the first possible opportunity, I have to admit there were a few positive aspects to rural life—I had the chance to shine in practical, concrete ways and I enjoyed the closeness of farm families and the sense of community and caring for others. I am not sure that an urban upbringing would have provided the same benefit in those regards. I could not quite articulate it then, but in hindsight, I believe what made me feel most stifled was the cultural isolation, the absence of intellectual stimulation, and a lack of contact with ideas and other cultures.

*Between 1953 and 1962 (when I left Korea for America),
our family moved from one rented room to another so many
times that it is impossible to remember them all. I would prefer
to be lost in the folds of an ever more evanescent past, rather
than remember all those crowded rooms. However, it is still palpable for me what I longed for in those dark nights, the silence
broken only by the rough breathing of my siblings in sleep: our
North Korean home that we left at the crack of dawn in 1945.
Strangely enough, that is what I craved in my soul, more so than
our home in Seoul bombed by the United States and Republic of
Korea. Of all the rooms in which our family lived, there was one
in Wang Sib Ri, a lower-middle-class neighborhood in Seoul,
that I can't forget because of my maternal grandmother who died
there. I believe we lived in that room for a few years. I recall
how my father was always engaged in urgent whispers with the
landlord, no doubt trying to persuade him to sell the house and
go into business with him. My father had been destroyed by the
war, never again able to find a way to use his business acumen.*

~ D S K-G

*The Gibson family at the farm: Don on his father's arm and David
holding his mother's hand*

Clockwise from top left: David and Don with Mom; Don, age 2, at the water pump; Dad reading ; seventh birthday; and at 11 years of age in 1949

Don at about 12 years old

From the top: Four friends in 1956; working hard for the 4-H Club in Tennant; back on the farm in 1962 with foster sister and her friend

Graduating with an MA from the University of Iowa, 1967

Indianola, 1956

PART III

From American Way to American Dream

From Cornfields to Simpson College

As my high school days were drawing to a close, perhaps by the end of my junior year or most certainly by early senior year, I knew that I had to leave home and strike out on my own. But where to? The only guiding star was my fierce desire to learn more about history and humanity. So the thought occurred that perhaps I should go to college.

Being the first person in my family to do so, I didn't know much about how to proceed. There was one kid from Tennant, a couple of years ahead of me, Donald Plumb, who everyone thought was brilliant in science. He had gone to college. But his parents were rich, engaged in a hybrid corn operation. I wasn't brilliant in science. I wasn't even that much interested in science. And my parents were not rich. So what was I thinking? What kind of education beyond high school was I seeking? And to what end?

In search of meaning and purpose, and in the absence of anything else, I gravitated toward religious fundamentalism. In my final months of high school, I became hyperactive in the Methodist Youth Fellowship. In a frenzy of energy, I organized the Easter sunrise youth services, and initiated a bulletin board at the church full of constantly changing, religious admonitions. Still just a kid, I sought and obtained a lay preacher's license from the Methodist Church and delivered three sermons in Tennant and one in Shelby, a much bigger town (500 people as opposed to ninety-five). The idea came to me that if I chose the ministry, it would provide both a means of escape and an end for which to strive. It was settled in my mind. I would go to college to become a minister.

Selecting a school was easy. I knew of one only, because I had attended Methodist youth camp there the previous summer— Simpson College, a Methodist Church–affiliated school located in Indianola. I never visited any other campus. I didn't send away for college brochures, never consulted a guidance counselor (we didn't have any). The thought of another college never crossed my mind. The concept that entranced me was *college* itself, pure and simple. College equaled escape. Simpson was not competitive. There were no arduous entrance exams, high school grades sufficed. My parents and I never even discussed any of this. They accepted my decision and had no advice to offer.

I enrolled at Simpson in the fall of 1956 with the full intention of becoming a minister in the Methodist Church.

My parents didn't drive me to college. I rode along with a girl from Harlan, Linda Hammes, who was also starting at Simpson. Her parents drove us to Indianola. It was not that my mom and dad were not interested. I had just entered a world about which they knew nothing, and they felt there was no way they could help me. I wrote them often that freshman year and even sent them copies of the college newspaper, *The Simpsonian*, which I'm certain meant nothing to them.

I lived in what was called the freshman dorm my first semester, a plain structure of no architectural interest whatsoever. My room-mate was a fellow named Charles Burton, who came from a small town—though much larger than mine—in southern Iowa. He too aspired to be a Methodist minister and perhaps that is why they assigned us together to this miserably small room, measuring perhaps eight-by-ten feet, with one closet and the bathroom far down the hall. I didn't mind the close quarters. It was simply a totally new experience, just like about everything else at college.

After twelve years in a single building that housed all twelve grades, here I was on an actual campus with separate buildings for separate activities. The very idea of that expanded my imagination. Every single day, some event or observation, large, small, or in between, widened my horizons. I was like a sponge, soaking up ideas and impressions.

Still, that first semester was harrowing. I was convinced I would flunk out, that I wouldn't pass muster. Many nights I couldn't sleep at all or would wake up drenched in sweat. So when first semester grades were released and I received a 2.8 GPA, I was elated. The grades were posted on the door of the dorm counselor's room for all to see. Relief flooded through me. I had feared Ds and Fs. Maybe, just maybe, I was cut out for the life of the mind after all.

Simpson had a core curriculum called the Vital Center, which had been introduced by the president, William Kerstetter, a few years earlier. It required all students, before declaring a major, to take a prescribed set of courses: western civilization, Far Eastern thought and culture, philosophy, psychology, and introductory science. It was a marvelous idea, and that introduction to various disciplines and ways of thinking was something I really needed. I think we all do. I strongly believe that a broadly based liberal arts education is the best possible preparation for life and work.

I augmented the core curriculum with a German language course, having been advised that German would be helpful were I to pursue the ministry. I also added a second elective, called Introduction to the Ministry. And I enthusiastically joined the college Methodist Student Movement (MSM) and became a counselor for a youth group at a rural church a few miles from Indianola.

That 2.8 GPA filled me with enough confidence that, by my second semester, I looked beyond the classroom and began to take an enthusiastic interest in extracurricular activities. In the spring, I played Chaplain de Stogumber in the campus production of George Bernard Shaw's *Saint Joan*. My parents actually came to see me in the role. The theater critic from the local paper dubbed me "a promising newcomer," and I was inducted into the Blackfriars campus theater group. I also started writing for the school newspaper.

Then I joined a fraternity, Sigma Alpha Epsilon (SAE), but not for very good reasons, I must admit. It seemed the thing to do if one wanted to avoid being seen as a nerd. During my sophomore year, I lived in the frat house and even attended an SAE national convention in Oklahoma City. The 1950s were the height of the Greek craze on college campuses. I tried to fit in, but failed. Life there was entirely social—there was nothing intellectual, no late-night bull sessions on ideas. The most intellectual the fraternity ever became was in maintaining files of previous tests and written reports. Certain professors were known to use the same exam and essay questions repeatedly and the fraternity dutifully filed and provided them to members. I just thought that was unfair. Yes, I was naïve. And also a nerd, I guess, at least in that sense.

I also became disillusioned when I discovered the fraternity's inherent and explicit, if deceptively defended, racism. When I raised the question about admitting blacks, I was told that SAE did not exclude any groups and the only rule was that a person had to be socially acceptable throughout the fraternity. That meant, as I quickly figured out, that a person had to be socially acceptable in the Deep South, since SAE was national. I was disgusted, even felt a bit betrayed. It took me a few years to realize the full extent of my revulsion.

Finally, I resigned from the fraternity, though I learned that doing so was not so simple. You couldn't just quit. There had to be a trial under official rules. The resigning member had to be officially excluded or rejected by SAE. After all, no member would voluntarily leave the brotherhood. In Evanston, Illinois, at SAE headquarters, there was a large book that held all official records. On the page listing ousted members, the word EXPELLED is stamped in huge, red letters. I am on that list and am proud of it.

So for better and for worse, intentionally and also inadvertently, my undergraduate years were largely ones of experimenting with ideas, exploring other ways of thinking, and beginning to define and refine my own philosophy and values in life.

This was all for the good. My college experience, however, had a major consequence—it rather quickly undermined my resolve to enter the ministry. I recall when I was new at Simpson walking eagerly to the dormitory lounge to watch a Billy Graham television crusade. (TV was then still relatively new.) Already, just a few months into my college education, doubts were beginning to surface. I didn't say anything to those around me, but I knew inside that my new life with its new vistas was beginning to erode what I had thought I believed. It was my course in western civilization, perhaps more than any other, that gradually moved me far away from any ministerial thoughts. In that class, I learned about the Greeks, the Romans, medieval society, the Enlightenment, the scientific revolution, the Renaissance, and the Reformation. Those ideas, movements, and events were totally beyond anything I had ever thought, heard, or dreamed of. I was transformed, but also more than mildly confused. Too much change was happening too fast in my head.

In my sophomore and junior years, a small group of us tried to establish something more intellectual in our lives. We started meeting in the old chapel building in a room on the second floor that had several ragged easy chairs and an equally ragged sofa. But we thought it was appropriately cerebral and sophisticated, *à la* New York City's Greenwich Village, which none of us had ever laid eyes on, of course.

George Washington Carver had attended Simpson (1890–1891) and took art classes on the third floor of that same chapel building. That floor was closed, but one afternoon after ascertaining that nobody was watching, I mounted the stairs, albeit with some fear. True confession: I had to break through a door to get in. There was, of course, no trace of Carver, just a lot of accumulated dust and abandoned shelves and crumbling books. But it was a precious, almost sacred, few moments for me. I felt I was alone with the spirit of one of the great African Americans, nay, one of the great Americans.

Carver once said, "At Simpson, I learned that I was a human being." In a far different sense, so did I. I learned that I was, or could be, an intellectual being. And our little band of brothers—unlike my fraternity brothers—was crucial to that awakening. There were three of us: Wayne Osborne, David Allyn, and me. We would designate a topic and invite some faculty members to join us for discussions. It wasn't especially well organized, but it taught me that I could engage with my professors on relatively equal terms, and that I possessed the intelligence to grapple in a meaningful way with scholarly topics. What a revelation. It was huge for me in my evolving sense of who I was as a human being.

Freed from Ministry

THE ONLY RELIGIOUS FIGURES I KNEW about when I entered college were Billy Graham, Norman Vincent Peale, and Billy James Hargis. These men allowed no room for ambiguity, or for the excitement of discovery and argumentation. They were dogmatic about their absolute certitude, the absence of any grey areas, the belief that there is only one answer to any and all questions. No room for debate or indecision or even reflection. And all of those answers, of course, could be found, must be found, in the revealed truth in the Bible, especially the New Testament.

Increasingly, the idea of revealed truth struck me as incompatible with what we as humans knew and could know. I could not accept the literal reading of the scriptures as absolute truth. During my years of religious enthusiasm as a teenager, I had read the Bible over and over again with ardor, often by flashlight under the covers after my parents had decreed lights out. Now in college, as I reflected upon my reading, I saw too many seeming contradictions and verses open to interpretation, though I certainly couldn't call myself a Biblical scholar. I began to see the scriptures as poetry, allegory, parable—insightful, evocative, and truthful, for sure, but not the dictates of an omniscient and omnipotent God.

More and more, I came to see the religion that I had known, the religion I grew up with, that I went off to college with, as narrow, pietistic, and hostile to the inquiry, experimentation, and free thinking that I now so urgently sought. Had I become acquainted with Paul Tillich, Reinhold Niebuhr, Dietrich Bonhoeffer, or others of that ilk, those who were not afraid to make Biblical messages relevant and applicable to the human mind and condition, I might have seen it differently.

During my sophomore year I received an invitation from the divinity school at Northwestern University to attend a two-day, all-expense-paid meeting for pre-ministerial undergraduate students. I accepted with some enthusiasm. For one thing, it was my first time on an airplane. Also it was a chance to visit Chicago, a real big city. Once there, I met a fellow SAE member and we ended up at a Northwestern frat party, replete with sports and drinking. I enjoyed the beer and toasted my friends several times. However, I did not feel at home with all those pre-ministerial friends and activities. On the last evening, I walked out to the end of a dock on Lake Michigan and sat on the edge alone, deep in thought, immersed in the water, the sky, and my own future. I decided once and for all that this was not the path for me.

My mother was extremely disappointed that I wasn't going to pursue my ministerial ambitions. I was never able to explain to her why I changed my mind. Well, I could have, I guess, but not in terms that she was ready to accept. Then again, perhaps here as elsewhere, I underestimated my mother.

So I left religion and never looked back. Decades later, after I was married, working for the federal government, and living in DC, I was sifting through old papers one day when I came upon a forgotten letter I had received in 1957 from Walter Muelder, dean of the School of Theology at Boston University (BU). I was still a pre-ministry student then, and Muelder was writing to urge me to consider BU for divinity school. In the small world department, several years after he wrote me, Muelder was Dai Sil's mentor. And twenty-two years after that letter, he performed our wedding ceremony at his Massachusetts home. I could not believe this amazingly coincidental link between Dai Sil and me. I couldn't help but wonder—had I in fact gone to theology school in Boston in the 1960s while Dai Sil was there pursuing her PhD, would anything have developed between us then? Or were we simply destined to meet at a later stage of our life? I wrote Dean Muelder and enclosed a copy of his letter. I told him how I very nearly entered the ministry, and why I rejected it. He wrote back that he thought I was a victim of fundamental Christianity. Maybe ministry was not meant for me. I never really had the calling.

I did have strong feelings about paying for my own education. It was important to me that I be as independent as possible. My older brother received quite a lot of financial support from my parents. But then he stayed on the farm and followed the family tradition. College was something else, beyond their understanding. So other than a few loans from them that I later repaid, I was on my own and felt comfortable with that.

The summer before college, I worked for the Squealer Feed Company in Harlan in order to earn money for tuition, room, and board. That was my first job off the farm. I operated a forklift, moving pallets of feed sacks. Once a week I'd drive a truck to the rendering plant a few miles away and scoop processed meat into it. A rendering plant is a disgusting place where unmarketable livestock (cattle and hogs) are boiled and then ground into a fine powder, which is used for feed supplements. Usually, the animals had died from one disease or another. I found that somewhat worrisome, but I confess that I never protested to anyone in authority.

During the school year, I waited tables at the college and took odd jobs such as helping movers load and unload furniture. I remember one embarrassing moment. I'd been called by a moving company to help them out on short notice. I ran right over and pitched in. Things were going pretty well and then the back of my pants split completely open. I just kept on carrying furniture and endured the stares from the family. I needed the bucks.

The following summers, I worked for Western Engineering, a road construction company based in Harlan, on jobs that had me traveling to sites throughout western and northern Iowa. Because I was a farm boy, the supervisors assumed, sometimes mistakenly, that I could handle all kinds of earthmoving equipment. So I drove trucks, operated front-end loaders, and manhandled a dirt-packing machine called a sheep's foot. Western Engineering constructed asphalt roads. The work was physically demanding and once the job nearly killed me—because I fell asleep operating some sort of road-building implement and hurtled down a thirty-foot embankment, barely missing a much deeper crevice.

That happened in 1958. After that, I was scared to go back to work, but I did on the strength of what my father had done for me a year before. Driving my father's Model A Ford, I had rolled it end over end, and the county sheriff told me at the scene of accident that I should be dead. But more than anything else, what I carried away from that potentially fatal accident was what my father did. Arriving at the scene, he simply asked me, his eyes full of concern, not anger, "Are you okay?" Then he took me to the car he came in and, as I was about to sit on a passenger seat, said, "No, you drive" and threw me the car key. That memory enabled me to go right back to work.

Road construction was long hours and low pay, a nonunion operation. But at least I was able to earn enough to pay for most of my college expenses. The men were a rough but jovial lot and I was teasingly (and, on occasion, resentfully) labeled the college boy. I didn't much mind. In fact, it was a valuable experience. True, I had worked plenty hard on the farm, yet this was my first experience of what it meant to be part of the working class. With one big difference, of course—I was a short-timer. Come fall, the other men were still on the job, while for me, it was back to college and loftier aspirations.

A Turning Point

AN UNEXPECTED TURNING POINT IN MY EDUCATION came with one of my required classes, Thought and Culture of the Far East, taught by a retired Foreign Service officer named Clayton Lane. It was one of those big lecture courses with over 100 kids. About a third of the way through the term, Lane gave us an essay test. A week later, he entered the lecture hall loaded down with our blue books and proceeded to berate us for forty-five minutes about our lousy writing, our ignorance, our abysmal essays. He ended his tirade by noting that two essays stood out from the dismal pack and were, in fact, quite brilliant, erudite, insightful, and exceptionally well written. Knowing that couldn't be me, I sat forlorn, hoping I hadn't flunked. Finally, he announced the authors' names and mine was one of them. That moment utterly transformed me. I felt as if the load of inferiority I had over coming from rural Iowa had been lifted. I had been set free to march toward my own future, which was mine to create.

A short time later, Lane asked me to work as his research assistant, and he subsequently arranged for me to study for a semester in DC, my first trip outside the Midwest.

Thus, slowly, steadily, gradually, my college education took me, as it has so many others, on a fateful journey from the American way of my youth to my own version of the American dream. Mine was a childhood, you see, that had been largely immune from any concrete sense of the dream. Our vistas didn't stretch far beyond the horizon we could already see. We were indoctrinated with an essentially passive acceptance of the goodness, the rightness of the American way, whatever that meant.

Walking around the nation's capital, awed and inspired by its architecture and ideals, I was drawn to the notion that, as an American, I should be part of not only a personal, but also a national dream—one accessible to all of us—and that I should pursue a life course for its realization. The importance of political awareness started to stir my consciousness, binding individual dreams to that of society as a whole. I came to realize that I could not and should not isolate my welfare from that of my fellow citizens.

This was quite a revelation to me. Certainly politics had no significance in my childhood. They barely registered in my consciousness. I knew that my Republican parents voted against FDR every time he ran, four times in total. But I was too young, born in 1938, to have any recollection of that. Republican or Democrat, politics and politicians were not a topic for daily conversation in our household. My father once told me that the only good program the federal government ever concocted was the New Deal's Rural Electrification Administration. (The grid didn't reach rural Iowa until 1946.)

My earliest overt political memory occurred in November 1948, the day after the presidential election. I recall quite vividly asking the school-bus driver who had won. He said Truman and I was disappointed. But my interest was more like curiosity about the outcome of a sporting event than any real concern about public policy or the direction of the country. I knew that my parents didn't like Truman much, so that was the side I took.

A few days later, standing outside our farmhouse, my father commented that the American people had made a great mistake.

"Why don't we take it back?" I asked, believing naturally enough that my father would surely have the power to manage that.

"No," my father said, "the American people have made a mistake, but they must live with it."

I, of course, had no understanding of repeal or recall or anything else about our American political system, but that may have been my first lesson in democracy—that we should participate and also accept the consequences.

During my first semester at Simpson, still emulating my parents, I considered myself a Republican and even participated in a torchlight parade for Eisenhower. I thought I liked Ike, and proudly wore a couple of I Like Ike campaign buttons. But as my American dream evolved over the next few years, inextricably related to my intellectual pursuits, I became a Democrat. Why? Partially, it was simply the discovery of the amazing world of ideas, of cultural expression, of diversity, all of which seemed to me the diametric opposite of my isolated rural childhood. I was entranced for a time with the thought that being sophisticated meant being Democratic. Not a good enough reason, but I cannot deny that wanting to be sophisticated was part of it.

Reading and learning more about American history in college helped shape my newly discovered political philosophy. I studied the presidency of FDR and the expanded role assumed by the federal government in efforts to achieve a just society. I began to question the idea that America was, in John Winthrop's words, a city upon a hill, a new, different kind of nation that stood in stark contrast to the corruption of Europe.

The truth is, Americans had it easy, or that's how I saw it. This was a largely empty continent that we invaded and then we set about exterminating much of the native population. We were largely free from external threats. We could establish a new society without any feudal past or other historical constraints. To paraphrase

Winston Churchill, never has so much been given to so few as has been given to Americans. A vast open land with enormous natural resources, and only a few Indians to subjugate and kill along with the importation of many Africans to enslave and exploit.

I still remember how pained I was to read in detail about the awful and enduring racial injustice that seemed endemic in our society. At first, it made no sense. I truly could not grasp how and why race should be such a cause of division and strife. But deeper study finally made it manifestly clear. And also made me manifestly angry. Inevitably, I came to realize that enormous race sins had been perpetrated against Native Americans and African Americans, and these sins were compounded by the corrupting influence of wealth and economic and social disparity. The way I saw it, we created oppression and then used its results to justify further exploitation. This was nowhere close to what I believed the American dream to be.

The issues of civil rights were definitely the first step in my political evolution. I never personally met an African American until I went to college. None lived in my home county. During my teens, I'd been in Omaha a few times and seen the massive stockyards, with cattle in tiny pens waiting to be slaughtered and sold to the highest bidder. I later learned that only African Americans were hired to kill the animals. In 1954 when I was a sophomore in high school, the news reported *Brown* v. *Board of Education*, the landmark Supreme Court case that mandated integration of public schools. As a junior, I heard about the murder of Emmett Till in Mississippi in 1955. To a farm boy who had a natural belief that all human beings were equal, the news was shocking and frightening. What is going on? I was stunned, confused.

There was no one I could talk to about any of this. No one I knew seemed to share my interest, my concern, my fury. Many years later, my dad told me that he himself had seen hooded members of the Ku Klux Klan in Logan (the county seat) gathered to take a stand against Catholics as well as Negroes. He also told me how a group of young men in Portsmouth in 1917 painted the names of so-called slackers on buildings in town, supposedly because they weren't fighting in the war against Germany. But Dad thought the real reason was because slackers were German. Portsmouth had a large German population, mostly from the Rhineland, meaning they were also Catholic. Equal opportunity prejudice. (I still recall the date, September 5, 2003, when Dad told me of these events during my nightly phone call to him, but I failed to ask him when all this happened. My guess is that it was in the 1920s.)

I remember that while I was at Simpson, on a visit home one weekend I attended Sunday School at my mother's Methodist church and responded—adamantly, but quite calmly—to a teacher's remark that Negroes were inferior. The following day the Sunday school superintendent drove all the way out to our farm to hand me a stack of about eight books. "These demonstrate," he declared, "that the inferiority of Negroes is clearly proclaimed in the Bible." My parents were appalled and embarrassed. My mother, in particular, felt that I had shamed the family. I never even glanced at those books, let alone read them. Now I kind of wish I could remember at least their titles. I'd be mighty curious to see the minister's sources.

With so much explicit prejudice on my home turf, it required immersion in a world beyond the cornfields of Iowa to transform my life. The transformation took root at Simpson, my small Methodist college. Simpson College not only changed my worldview, but actually defined my life, charted its course, and put me on the road to decades of political activism. Though I did not have the kind of direct experience of war that Dai Sil had to endure, there were other kinds of wars within America in which I became heavily involved.

By the time I walked down the aisle to receive my diploma at Simpson, I had not completed the task of becoming the person I wanted to be, but I had come a long way, a great deal farther than I could have imagined just four years earlier. College literally opened my eyes and was in a very real sense the beginning of my life, or at least my life as a thinking, sentient, and sensitized human being.

By 1960, I had become enough of a liberal that, during the presidential primary season, I considered John F. Kennedy too conservative and cast my lot with Hubert Humphrey. I cried with Humphrey when he lost the West Virginia primary. I couldn't abide Richard Nixon, of course, and eventually was won over by Kennedy, for whom I voted in November 1960, the first election in which I was eligible to vote. JFK's stirring inaugural address instilled in me, as in so many others, a fervent commitment to public service as a vital way of joining in the pursuit of the American dream. And that is something I have never lost.

I was deeply into what our missionaries tried to instill in us: for the sufferings of this world, glory in heaven. I literally summoned the image of heaven with all its splendors. And yet, the more I learned about Christian teachings, the more my mind began to rebel. How could such an omnipotent and omniscient God allow so much evil in the world? I swam in an endless sea of confusion, trying to grasp a straw that I could hang onto. But no answers were forthcoming from the church pulpit, nor from the adults around me who pushed blind faith in God. After I graduated from Ewha High School, I persuaded myself that going to the Methodist Seminary would enable me to wrestle with my doubts. I convinced myself that I was taking a path loftier than philosophy—theology—to encounter God in the depths of myself, and to demand answers for the world he created, even while clinging to Him for love and protection.

~ *D S K-G*

Don in the sixties

PART IV

Into the World

∽

My First Job

IN MAY 1960, WITH COLLEGE GRADUATION JUST DAYS AWAY, I was clearly in the camp of the undecided when it came to my immediate future. I variously applied to the Navy's Officer Candidate School, to graduate school at Kent State University in Ohio (only because I knew a professor there), and for several different high school teaching positions. The Navy accepted me and I was ordered to appear at Newport News, Rhode Island on July 5. I also received a job offer from Andrew High School, just south of Dubuque. Kent State said yes as well. I had really thought none of it through. I was just flailing around.

Joining the Navy would have committed me for four years, and I was way too uncertain about what I wanted to do with my life to tie myself down like that. Nor did I feel ready for the rigors of graduate school. But I did rather like the idea of an adult job and finding out if I really wanted to teach. So I headed east, or at least as far as eastern Iowa. In retrospect, it was the absolute correct course. But I can't take much credit; a lot of it was dumb luck.

Andrew was a town of roughly 300 souls, heavily dependent on agriculture for its survival, with a handful of stores scattered along its lone main street. Located south of Dubuque, a few miles from the county seat of Maquoketa and north of Clinton, it was the hometown of Ansel Briggs, the first governor of Iowa in the mid-19th century. That was its sole claim to fame, but a pretty good one. I could see Briggs's small, oblique tombstone from my classroom window. The school had about 100 students and ten faculty members. I became friendly with the principal, Dean Penney, the coach Keith Brown, and the music teacher whose name I no longer recall. At the urging of Dean and Keith, I joined a bowling league with them and their wives—and I competed reasonably well.

There was one other first-year teacher, whose name I've also forgotten, but he didn't last the year due to some kind of unexplained mental illness. We first met at a picnic in late August to welcome new faculty, which was held on a farm just outside the town. I liked him as well as his wife, but apparently he was so frightened of standing in front of a room of teenagers that he just folded. His wife made a spectacular Hungarian pastry and I spent a few pleasant evenings at their house. His collapse sobered me, but I also found strength in it. He was as young and inexperienced as me, but I persevered.

The music teacher quit as well, going off to sell life insurance. Wish I could remember his name, but I recollect well spending election night 1960 at his home in Maquoketa watching the returns. We were all keyed up because we badly wanted Kennedy to win, but it was so close that, when I finally decided I had to leave at 2:00 in the morning, the result was still unknown. I was only twenty-two years old, but I was exhausted and had to teach four classes the next day. Thank goodness, before I left for school in the morning, I learned the happy news. It felt mighty momentous.

I was assigned to teach four subjects: U.S. government, American history, world history, and German. The most challenging of the lot was German. I'd had a total of three classes in college—that was it—and not a single course on instructional methods. I didn't know the first thing about teaching a foreign language and ordered a textbook that I subsequently learned was frightfully out of date. I knew no methodology whatsoever. The textbook was even written in Gothic script, which I later discovered had been banned in Germany after the fall of Nazism. Oh well.

I also kept score at school basketball games, chaperoned a hayride, organized a mock election in the gym for the Nixon-Kennedy race, cataloged the tiny school library with the help of some student volunteers, and delivered the commencement address.

I thought a teacher was supposed to teach from textbooks, so I was tied to them. Plus I didn't really have the time to prepare anything fresh or different, had I even been so inclined. But over the course of that year, I came to despise those books. They were just plain boring, based upon the expectation that pupils were to take in facts and regurgitate them. That was it. Any kind of reflection or analysis was discouraged. The excitement of ideas, the pure love of learning—these values weren't exactly anathema, but also they simply weren't a consideration. This couldn't be right.

So out of necessity, I began to develop a kind of educational philosophy of my own. By my second term, my students received an impassioned lecture that expressed disdain for textbooks and proposed an alternative route to serious and stimulating learning by escaping the stultifying, old-style approach to curriculum. I revised and devised all my own methods. I learned how to say "I don't know" in response to a question from a student. And then to ask, "How do we find out? Where do we look? What sources are there?" That was a critically important lesson and one that I have used ever since. And an amazing thing happened. I began to genuinely enjoy teaching, and at least some of my students began to flourish.

Nonetheless, I did flunk three of them in government, an apparently unheard of action. I was asked by the principal, gently and firmly, to teach a special summer session to see if they could pass. The clear message was that they should pass. I complied and they did. But the entire experience was new to me. I felt ambivalent and even confused and wondered about life ahead. What more challenges and conflicts will be waiting for me?

Well, I experienced a similar event soon enough. I boarded in a single-parent household—a working-class mother with two high school age children. I had a small room, paid a small rent, and largely felt comfortable there. The daughter, the youngest of three siblings, was also in the 8th grade. She was a lazy and noisy student who rarely studied, did mediocre work, and talked constantly. I gave her a D in deportment (yes, those grades were required back then). The morning after the grades were released, I was subjected to a loud and abusive tirade from her mother at the breakfast table.

In the end, if I were to evaluate my own performance as a novice teacher, I guess I would have to say that I was not especially effective. I was just too inexperienced and would have benefited from some expert guidance and perhaps some training in pedagogy. I worked hard and may have helped a few kids. But I was green, very green and ill-prepared, but also genuinely eager. Meager skill, great attitude. But in that one year, I learned a lot. I learned I had the potential to be a quite good teacher and that I enjoyed it. It brought me true joy to watch a student catch an idea and run with it, play with it.

During that year in Andrew, I felt as if I became an adult. I earned $4,000, and bought a car from my father, a 1957 Ford—a big deal for me.

Two weeks after the school term ended and a month after I'd signed a contract to teach again the following year (at a whopping annual salary increase from $4,000 to $4,200), I was cataloging books in the school library when I was summoned to the office to receive a phone call. It was from Joe Walt, my mentor at Simpson. He was calling to offer me a teaching position at Indianola High School. I was thrown into an agony of indecision. I was thrilled at the prospect of leaving sleepy Andrew and returning to a college town with more intellectual, social, and cultural excitement, but I had signed a contract. What was my ethical obligation?

I was in desperate need to consult someone. The only person who came to mind was Reverend Elwin D. Farwell, who was now in California. I had met him in Andrew, where he was a local Lutheran pastor, and was impressed. He had spent several years as an agricultural missionary in Latin America and Andrew was his first pastoral assignment. We met because he attended my German class. He then invited me for dinner and we became friendly, if not friends. I was pleased for him when, in the early spring of 1961, he was appointed as the first dean of the college at the new California Lutheran College in Thousand Oaks, California.

Well, I called Reverend Farwell for advice. He immediately recognized my dilemma. But he assured me that the people at Andrew High School would understand my need to go to Indianola, though they would be sorry to lose me. After all, he said, contracts exist for people, not the other way around. He urged me to accept the job in Indianola. That is the only time in my life that I have sought counsel from a clergyman. Looking back, I suspect he was advanced enough in his thinking to embrace what was to be called situational ethics.

Reverend Farwell helped me to realize that I was a young man starting out my life with the door open for exploration. Put in that light, I could see the cons of living and working in a community so shockingly similar to the one I had escaped. I could have stayed, could have become a solid and respected citizen, probably would have eventually been appointed superintendent of schools. But no, I thought, there must be something more. And although that "more" was likely rooted in personal ego and ambition, rather than any commitment to help my fellow human beings, I convinced myself I could do more good in the world if I found a way to paint on a larger canvas. How many other times did I make that decision for those reasons? Even now, I realize how difficult it is to distinguish between personal ambition and a desire to serve the larger society.

Indianola High School

SO OFF I WENT TO INDIANOLA, and there I indeed learned how to teach and to love doing it. Once again, I taught world history and German, and also a course called social studies, the intended content of which baffled me—something about teenagers and adjustment. I was quite miserable teaching social studies. Thankfully, the assignment lasted only one year.

But if social studies confounded me, I both adored and excelled at world history. During my first couple of years, I relied too much on so-called objective tests that use true/false and multiple choice questions. But I quickly learned that those types of exams encourage students to simply memorize and regurgitate facts, rather than engage in what we now call critical thinking. My goal was to explore the "why" of history, the questions of cause and effect. And also to emphasize that history didn't have to turn out the way it did. "Nothing is inevitable," Eric Foner once wrote, "until it has happened." That statement is absolutely crucial to my conception of teaching history. And its opposite is precisely the great failing of so much secondary-school instruction.

I began to use essay exams almost exclusively, including an invention of my own—the one-sentence essay. I would pose a broad question and demand that they answer it in just one sentence. That produced some ridiculously long and awkward constructions, but I was trying to teach students how to home in on the key point and how to deploy topic sentences. One of the compliments I received with some frequency from former students—and one which makes me proud—was that I had taught them how to write. I also made frequent use of chronological-order questions, where I would ask students to place four or five historical events in the correct order. I wasn't asking for dates (I promised at the beginning of each course that I would never ask for a year, a month, or a day). Rather, this was another way of getting them to think about cause and effect. The Crusades, for example, helped lead to the discovery of America by Columbus.

Of course, not all facts are equal. For example, I would tell my students, that the first president of the United States, technically speaking, was John Hansen. He was president of the first assembly of delegates convened under the Articles of Confederation. It was a one-year term and the president had almost no authority. So being the first president wasn't meaningful in the sense that we normally accord such meaning, and it isn't worth noting, or certainly not emphasizing.

Though I didn't read Milan Kundera at the time, I recently came across what he wrote about the fog of history in his essay "Paths in the Fog," which is included in a collection of essays, *Testament Betrayed*.

> Man proceeds in the fog. But when he looks back to judge people of the past, he sees no fog on their path. From his present, which was their faraway future, their path looks perfectly clear to him, good visibility all the way. Looking back, he sees the path, he sees the people proceeding, he sees their mistakes but not the fog.

That captures part of what I was trying to convey in teaching history.

During my first year teaching in Indianola, I concluded that the school's world history textbook was not only inadequate, but also strongly undermined the thrust of my instruction. I talked to the principal, Louis Smith, and asked if I could simply dispense with the book. I offered to personally buy, from my own funds, what I considered to be more relevant books (in paperback to keep the cost low). Smith was reluctant, understandably I suppose, and proposed a compromise. I would hand out the textbooks to students at the beginning of the term, but I could then announce that nobody had to read them. That was acceptable, and so we agreed.

Just what was wrong with the textbook? you may wonder. Well, let's put it this way. Its only positive features, from my perspective, were the large and colorful illustrations. The narrative was superficial and sketchy and it emphasized nothing beyond the memorization of facts. There was no sense whatsoever of alternative interpretations or competing responses to the question "why?" that was so central to my approach.

To underscore my emphasis upon analysis and interpretation, I would open each term of my world history classes with a lecture on historiography, essentially the philosophy of history, comparing and contrasting how different historians such as Marx, Toynbee, and Gibbon, among others, would interpret macro history. I would also point out how religious, environmental, and geopolitical approaches could shape one's view of history. Then I'd explore with the class how history can be influenced by both personal and impersonal forces. I warned them against the Rationalistic Fallacy, the assumption that historical events are determined primarily by human reason. "Sloth and ineptitude," I argued, "have much to do with the unfolding of history." And I loved citing Hans Zinsser's delightful book, *Rats, Lice, and History*. It was Zinsser's belief that disease and plagues have had a profound and largely ignored impact on the course of human events.

The students responded to my lecture remarkably well. At various points throughout the term, I would ask them to consider how the period we were then studying might be interpreted by one of the historians I had initially mentioned. Lively discussions often ensued. I wanted to stress that history is a matter of interpretation, but not that it is entirely subjective. There are rules of evidence.

I also introduced them to the German concept of weltanschauung, meaning worldview or the way one sees, perceives, and comprehends the world. I wanted them to realize the importance of trying to comprehend how various peoples viewed the world, from their limited perspective. I wanted them to understand that their own limited perspective as young people in the 20th-century American heartland was not universal. How did the Greeks, the Romans, or the Native Americans view the world? How was their understanding of the world different than ours, and why?

To my (pleasant) surprise, it turned out that I was popular enough that a small group of students, seven or eight, asked me to teach a reading seminar during the summer. We met once a week at the school to read and discuss such heady tomes as Plato's *Republic* and Erich Fromm's *May Man Prevail?* I wasn't paid, nor did I expect to be. For the most part, the parents were greatly appreciative.

I have to confess that the one area where I didn't fulfill my prescribed duties was in preparing advance lesson plans. Those were required, I presume, both to induce the teacher to plan ahead and to provide a blueprint for a substitute teacher, should one be required. Lesson plans were due at the end of the term. So I'd spend the last week making up plans for what I'd taught the previous four months.

To be sure, I had detractors. I was denounced at a local meeting of the John Birch Society for failing to bow my head during a prayer meeting at a parent/teacher banquet. There was some considerable grumbling over the fact that I taught about religions other than Christianity, and also that I presented the theory of evolution as part of the intellectual history of the 19th century.

I have two favorite stories from my days at Indianola High. At the end of one school year, I handed out the requisite forms that asked students to evaluate their teachers. Their responses were, as usual, quite positive because kids understandably believe that a negative appraisal might be used against them. The forms were anonymous, but one girl insisted upon signing her name anyway. She planned to study medicine, and she was, apparently, quite accomplished in math and science but seemed to have great difficulty with the ambiguity of history. She wrote, "I hope Mr. Gibson is my patient sometime and I will cut his tubes." Indelicate, but convincing.

Then there was the time at the end of one first semester, when the guidance counselor informed me that she had urged a boy named Tommy, who was flunking world history, to switch to a different course for second semester. It was certainly true that the way I taught it, world history was an exceedingly tough class, virtually college preparatory, though not officially acknowledged as such. But Tommy insisted he didn't want to switch. "Why on earth not?" the counselor pleaded. "Well, Mr. Gibson is so excited about something. I just want to find out what it is." I raised his grade.

Indianola was a magnificent experience for me. To this day, I sometimes think that the most important thing I've ever done professionally was teaching high school. And I sometimes wish I had spent my whole career at it.

When I taught high school, the highest compliment people could think of was, "You are too good for high school teaching." I was always distressed by that comment. And I think it is an all too eloquent explanation for why so many of our schools are failing. That attitude still prevails today, and it stands as an indictment of our society and its priorities. If I could do it over, I think I'd spend my life in the classroom.

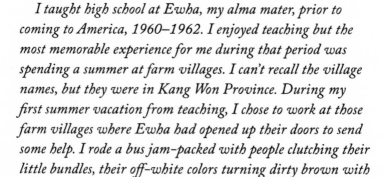

I taught high school at Ewha, my alma mater, prior to coming to America, 1960–1962. I enjoyed teaching but the most memorable experience for me during that period was spending a summer at farm villages. I can't recall the village names, but they were in Kang Won Province. During my first summer vacation from teaching, I chose to work at those farm villages where Ewha had opened up their doors to send some help. I rode a bus jam-packed with people clutching their little bundles, their off-white colors turning dirty brown with

dust. That summer, I learned firsthand that our farmers' diet consisted of whatever vegetables they grew themselves and rice mixed with barley. That was it. Nowadays, that mostly vegetable diet sounds like health food, but back then it was for the poor—meals without meat were only for the poor. Moreover, there was never enough rice. So they had to augment it with a large quantity of barley. Even then, they did not have enough to fill their stomachs. They sold grain, vegetables, eggs, and meat at the market, but they never bought any food there. The only thing they bought or exchanged were farming tools or other necessities, like a small piece of red silk, not for clothing, but to make a ribbon for their daughters' braided hair.

~ D S K-G

My Civil Wars

I AM NOT A VETERAN IN THE CONVENTIONAL SENSE, yet I assert and confess with some satisfaction that I did serve as a kind of warrior on behalf of my homeland. My wars were not with foreign soldiers on a physical field of battle, but rather with the ultimate failure of my own society to put into practice the dreams, promises, and opportunities that it so proudly and even arrogantly proclaimed were attainable for all.

I was first drawn into these wars through my intellectual passions and ideas. My ideological journey really began with that freshman western civilization class at Simpson. I found that I was passionately attracted to German romanticism, ancient Athenian philosophy and drama, the French Enlightenment, and Marxism/socialism.

Then during my teaching stint at Indianola, I became more politicized, but initially not in an activist sense. At that point, I was still muddling around with concepts in my head about a just society, about democratic processes, and social-economic justice. I was, and remain, a voracious reader, and I consumed all the books I could find on such topics, from classical theory to contemporary commentary. I delved heavily into Marxist, socialist, and anarchist thinking, which led me into American protest thought—people like Henry George, Ida Tarbell, John Steinbeck, and Upton Sinclair, as well as Eduard Bernstein, Rosa Luxemburg, and other leftist critics and thinkers. I read Karl Marx, Friedrich Engels, Mikhail Bakhtin, Pierre-Joseph Proudhon, John Maynard Keynes, Charles Beard, John Kenneth Galbraith, Erich Fromm, and many others.

The insightfulness and cogent logic of Marx impressed me greatly back then, and indeed does to this day. His philosophical essays of 1948 really hit home. I am still strongly influenced by Marxist thought and without reservation I believe that any scholarly inquiry in any humanistic discipline must encounter Marx. Ultimately, however, I decided that Marxism itself, i.e., revolutionary socialism, is not a plausible philosophy when put into practice.

As I read more, I came to believe that Eduard Bernstein and the English Fabians had a more realistic answer. They argued that true democratic socialism—social democracy—could be achieved through the democratic process and by education and advocacy. Perhaps, perhaps not. This might be yet another compromise with the capitalist forces. But, in fact, my political philosophy was evolving to a belief in regulated capitalism, a different version of the welfare state. In other words, the central government must play an active, at times even aggressive, role to insure fairness and justice. Regulated capitalism is based upon the simple democratic principles that each individual has equal rights and an equal chance and that the government should, if necessary, help ensure that is the case in practice. It is a pragmatic philosophy, but built firmly on a theoretical base of economic justice, equal opportunity, equal access, equal education.

A turning point in my life—that helped move me from armchair observer to activist—came with the 1964 Lyndon Johnson

v. Barry Goldwater presidential race. I was terrified of Goldwater because, to me, he represented an explicit rejection of precisely the vision of a progressive society I had come to embrace. I also saw this election as a kind of final referendum on FDR's New Deal. Although Eisenhower had been the first post–New Deal Republican president, he hadn't contested its fundamental principles and programs. In fact, he had in effect accepted them as a basic part of mainstream America. But now Goldwater was launching a direct assault on the New Deal and everything it symbolized.

I was twenty-six years old, and I saw America at a crossroads facing a momentous choice. The people could endorse social progress and move forward toward a just society, or they could lurch backward, embracing barbarity, exclusion, repression. The options seemed just that stark and dramatic to me. For the first time in my life, I made the leap to political action, albeit strictly as a part-time volunteer. I kept my day job at Indianola, and signed up with the Warren County Democratic Party. In my off-hours, I organized the local party's first-ever door-to-door canvass and coordinated its election day Get Out the Vote campaign.

I think I was effective, though if pressed I certainly couldn't measure the results of my efforts. But the whole experience was a crucial awakening. I had the ability to motivate and organize other people in pursuit of a common goal.

On the night of the election, I recall standing outside the house of a family named Cole (defiant Republicans) and thinking that the real victory was that we had defeated, once and for all, attempts to destroy the welfare state in America. I could not have been more mistaken, of course, given the subsequent election of Reagan and Bush Jr. But in the autumn of 1964, I felt ebullient, affirmed, and confident in the future, both my own and the nation's.

Yet the persistence of racism and poverty, as well as the imperialist war in Vietnam haunted me. If I was, as a sheltered teenager, startled to discover the reality of racism, I became downright furious as I learned the depth and pervasiveness of racial prejudice. This was not the America I loved. The more I learned, the more I struggled to understand how racial injustice could be so grotesquely entrenched in a nation that proudly proclaimed and celebrated inalienable and equal rights for all. Growing up in rural Iowa, I thought I was disadvantaged, but once I became aware of the massive oppression of African Americans, I realized how minuscule my own disadvantages had been.

And so I came to the Civil Rights movement. As usual, my path to understanding and activism was fueled by reading. With growing passion, I took in the words of W.E.B. DuBois, Frederick Douglass, and A. Philip Randolph, and I followed every move of Rev. Martin Luther King Jr. In that electoral summer of 1964, I traveled to Mississippi to register black voters. While I never personally experienced the widespread violence that occurred, I certainly faced intense white hostility such as I had never previously imagined. Curiously, I did not feel intimidated, though I was frightened much of the time. Instead, I felt invigorated, convinced that I was doing something of importance, something far better than I had ever done before. The Civil Rights movement was, and remains, the quintessential expression of the American dream.

The New Deal coalition put together by FDR (though Eleanor had as much to do with it as Franklin) was highly successful, but also exceedingly vulnerable. That unlikely coalition consisted of the Democratic southern states—the so-called Solid South—along with industrial laborers (who directly benefited from the New Deal programs) and African Americans (who also benefited). In large part, the supporters of FDR were members of groups that had been oppressed by the rampant capitalism that prevailed in the United States since the late 19th century. The one exception was the Solid South. Southern states voted solidly Democratic because the Republicans (that is, Abraham Lincoln) won the Civil War. Southern support for FDR was tenuous but lasting, because FDR did not challenge southern attitudes about race and segregation (much to Eleanor's dismay).

In the end, it took a southerner, Lyndon Johnson, who came late to the cause, to sign the Civil Rights Act of 1964. Johnson fractured the Solid South and told his then-aide Bill Moyers that he had probably sacrificed the region, a democratic stronghold, for a generation. Johnson underestimated the impact of his action. It lasted far longer than a generation.

My fervent absorption and involvement in the Civil Rights movement led me to another pressing political issue, the war in Vietnam. By early 1965, I began to have serious questions about U.S. engagement in Southeast Asia. Lyndon Johnson had promised during his 1964 presidential campaign that he would never send American boys to fight in a land war in Asia. I chose to believe him, primarily because I was so enthusiastic about his Great Society and, in equal measure, so scared of a Goldwater presidency. I was enthusiastic about Head Start, Medicare, Medicaid. I believed, and continue to believe, that LBJ was a masterful, purposeful president, a leader of principle. But sadly, tragically, he was utterly beyond his reach when it came to foreign policy, and surrendered to the simplistic verities of cold-war propaganda.

At Boston University, I had my topic. I wrote my dissertation on the Doctrine of Man in Irenaeus of Lyon. I was drawn more and more to what Irenaeus had to say about man, his emphasis on dynamic becoming over static being. My one big regret about my dissertation was my limited knowledge of Latin and Greek, not to mention an equally inadequate understanding of the ancient world, Christian thought, as well as other worldviews. I did what I could and I got my PhD. What did happen to me during seven years at BU? As I used to tell Don, I didn't live, I studied. Going to classes, reading at the library between classes, and eating my two hard-boiled eggs and carrot sticks for lunch were my daily activities.

~ D S K-G

Campaigns and Protests

IN THE FALL OF 1965, DURING MY FIRST YEAR OF GRADUATE SCHOOL at the University of Iowa, I joined twelve other students on the Pentacrest (an ensemble of buildings on the campus—one that was the state capitol building until the 1860s, when the capital was moved to Des Moines, and four that were built around 1900—that was given its name by means of a little naming contest) to protest the war in Vietnam. I remember there were students who mocked our protest. One stood on the sidelines with a gas can and a matchbook, holding a sign that read "free gasoline and matches for peace freaks." Another handed out IBM computer cards that said, "Forget this nonsense; support the Hawkeyes." It so happened it was the Saturday morning of a home football game. It was a small demonstration that met opposition by our fellow students, but it ignited my passion to oppose the Vietnam War. And it was the very beginning of my long protest.

Spending far too little time on my studies, I opted instead to organize a group called Priorities for National Survival. We placed professors in TV and radio shows to speak about grotesque distortions of national interest, and we also scheduled them for speeches at Rotary Clubs and the like throughout the region. The essential idea was to take our antiwar protests beyond the ivied campus to the broader public in small towns throughout Iowa.

Even though I was in grad school and supposedly preparing for comprehensive exams, I spent several weeks traveling all over the state, attempting to gather support for the movement. I appeared at labor union meetings in Waterloo and Dubuque, caucuses in Des Moines, and wherever I could find an audience.

In 1968, prior to starting my doctoral research in Germany, I was offered a one-year teaching job at Simpson College and I decided to accept. (Oops, I jumped from 1965 to 1968. For a fuller, more systematic accounting of my graduate studies at the University of

Iowa starting in 1965 see the chapter entitled "Back to School," which begins on p. 135.) At Simpson, one morning in January, Joe Walt called to tell me that two women from Grinnell College who were working for Eugene McCarthy's presidential candidacy were in the faculty lounge. He asked me to go talk with them. "Nobody seems to be interested," he said, "and it would be a courtesy. You might even learn something." Well, it changed my life.

One of the women was Bea Wall, who was married to Joseph Wall, legendary history professor at Grinnell. I forget who the other one was. It wasn't anything in particular that either one of them said that persuaded me, but our spirited conversation just caused me to consider where I really stood in the political spectrum. And I concluded that McCarthy's renegade campaign against the war and against LBJ suited me perfectly. Curiously enough, it felt like a return, in the best possible way, to the conservatism and optimism of my small-town roots. We must and could, I thought, end the war and achieve civil rights, working through our constitutional system. In the forty-plus years since, I have never shifted from that line of thinking.

The upshot was that I became the Iowa state coordinator of the Eugene McCarthy for President campaign. We stacked the caucuses with McCarthy supporters, the first such use of Iowa caucuses in what has now become a national phenomenon.

When Bobby Kennedy announced his candidacy in March 1968, I retreated into my apartment for a long weekend of contemplation and soul-searching. I believed that Bobby had a better chance of being elected and that he would be a better president. McCarthy had good values and good judgment, but I feared he lacked the decisiveness and toughness that the presidency demands. Yet, I also felt it was important for both candidates to keep going until the convention in August. If we could attract a critical mass of voters who supported one or the other, we might just be able to combine forces and prevail over the Johnson-Humphrey ticket. With Kennedy's assassination in June, of course, that scenario never played out. And after his death, the air seemed to go out of the McCarthy campaign. We all kept working as hard as ever, but it just didn't feel the same. Victory seemed elusive at best.

In Chicago, that August, the evening before the Democratic Convention opened, I had just finished setting up our headquarters at the Drake Hotel. A group of us, all part of the McCarthy campaign, decided to go for drinks at a place called Your Father's Mustache, which we renamed Eugene's for the occasion. We bantered and joked and we tried to stay upbeat, but then around 11:00 p.m., Peter Paul & Mary arrived and serenaded us with "The Impossible Dream." Indeed, impossible to contain myself—I cried openly. We knew we couldn't possibly win at this convention in this city.

A couple of days later, just after we lost the peace plank in the party platform, we got word in the afternoon that there were demonstrations in Grant Park. We all headed over there. By the time we arrived, things were at a fever pitch—frustrated protesters were massed, cars packed the streets, the police lines went on forever.

I remember getting into an angry, irrational argument with some young Bobby Kennedy supporters who blamed our defeat on McCarthy's failure to support Bobby back in the late spring. What in the hell would that have done? Walking up to a police line with my fellow campaign worker Sue Kaul, I asked to be let through. The policeman I approached, appropriately enough, said politely that going through was not permissible. I clenched my fist and was about to hit him—me, who did not believe in physical fights and was also no good at them, about to hit a cop!—when Sue pulled me back. I was that angry and I had lots of company. The angrier I got, the more helpless I felt. What could I do to bring some purpose and direction into the next course of action?

That evening, the revered activist Allard Lowenstein (who was elected congressman from New York the following year, but sadly served only one term) called a meeting at the Drake Hotel with the announced purpose of forming a third party, one whose fundamental goal would be to run against the Vietnam War. I pondered for a while and then decided to walk over there alone and check it out.

Several hundred people had gathered and a lot of passion emanated from the room. Outside in the hallway, I ran into Paul Newman, also alone. We glanced at each other and then started chatting. I knew he had been very active in the McCarthy campaign and I explained my role. We walked through our mutual anger about the war, our frustration with Johnson and Humphrey, and how we both agonized about the prospects for a third party. We went on for thirty minutes or so, neither of us saying anything of great consequence, and gradually we realized and acknowledged that we were thinking the same thing—a third party wouldn't work. It couldn't win in the general election. And although Humphrey had been hopelessly compromised by his association with Johnson, he was a decent man, whereas Nixon would be frightful. We shook hands. Newman said, "Keep up the fight," and we parted company. I walked out alone, feeling sad but encouraged by Newman's piercing blue eyes that drew me in as a like-minded citizen engaged in the same cause. I was not alone.

The next day, I was wandering morosely around Lincoln Park in the wake of the riots and saw Mary Travers (of Peter Paul & Mary) also wandering about, aimlessly picking up papers left strewn on the ground as if to bring some order to it all. It was an incredibly poignant moment for me.

Later that week, the second to last night of the convention, the McCarthy team gathered for the last time at our Drake Hotel headquarters. The mood was bleak. We were depressed and drinking more than we should, not knowing what to do. Unannounced, Harold Hughes, the governor of Iowa and the man who had placed McCarthy's name in nomination, walked into our suite. I was stunned and delighted. He sat and talked with us for about an hour. He spoke of his own dismay at the defeat and also at the rioting in the streets (later characterized by the Kerner Commission as a police riot). But his disappointment notwithstanding, his message to us was that we dare not be broken by this loss. The war was continuing and so was injustice, and that meant we must fight on.

The following morning I was scheduled to address the Sigma Alpha Epsilon Leadership Conference. I had agreed to do so weeks before, not anticipating—actually not even thinking about—the intervening events. I dreaded doing it. I had no prepared remarks and no idea what I would say. This was a group of elite, wealthy white men. How could I possibly articulate the causes that meant so much to me in a way they would understand?

I was scheduled for a session on national politics, where I would represent the Democratic Party and two other speakers who were fraternity members would stand one for the Republicans and one for George Wallace. Wallace, of course, was running for president as an independent. We all made our way to the dais. My old professor, Joe Walt, who had roped me into this to begin with, did the introductions. He made some generous remarks about me, specifically mentioning my work at the convention that week. When I stood up, to my great surprise, I was greeted by a sustained standing ovation. It rocked me back on my heels. I recall not what I said after that, but it was another turning point. It shocked me out of despair and back into the fight.

Back in Iowa a week later, I received a call from Edward Campbell, chief of staff for Governor Hughes, who wanted me to join the Hughes for Senate campaign. I readily agreed. Campbell asked me to work only part time, but I knew myself better than that. I would just work full time and receive part-time pay. I think the Hughes people principally saw me as a symbol of McCarthy, a means to attract those votes. They wanted my name more than my actual effort, which didn't bother me. I fully understood. I had drunk the political campaign Kool-Aid and I was hooked. My scheduled return to grad school that autumn would just have to wait.

The Hughes operation got a bargain, if I do say so myself. In fact, they probably got more than they bargained for. I was a veritable whirlwind, opening a storefront office in Iowa City, issuing position papers, recruiting dozens of volunteers, and touring pretty much every college campus in the state by way of an Iowa National Guard airplane. (Back then, that wasn't considered a violation of campaign finance rules.) I worked closely with Vance Bourjaily, a novelist from Iowa City who had drafted Hughes's address at the convention placing McCarthy's name in nomination. That was a delightful friendship. Vance was as much of a romantic as I was, and we often fantasized together about a White House dream team that was never to be. It consisted primarily of our heroes who had been assassinated in service of the cause—JFK, RFK, Medgar Evers, and Martin Luther King Jr.

I liked Governor Hughes, and, as important, deeply respected him. He was a small-town Iowa boy and a soldier in World War II, where he fought in the Italian campaign and then returned to the life of a truck driver—and an alcoholic. One time on the campaign trail, he recounted a morning when he woke up in a Des Moines hotel and had no idea how he had gotten there.

That incident and other alcohol-related disasters brought him to the brink of suicide and propelled him into recovery. Once he had reclaimed his life, he got into politics, stirred by his involvement in the trucking industry. Working as a manager of a local trucking business, he became sharply aware that little independent truckers were not getting a fair deal from the State Commerce Commission. He eventually started the Iowa Better Trucking Bureau and went on to serve on the state commission, which brought him in contact with the federal Interstate Commerce Commission and national politics.

He ran for governor in 1962 and won. I was then a high school teacher and heard him delivering a campaign speech in the auditorium of the Indianola Methodist Church. In forthright language far from characteristic of a politician, he announced that taxes would have to be raised to meet public needs. It was such a shocking statement from a politician. It could have been a political suicide—he wasn't even an incumbent. But his candor and integrity seemed to resonate with Iowa voters.

During his 1962 campaign, he also revealed to the public that he was a recovering alcoholic and that he was a supporter of liquor by the drink. In Iowa at that time, liquor and wine could be purchased at state stores by the bottle, but, except for beer, could not be served by the drink at restaurants or bars, although the law was largely flouted. Hughes promised that if he were elected, he would close down all illegal bars until the legislature voted in liquor by the drink. That position didn't hurt his appeal with Iowans. Once in office, he threatened to send state troopers into every tavern in the state and shut them down if liquor was being served. The legislature quickly complied.

One of the most fascinating aspects of Hughes was his political and intellectual evolution. Early on as governor, he toured a blighted African American neighborhood in Waterloo. Again displaying his disarming candor, he admitted to the media that he had never known that such poverty and deprivation existed in America, much less in Iowa. It is, to put it mildly, highly unusual for a politician to publicly confess ignorance of anything other than, perhaps, an allegation of infidelity or corruption. But Hughes took the public along with him as he learned and developed, and they respected him for it. I don't know if the same would be true today. Perhaps those were more innocent times.

As governor, Hughes also found himself having to preside over the government-mandated closing of the state's Amish schools, which were not in compliance with official regulations for public education. It was widely reported that he was anguished by this experience, and I think it helped move him toward a deeper understanding of cultural diversity.

But it was the Vietnam War, more than any other issue, that brought him national attention. Lyndon Johnson in the 1960s was waging the war in full fervor. Hughes, then chair of the Democratic Governor's Conference, was a guest at the White House and reacted in anger to the president's statements about the war. I believe Hughes said that he would not be "the bangle on the horse's tail." Of course, for me personally, his strong opposition against the Vietnam War brought him closer to my heart and mind.

Cold Turkey and Vietnam

AFTER MY STINT WITH THE HUGHES CAMPAIGN in 1968, I went back to Iowa City ostensibly to complete my doctorate—at long last—but Vietnam never left my mind. I quickly got involved in planning for the Moratorium to End the War in Vietnam, which was organized by some folks I had worked with during the Mc-Carthy campaign—David Hawk, Sam Brown, and David Mixner. I became the principal organizer for the state of Iowa. The idea was to coordinate a giant strike throughout the country as a powerful protest against the war, followed by a massive march on the White House. Half a million demonstrators rallied on November 15, 1969. They were entertained by Pete Seeger, Arlo Guthrie, Peter Paul & Mary, and others. There were also demonstrations in a number of major European cities and Australia.

I worked on Moratorium through an Iowa City group I had cofounded, Priorities for National Survival. Simultaneously, Richard Cohen, a student at Simpson with whom I had worked on the McCarthy campaign (who went on to become a producer at *CBS News*, a best-selling author, and a lifelong dear friend), brought in a clever idea for pre-Moratorium publicity. A movie called *Cold Turkey* was filming on location in Greenfield, Iowa. Richard drove up there and recruited some of the cast and crew to participate in a rally on the Simpson campus. Norman Lear, then a little-known director, and stars Dick Van Dyke, Pippa Scott, and Jean Stapleton agreed to appear. At a cocktail party in Cohen's apartment immediately beforehand, Jean Stapleton sidled over to me and confided that we shouldn't be too surprised if Van Dyke didn't show. "He is probably drunk in some bar in Des Moines," she sighed.

The rally was a huge success. The hall was packed and a number of reporters and, we learned later, several FBI agents were in attendance. Happily, Van Dyke arrived a few seconds after the other dignitaries had gathered on the stage. He slipped into a chair next to me. We shook hands and then he leaned over and asked if he could bum a cigarette. The movie *Cold Turkey* dealt with an entire town that was trying to quit. "Sure," I said, and we both lit up.

During 1969 and 1970, I was also heavily involved in organizing the Iowa Democratic Coalition. It was an ill-advised effort, but I personally benefited through meeting more Iowans. I traveled extensively, all at my own expense, to meet with Democrats and labor officials to advocate our cause. I went to Cedar Falls, Des Moines, Dubuque, Mason City, and Burlington.

During those years, I guess I became what we now call a talking head at various events and on regional radio and television, as a representative of the day's leftist causes. That was okay by me. I actually rather enjoyed it, although I do recall one invitation I declined. I was asked to speak on behalf of the counterculture as an advocate for nude bathing, marijuana smoking, and such. That was not my shtick. Then there was the evening I was branded a sexist pig at a meeting of Students for a Democratic Society, an iconic group of radical activists. The room was packed and the meeting well underway when a distinctly pregnant woman came in. I stood up to give her my seat and was immediately and roundly booed by the crowd. I still don't regret that action.

After the tragic Kent State killings in 1970, the University of Iowa, like so many other schools, shut down. I furiously met with students, arming them with literature and urging them to go home and work against the war in their hometowns.

In 1970, I felt it was time for me to return to my studies. I somehow managed to pass my comprehensive exams, and left for Germany to do archival research on the 1932 elections and the Nazi successes.

*When I went to Mount Holyoke College to teach for a year
in 1969, still on a student visa but taking advantage of what
Immigration called the practical training period, I lived in one of
the dormitories. It was the end of the 1960s, but plenty of the kids
got involved in antiwar protests. Night after night, students met
in the dormitory to discuss the serious matter of their grades. They
wanted the faculty to make contingency plans, so that students
who participated in the protests could make up lost work without
penalty. I would sit there with a wooden expression, careful not to
betray my real feelings.*

*One night a student asked me, "Ms. Kim (all faculty were
addressed as Ms. or Mr., rather than Dr.; everyone had a PhD),
we'd like to know what you think."*

"Oh no, you don't want to know what I think."

"Oh yes, we do," more voices joined in.

*Thus put on the spot, I spoke up. "You should know that I come
from Korea where students put their lives on the line when they
protest. Two years prior to my departure in 1962 for America
for my graduate studies in Boston, there was a protest movement
that is generally known as the April 19 Revolution. Spearheaded
by students and labor groups, that revolution overthrew the first
American–backed president of South Korea, Syngman Rhee, and his
government. I can still feel the blood spilled by the students. If you
are so worried about what will happen to your grades, I suggest that
you go back to class and study, and not worry about protests."*

*After that night, they never again asked what I thought. They
were more than content to let me remain an inscrutable Asian
woman.*

~ *D S K-G*

The farm in Iowa

Ramsau, Bavarian Alps

PART V

Into the Unknown

Someone from Iowa Gets a Fulbright

IN 1962, I WAS TEACHING GERMAN AT INDIANOLA High School. And as a history major, I was most ill prepared to do so. In an effort at self-improvement, I had attended a special study program at Montana State University in Bozeman the previous summer. My German skills improved, but not enough for my taste. Then, I learned about the Fulbright scholar program for summer study abroad and eagerly applied. To my delight and surprise, I was accepted. The award paid all expenses for a two-month course in Germany. I was immediately a big fish in the small pond of Indianola, my name and accomplishment featured in the local newspaper. I was flattered, honored, and I must admit a bit frightened. Me, an Iowa farm boy going to Germany on the Fulbright program? Can I handle it?

All year long, I'd had fantasies of dating Genelle Morain, the school's French teacher. She was ten years my senior, but good looking, I thought, and she and I worked closely together pioneering the introduction of modern foreign languages in the school. A week before I was scheduled to depart for Deutschland I asked her out to a movie. She accepted, and we arranged the date and time. In retrospect, I think she must have engineered the invitation, because when I arrived, quite nervous, to retrieve her for our date, I was greeted with an eruption of "surprise!" All of my friends and colleagues had assembled to throw me a farewell launch. I was astonished, thrilled. It was a great party, and a memorable send-off for my exciting adventure. But I was deeply disappointed. I had really wanted some time alone with Genelle. I tried to persuade myself that perhaps it was for the best. After all, she was an older woman. A romance with her was not to be. Perhaps there was another woman waiting for me. Still, I remained disappointed for a long while.

Just before I decamped, I stopped in Tennant to see my parents, wanting to share my excitement and dreams for the future. I hoped to convey what a big deal it was for an Iowa farm boy to go to Germany on a Fulbright scholarship. I wanted them to tell me how proud they were. They were pleased that I was so excited, but they didn't have any idea what a Fulbright was. Nor did I try to explain. Thinking back, I should have explained, but instead I just felt sorry for myself being unable to share the joy of this singular event in my young life.

In any event, in early June 1963, I flew to New York and arrived at my hotel in the late afternoon. It was my second visit to the Big Apple (I'd come in 1959 on a college trip). I was more intimidated this time because I was alone. With some trepidation, I made my way to the hotel dining room and ordered dinner at a cost that was extraordinary for a young man from Iowa. I knew I should enjoy it, but I simply could not.

Later that evening, the Fulbright grantees gathered in the hotel ballroom and endured a series of speeches from various Washington dignitaries. By then I had recovered from my gloomy fear and was feeling quite satisfied with myself, that is, until one speaker commented on the dire need for applicants from underserved parts of the nation.

"We seem to attract candidates only from the two coasts," he lamented. "It's gotten so bad that whenever we receive an application from someone from, say, Iowa, we just give them a grant."

Needless to say, that didn't sit well with me. But I consoled myself with a pragmatic rationale: What does it matter? I got a Fulbright. Iowa did me a favor!

Germany, JFK, and Me

THE NEXT DAY WHEN MY PLANE TOUCHED DOWN at the Cologne/ Bonn airport, I was filled with exhilaration. I was stepping on foreign soil for the first time. Eighteen years had passed since the end of World War II. That seemed like a long time to me then (now I realize what a blip on the calendar it actually was). As we were whisked into the city, I noticed armed soldiers stationed all along the highway. It turned out that the military was there because President Kennedy was scheduled to arrive just two hours after our plane landed. That was a historic visit, the first by an American president since the end of the war.

I had not anticipated the overwhelmingly enthusiastic response of the German people to JFK. Nor, for that matter, had anybody else. It was Kennedy's charm, charisma, and youth, but Germany was also eager to rejoin the community of civilized nations after the horrors of Nazism and the Holocaust. Germans hailed this visit by the dynamic so-called leader of the free world as an enormously important symbol of their acceptance into the world community.

Cologne was only the president's entry point to the country, but the crowds lining the highways several miles from the airport to the city were huge. In the city, where the president gave a brief speech, more crowds were crushing and screaming their approval. In one humorous incident, a resourceful chap raised a can above his head and yelled *heisses wasser* (hot water) as he deftly moved through the crowd. I doubt if there was any water, hot or cold, in that can.

A massive reception was scheduled for JFK the following afternoon in Berlin, in front of the Brandenburg Gate on the border between West and East Germany. I had just arrived in Cologne myself, but I was so inspired by the joy of the German crowds—and such a Kennedy fan—that the next morning, I abandoned my Fulbright group, took a taxi to the airport, and flew off to Berlin. I just had to be there when the president spoke.

President Kennedy spoke from a platform erected on the steps of Rathaus Schöneberg, and most of his speech was in English, but in a famously dramatic flourish, he proudly asserted, "Ich bin ein Berliner" (I am a Berliner). The Germans fervently and rightly interpreted that statement as meaning that Kennedy—and America—stood firmly with Berlin, which was an island in hostile waters, totally surrounded as it was by communist East Germany. The rest of West Germany was more than 100 kilometers away. What the Germans also understood, but politely ignored in the popular line is that Berliner is also the name of a quite famous German pastry.

The president's words weren't all that profound and his famous speech was not delivered at the Brandenburg Gate, but his poise, confidence, and delivery drove the enormous crowd wild. It was mesmerizing and deeply moving. And that single experience on my first full day in a foreign land was really the foundation, the stimulus, for my lifelong commitment to public service. I shall never forget it, and shall never regret it, though I could ill afford the travel expense.

Unable to find a hotel room in Berlin, I had to take a late-night flight back to Cologne and then sleep on an airport bench until dawn.

Early in the morning, I made my way to our designated hotel in Cologne (Köln), a city on the river Rhine, built originally as a Roman colony. The hotel was pleasant, functional, and amazingly clean. But then, Germans are notoriously neat and sanitary. Some wag once told me that if you fly low over Europe, you can immediately recognize the French-German border, slovenly on one side, pristine and orderly on the other.

I remember taking a tour of the city and being astonished by the fact that everyone was speaking a foreign language. Such a rube I was. After an orientation session, my group of language teachers was dispersed to various sites throughout the country. I was sent to the Hanseatic City of Lübeck. (Around 1400, more than 160 cities along the north coast of Europe were members of Hansa—which means withstand the wind—a confederation of merchants guilds and market towns and cities that played an important mercantile and defensive role in medieval Europe.)

In Lübeck, I was assigned to live with a German family. I do not recall the name of the mother, but she fit the stereotype of the German hausfrau, pleasant but dominant. I was given my room and served breakfast (frühstück) each morning. The rest of the time I spent in classes and on tours of the city.

I did go with the hausfrau one evening to hear the remarkable Willy Brandt deliver a speech. Brandt was then the mayor of Berlin, and he went on to become chancellor of West Germany. He had resisted the Nazis, and had to escape late at night on a small boat to Sweden. As mayor, Brandt was a major voice for democracy and freedom. I found him spellbinding, but the hausfrau was mildly disapproving of his liberal leanings. Actually, she never really explained how or why she disagreed with Brandt. But it was clear from other conversations and comments that she disapproved what she viewed as Germany's rush toward modernity, and its casual rejection of traditional values and practices.

After three weeks in Lübeck, I rejoined our little band of American teachers in Munich for three weeks of intensive instruction in German grammar and culture. We attended classes part of the day, but most of our time was devoted to cultural immersion. For me, at least, it was a colossal success. We explored the city exhaustively. I particularly enjoyed the cathedrals and coffee houses. We also took side trips to Vienna and Berlin. In Berlin, I saw the play *Der Stellvetreter (The Deputy)* by Rolf Hochhuth. It was a riveting indictment of Pope Pius XII for his complicity with the Nazis, and the only play I have ever attended where there was no applause at the end.

At the end of the summer, we had two weeks of free time, which I used to hike through the Black Forest and visit the cities of Ulm and Innsbruck, as well as to visit a friend from my student days at Simpson in Basel, Switzerland.

My first trip abroad. It opened my eyes and mind to an astonishing degree and set my life's course more than I could have ever imagined. I could literally feel my world of ideas and culture expanding.

Back to School: University of Iowa

AFTER FIVE YEARS OF TEACHING HIGH SCHOOL, my desire for more knowledge and insight into true scholarly pursuit compelled me to return to school myself and pursue a PhD in history at the University of Iowa. In the fall of 1965, I arrived in Iowa City with much the same anxiety and fear that I had my freshman year at college. Almost ten years had passed since then and I had more experience behind me, but I still felt nervous about pursuing graduate studies at a large university. I was puzzled at my own fears, but they were there and real. Perhaps I was too eager to excel.

I located a one-bedroom, second-floor walk-up just a few blocks from campus and converted the aging Victorian turret into my bedroom to give myself much more living space. I was actually quite comfortable there. Although I had a car, I rarely needed it. Most of my life was within easy walking distance.

I intended to write my dissertation on some aspect of modern German history. I was profoundly interested in the paradox of how a country like Germany could produce such a rich cultural history with giants like Freud, Marx, and Nietzsche, and yet also give birth to the beyond-monstrous horror of Hitler and the Third Reich. Looking back, I am inclined to believe I would have been wiser to pursue my degree in American history, given my intense interest in our politics. Moreover, I would have escaped the added burden of tackling scholarship in a foreign language. Trying to become fluent in German at the same time I was conducting research delayed my progress and frustrated my ambition.

During my first year, I was an intense student, consumed with my studies and largely shunning any social life. After every lecture course, I would return to my apartment and type up my notes, adding comments to clarify their meaning. Still not content, I would also run to the library to double-check facts and gather added information. As a result, I earned all As and qualified for a University teaching and research fellowship, which was the most prestigious financial support package at Iowa. I was even recruited by several professors to participate in their reading seminars. That boosted my spirits, knowing they considered me articulate and well read.

Then my studies were interrupted by an unexpected invitation to teach a year at Simpson, which led me to managing those aforementioned political campaigns and the protest movements against the Vietnam War. By that time, I had gained support and even some respect as a promising student from a few professors who made my leave possible.

So when I returned to the University of Iowa, I had quite a bit of experience in politics, but it was time for me to concentrate on preparing for my comprehensive examination. I was frantic and often felt discouraged and depressed, notwithstanding the excitement generated from delving into modern European history. Occasional visits to bars and long walks through the campus helped to revive my enthusiasm, but I was often on a roller coaster struggling with recurring downs. During that period in the early 1970s, a close friend gave me a Joan Baez album that featured the song "One Day at a Time," which was remarkably calming to me. It encouraged me to focus simply on the texts to be read that day and not the huge, somewhat imagined task of passing the exam. It worked.

I passed my comprehensive exam "with distinction" and was ready to proceed to the dissertation stage. I prepared a written document about my research approach for a meeting with four professors—three in history and one in political science, as my dissertation required the use of electoral analysis. They were to question and comment on my paper, but we spent almost as much time talking about politics as we did about my dissertation. That's how it was in the early 1970s when campuses and, for that matter, the entire nation, were in turmoil. My professors were fascinated and bewildered by it all. And I think they saw me as a kind of political war veteran and were eager to discuss politics with me more than my paper. As we finished the meeting with warm handshakes, I hoped that they were impressed by my paper outlining my research approach, not just my politics.

So it was that, in May of 1971, I packed my bags and headed abroad for an extended sojourn amid the annals of German electoral history. The first year of my research was to be paid by a University of Iowa fellowship, and the second by the Stiftung *Luftbrückendank* (the Airlift Gratitude Foundation). In June 1948, after the Soviets cut surface traffic to and from West Berlin—planning to gain control by starving out the population and cutting off their business—the Truman administration provided daily airlifts that brought food and other essentials into the city. In appreciation, the foundation was established to provide scholarships for the sons—although not the daughters—of American pilots in the airlift. By the early 1970s, they had run out of qualified sons, so they enlarged the pool of eligible students—to my benefit.

Growing up, my father woke all eight of us children—six boys and two girls—at 5:00 every morning to conduct a family service, complete with hymn singing and prayers. He told us to dream of an unrestricted future, a future not circumscribed by any border or ocean or mountain. He told us to get as much education as we wanted and that he would support us. During those predawn services, my father invariably ended his "dream" sermon with these words: "Think of what your cousin Dae Won did. She went to America. You can, too, if you work for it." Well, Dae Won came to my graduation. She arrived with a Swiss gold-plated watch as a gift. Everything in life has its own time, I thought.

~ *D S K-G*

⚭

Bremen and Seig Heil

From Iowa city, I flew to New York and boarded a University-chartered plane filled with undergraduates embarking on a European adventure. When we landed in Cologne, my mood was quite different than it had been on my earlier Fulbright trip. This time, I felt pressed by a somber sense of responsibility, and worried that I might not be sufficiently well prepared for the research tasks I had set myself. And yet, history geek that I was, I was also undeniably exhilarated at the prospect of unfettered access to primary sources and the thrill of intellectual discovery.

The central question for my dissertation was: Who voted for Hitler and why? To obtain some answers, I proposed analyses of which demographic groups had voted for the National Socialists—the Nazis—based on the assumption that one could accurately determine exactly who had cast their votes for the Nazi Party, as well as other parties, by identifying the demographics to which they belonged.

I intended to begin by burrowing into West German archives and statistical files to study the elections of 1932, which brought Hitler to the brink of power. There had already been considerable scholarly research on the subject, perhaps most notably William Sheridan Allen's *The Nazi Seizure of Power: The Experience of a Single German Town, 1922–1945*, an exhaustive and insightful study of the Nazi victory in one small town in northern Germany. My work was to be a quantitative study of the elections of 1932 as they played out in a major city—a task no scholar had yet addressed. No historian to date had analyzed data at the precinct level, as I set out to do. Despite my concern as to whether I was adequately equipped to engage in complex quantitative methodology, I was determined to try.

My Iowa advisor, David Schoenbaum, had arranged an introduction to the chair of the political science department at the University of Mannheim who, in turn, graciously instructed one of his assistants, Dieter Roth, to help me out. And indeed he did.

Dieter set me up with an office, a telephone, and my own letter-head stationery. The office was in a rundown abandoned hotel with an antiquated elevator, but still it was more than satisfactory for my purposes. It was right next to the train station (bahnhof), with easy access to bookstores and restaurants and just three blocks from the residential hotel where I was staying.

From that office, I forged ahead to identify a city with adequate records. I sent out letters of inquiry on the letterhead stationery to more than thirty cities to inquire about their holdings and to iden-tify the urban center I would study.

Mannheim is a largely uninteresting industrial city located on the river Rhine, though it does have an enormous 18th-century palace, once the seat of the elector of the Palatinate (Pfalz) and now the home of the university. (As a curious footnote in my life, years later Dai Sil and I lived in New Paltz, New York, named after the Pfalz by the French Huguenots who fled to Mannheim before migrating to America.)

German cities in the Weimar era (1919–1932) had compiled and maintained *adressbücher* (address books) that included the name of every household, the number of residents, the occupation of the head of household, and whether the domicile was owned or rented. But, as I learned, these *adressbücher* and other data—in-cluding election results—were hard to find. Because most major German cities came under severe bombing during the war, very few statistical offices survived. The Germans did a marvelous job of protecting fine art, often transporting it to salt mines in the eastern part of the country. But statistics were a lower priority, and many documents went up in smoke.

Thus, the replies to my inquiries were disappointing, but I gath-ered the few promising responses, headed to the train station, and visited ten different cities to examine their materials personally. One of the stops was Bremen, which I determined to be the best bet for my research. A member of the Hanseatic League in the Middle Ages and a leading world trade center, Bremen had a sophistication and awareness of the larger world that was somewhat rare in those times. It was not the typical German city I had hoped to study, but it did have the best stats and records. So I arranged to settle in.

Bremen is a pleasant but woefully unexciting city, although it does have a marvelous cathedral that took a thousand years to build, as well as a statue of the Stadtmusikanten (the city musicians of mythical, Grimm Brothers storytelling fame) in the main square, in front of the rathaus (town hall). Intriguingly, the basement of the cathedral houses the mummies of Swedish military officers who served in the Thirty Years War in the 17th century (1618–1648). Transportation was difficult in those chaotic years, so the bodies of the brass were stored in the cathedral's crypt for safekeeping. For reasons that were never explained to me, they mummified naturally. At the beginning of the 20th century, the city fathers placed a dead turtle in the basement and it mummified as well.

I located a room for myself on Schwachauserherr Strasse, number 108. The street was lined with aging 19th-century mansions, which once had been occupied by wealthy shipowners but now were in various states of falling down or being torn down. The best of the lot were rented by the room to low-income folks like me. I encountered quite a few Arab guest workers (gastarbeiter). I found them friendly and pleasant, despite our language barrier.

Every single morning, I'd get up early, down some strong coffee, and dig into my quest to unravel the profile of the Nazi voter. I needed a multifaceted approach for this task. In part, I had to study the content and style of Nazi party campaign appeals and activities throughout Bremen during the Weimar Republic, when Hitler rose to power. I also had to undertake a precinct-level analysis of voting statistics. For this task, the demographic data available through the *adressbücher* was the most valuable. Also helpful were election results broken down by gender—German women got to vote in 1919, and their votes were tallied separately. Following the onset of the Great Depression in 1929, Germany held a flurry of elections. There were five major elections in 1932 alone. I chose to examine the eight ballots that took place from 1928 (the last before the depression) through 1932.

If I was to understand the series of events that carried the Nazis into office, I had to examine the context in which those elections occurred, particularly in Bremen. For this, my sources, other than the raw statistics, were primarily secret police reports on meetings of the Bremen Nazi Party (thank goodness, they were no longer secret), newspaper stories on campaign activities, and political brochures and flyers. Bremen had six daily newspapers during that period and, as was typical, each had a pronounced political position.

I quickly discovered that the police reports were unprofessional and unreliable, but nonetheless fascinating. The authorities considered radical political activity a potential danger, but they lacked the resources to do much about it. The Bremen police recruited informants—generally from lower-middle-class and working-class neighborhoods—most of whom, I presumed, were unemployed or underemployed, and needed the few German marks they could earn as stoolies. They would attend party meetings and submit handwritten notes to the police. But the notes were never transcribed, nor were there any summaries or analyses by authorities. As far as I could ascertain, whatever data were collected were ignored. But in good Teutonic fashion, they were filed, retained, and still existed for me to review.

For the first half of the 1920s, Nazi party meetings were attended primarily by young and middle-aged men, most of them unemployed, and intensely bitter and angry about Germany's defeat in World War I, its loss of national prestige, and the imperialism of the French and the British. There was much resentment of the Weimar Coalition parties, which, it was vigorously argued, betrayed their own country when it was on the verge of winning the Great War. The men—and they were all men—who attended these meetings were rabidly consumed with the conviction that by 1918 Germany was winning the war, when the socialists and the Jews in wantonly surrendering gave the country a stab in the back (dolchstoss).

To put this in context, it helps to understand that World War I was never fought on German soil. France, Poland, and Russia suffered the most. Germans were deprived of food and resources, but never saw a foreign soldier. Adolf Hitler fought in France as a private in the German army and was injured—even temporarily losing his eyesight. He never fought in the homeland, however. This partly means Germans didn't fully understand World War I.

The documents about the Nazi party meetings were available in the State Archive (Staatsarchiv) of Bremen. I spent several months reading all the daily newspapers from the period and all the police reports. I recorded—on four-by-six index cards—voluminous notes on each and every gathering, rally, demonstration, and related legislative meetings.

I had to study for several days to learn how to decipher the handwritten notes of the informants, which were written in an archaic script. The archivist, Herr Olk, kindly gave me a graph with individual letters from the old and the modern script. Each weekday I would arrive at the archive when it opened at 9:30 and leave when it closed at 4:30 in the afternoon. In the winter it was dark both times.

It is relevant to note that those who joined the Nazi party or who attended its meetings were small in number, frequently less than a dozen. Only with the start of the depression in 1928 did affiliation and attendance numbers increase substantially. There had been some interest in joining the party prior to its 1923 beer hall putsch in Munich, an attempt to overthrow the government that was immediately crushed and resulted in Hitler's imprisonment. (It was in prison that he wrote *Mein Kampf*, the bible of the National Socialist movement.) But with the collapse of Hitler's putsch and his subsequent imprisonment, along with the revival of the economy in the mid-1920s, support for the Nazis waned.

By the late 1920s, the tenor of Nazi meetings changed. Having served several years in prison, Hitler now began to organize a national party and put Joseph Goebbels in charge of organization. All local and state parties were required to follow central orders. All campaign literature was centrally written. No exceptions were allowed. There was a shift toward active participation in electoral politics and a focus on recruiting working-class union members.

Hitler visited Bremen only once, in the summer of 1932. Local party meetings were full of chatter about the upcoming gathering, which was to take place in a football stadium. Goebbels's organizers were everywhere. I read a number of newspaper accounts, but learned the most from an interview with a woman who was a teenager at the time and the daughter of a wealthy shipowner. She and a friend went to the stadium on a lark, having heard quite unpleasant things about this lower-class rabble-rouser. They waited with thousands of others packed into the stadium. About a half hour after the rally's scheduled beginning, an airplane banked overhead. It was Hitler, announcing his arrival as if, one might say, from heaven. His language, this woman recalled, was initially garbled and almost incoherent. Then he caught his stride and delivered such an emotionally powerful speech about the German nation that the teenage girl and her friend could barely resist raising their arms in the Hitler salute and screaming *"sieg heil!"* So they did.

During the years from 1928 through 1932, Weimar Coalition governments were weak, compromising, vacillating, and ineffective. They faced difficult times: the devastating economic impact of the harsh peace terms forced by the Allied powers after World War I, the horror of international communism, the inability of the government or any of the other parties to deal with the depression, and the growing power of large businesses and banks—mainly Jewish owned—that were crushing small shops and workers.

The highest vote received by the Nazis was 37 percent in July 1932, and that percentage fell in November. Yet in January 1933, Hitler was appointed chancellor (kanzler) by President Paul von Hindenburg, an act allowed under the parliamentary constitution. The appointment was justified or rationalized by the fact that no coalition of parties could be mustered to form a government.

CRO

Documents, People, and Boxes of Findings

AFTER MONTHS OF ARCHIVAL RESEARCH, it was time for me to move to the next phase of my research: interviewing people. Initially, I thought that would have only marginal value, but I dutifully compiled a list from across the political spectrum of approximately fifty individuals who played a role in this period and who, I thought, might still be alive. The interviews turned out to be the most fascinating part of the entire project.

I took my list to an archivist who had been particularly helpful and asked if he knew whether any of these people were still around. His first response to one name on my list was immediate and amazing. "Karl Hartman is in the next room, doing genealogical research," he said. "He was in the Nazi party. Let me introduce you."

Hartman readily agreed to be interviewed, and I returned a few days later for a lengthy session, which yielded some fascinating information. Most interesting, though, was his response to my final question, which wasn't even technically part of my research.

"I noticed," I said, "that the Bremen State/City Council voted unanimously in the summer of 1934 to join the SS. Why was that?" That it had so voted surprised me, because Bremen was a sophisticated port city.

"Ah," Hartman responded, "it's quite simple, really. Hitler reorganized the administrative political structure of Germany, placing the free Hanseatic city of Bremen in *Gau Osnabrück* (the League of *Osnabrück*). *Osnabrück* was controlled by a rabid anti-Semite named Karl *Röver*. We joined the SS so that we could report directly to Berlin and avoid reporting to *Röver*."

A fascinating aspect I had not thought of: the reasons for joining the SS were far more complex than I had assumed, far beyond ideological support and anti-Semitism.

Another intriguing interview came through my brief association with a diva of the city opera, a woman from Philadelphia named Deborah Cook. We had a fine time together. Intrigued by my research, Debbie introduced me to an older Jewish couple who had owned four movie theaters in Bremen and then fled to England in 1938, eventually emigrating to Texas. In the late 1950s, they returned to Germany. Debbie invited all of us to her apartment one night for dinner, so that I could meet them and conduct an interview. She told me in advance that he loved Scotch, so, though it was a stretch for my fellowship budget, I arrived with a quality bottle in hand. The husband told me right away he preferred to converse in English. That lasted for all of one or two questions before he lapsed into German, which we spoke for the next two hours as well as in the next three interviews at Debbie's apartment.

I was fascinated by their case. They escaped the horrors of the Holocaust themselves, but nonetheless they returned to Germany where so many fellow Jews suffered the most inhuman persecution. Why? I wanted to understand. What was in their bones—because they were born and raised in Germany—did not mix or accommodate well with Texas, they said. When they lived in Germany before, they owned theaters, but they were not particularly keen about all the cultural aspects of their country of birth. However, in a strange way, life in Texas made them long for German culture. They learned English well enough to get along, but they were eager to speak German, their native tongue, and to listen to German music on German soil. They missed Germany—the land and its culture.

What about all those Jews who died such cruel deaths? What about all those children whose lives were cut short in the most brutal way? I pursued with question after question. Well, they were sad and mad about them, but still Germany was their land of birth and it has hopes of renewing itself from the horrors of Holocaust. I still think about my interviews with them and wish I could write more extensively about them after all these years, but my notes became ashes in our house fire.

Another revealing occasion was provided by a young couple who lived in my building, Roswithe Stark and Wolfgang Jehle. They invited me to a party at their place one evening, and we all sat on the floor eating fondue. I was seated beside Roswithe's mother.

She asked what I was doing in Germany, and I explained that I was studying the elections that brought Hitler to power. She was very quiet for a few moments and then, with tears in her eyes, told me that when she was a little girl, her father had been unemployed for eight years until Hitler gave him a job. I didn't quite know how to respond. But it was a pivotal moment for me. I experienced a moment of understanding about how a 1930s German might vote for Hitler. Hitler spoke most persuasively to Germans who felt left behind by history, economically threatened by industrial advance, and alarmed by what they saw as a breakdown of traditional morality. My insight didn't change the monstrous face of Hitler and the Nazis for me in a fundamental way, but my understanding of people who voted for Hitler was enriched.

After completing my research, my interviews and, yes, my agonizing efforts to make sure that my research was thorough and accurate, I returned to Mannheim, where I still had an office at the university, a telephone, and contacts with historians who might offer some advice here and there or at least some encouraging chatter over lunch. (My mentioning a telephone might sound a tad strange, but at that time in Germany, or perhaps anywhere in Europe, it could take up to a year or more to have a private telephone installed. I never had a phone in Bremen.)

Now that I had accumulated boxes and boxes of archival notes, what still remained to be tackled was the heart of the project: the statistical breakdown of Bremen's demographics. From that would emerge a profile of the Nazi voter by income, occupation, gender, and the like. This would reveal some answers to my question: Who voted for Hitler and why?

Following consultation with political science election experts at the University of Mannheim, I designed charts and recorded data on all 200,000 households in Bremen. I recorded roughly 2,000 households per day and dutifully kept those records. For several months, every morning at about 7:00, I carried a bundle of them from my hotel across the street to a sidewalk cafe where I would order breakfast and coffee and work through the papers, marking each household on the forms. After a sparse lunch, I would shift to weizenbier (an inexpensive and low-alcohol drink) and work throughout the afternoon. That would end around 6:00 when I would return to my hotel room, rest for about an hour, and then head off to the neighborhood restaurant/tavern for dinner and games of darts and Yahtzee with the locals. At a neighborhood bar with the unlikely name of the Bodega, I learned to play Yahtzee, which I played not as much to win as to not lose. Given my limited funds, I paid special attention to the custom that the loser had to buy beers for all. There were generally four or five players.

I made very few friends or even acquaintances in Mannheim, partially a result of my own shyness, but I also didn't have or couldn't find anyplace to meet people. I could go to bars or restaurants, but they were not easy places to strike up conversations. Nonetheless, I did find a neighborhood bar that quickly became my favorite, because it served a marvelous French onion soup, and the bartender, who was also the owner, was friendly and forthcoming with information about the neighborhood and the city. One evening, I inadvertently left my billfold at home and had no money to pay for my beer and soup. He graciously said not to worry about it and to bring the money some time later. I dutifully arrived the next evening, billfold in hand, only to discover that the bar was closed. The next evening, the same. Finally, on the third day, I read in the city newspaper that he had gone crazy, imagined there were ghosts in the bar, and proceeded to fire a handgun in all directions. The bar never reopened, and I still owe him a few German marks.

Then there was the time the guns were aimed at me. An anarchist group calling itself the Baader-Meinhof Gruppe was terrorizing Germany in the early 1970s. They were few in number, but they used the shock of violence as a way to force what they thought was democratic change in European society. One drizzly Sunday morning, with the archives closed, I decided to take a leisurely stroll in a nearby park. I wore a trench coat, but took no money or identification because I didn't expect to need any. I noticed an elderly woman eying me suspiciously, but I ignored it and headed down a deserted path. Within minutes, a police car screeched to a halt in front of me and four uniformed officers with guns drawn surrounded me, demanding identification. I responded in German that I had none. This one time, my American accent saved me. They quickly recognized that I was not, as they had strongly suspected, a member of the Gruppe. As quickly as they had appeared, they jumped back into their car and were gone. I was shaken, to put it mildly.

In the end, my research in Germany left me with an enormous amount of facts and information that could be churned into a couple of books, if only I was able to analyze and draw conclusions about the profile of Nazi voters. My exhaustive, monotonous research in Bremen and attempted analyses in Mannheim, aided solely by my own manpower, went nowhere and ultimately turned into ashes when our house burned down. In the absence of my handwritten notecards, which I'd toted around with me since leaving Germany, I am left with no conclusive results that would be acceptable to scholars. So all in all, from an academic point of view, my German experience left me empty and sad.

An American in Germany

IN CONTRAST, I GAINED QUITE A FEW BENEFITS from my German experience. I realized the extraordinary value of living and working in a culture different from my own. I admit that I was obsessed with my research and was not exposed to cultural and social life as much as I would have liked. Also, it was difficult to meet Germans from all social classes and walks of life. I readily confess that I felt more comfortable with the scholars, but that was principally a matter of our common interests and my German vocabulary. I didn't have the words to talk with factory workers or the expressions I would need to discuss dating or cooking. But

I had read and spoken enough about history and scholarship to converse confidently with scholars. Despite language barriers, I practically ate up and took every advantage of whatever contacts I had with people beyond the confines of my research, just as I had done long ago on the Iowa farm.

I liked German people. At times, they can match their Teutonic image and seem cold and hard to know. Americans see themselves as warmer and more friendly, but in my view that purported friendliness can be pretty superficial. What impressed me about Germans was how smart, well informed, and culturally sophisticated they are. I loved German music and theater. I appreciated the beauty of the land, especially the Black Forest.

Among my few cultural and historical explorations, I remember my visit to Worms in the spring of 1973. I was awed to stand in the cathedral where Martin Luther, a defrocked monk, confronted the Holy Roman Emperor and announced in 1520, "Hier stehe Ich. Ich kann nicht anders." Between Dai Sil and myself, we had five copies of Roland Bainton's *Here I Stand: A Life of Martin Luther*. Sometimes we fantasized about teaching a course together on Luther.

Not frequently, but once in a while, I was invited by German families to visit. While I was living in Mannheim in 1972, a gracious family invited me to spend Christmas Eve with them. We shared a delightful dinner in a beautiful room with an enchantingly decorated Christmas tree. Shortly before midnight, we all walked over to a nearby hilltop cemetery where the family's ancestors were buried. As we ambled slowly among the graves, I noticed with horror that many of the headstones were emblazoned with the Nazi swastika. It was deeply unsettling, and seemed even more macabre, given the beauty of the setting and the clear, crisp, serene night. I remember thinking to myself that German history for some time to come will remain a murky mixture of cultural achievement, natural beauty, and the horrors of Nazism.

If that experience at the cemetery left me sad and horrified, I had another experience that gave me hope. One day in Bremen, while I was researching in the State Archive, I went off to use the photocopy machine. In front of me was a middle-aged woman, and we got into a conversation. It turned out that she was an elementary-school teacher and she was reproducing her pupils' artwork, along with some she herself had made as a girl in the 1940s. The assignment, in both cases, was the same: simply to draw children. Her childhood drawings were cramped, restricted, clearly unhappy—whereas those of today's students were free-flowing and energetic. The contrast made her joyful, and I found that exhilarating. Despite all the horrors, I felt hope.

When my research had become increasingly tedious, I applied for a position teaching American history at the U.S. military base in Heidelberg, through the University of Maryland's overseas program. It was a great experience for me. Almost all of my students had served in Vietnam. Initially they were somewhat indifferent to learning, and just wanted to earn a few college credits or to spend a bit of time at something other than military drills. But as the class moved through World War I, the depression, and World War II, many of them became interested and even enthusiastic.Then we got to the war in Vietnam, and their bewilderment was total and quite poignant. I tried to be neutral and objective, keeping my own antiwar views out of the discussion. They indicated in both words and facial expression that they just couldn't understand what had happened, what was still happening. They had entered the military believing that America was right—if not always, most of the time—and that the Vietnam War must be right, too. But now it seemed that their fellow Americans had turned against the war and against them, the soldiers who were fighting on their behalf. They could make no sense of that, and yet, they could also see unmistakably that the war wasn't going at all well. Most of them, officers as well as enlisted men, did not espouse any pro-military doctrinaire or right-wing agenda. They simply couldn't understand what had gone wrong, and it was shattering to their worldview.

We talked at length about the nature of the cold war, the fallacies and exaggerations on both sides, the responses of Asian and African peoples to western imperialism, and the nature of wars of national liberation. I carefully explained, for instance, about

Ho Chi Minh and Woodrow Wilson—that when President Wilson arrived in France in 1919 to sign the treaty ending World War I, Ho was hopeful that he would help Vietnam. After all, Wilson had to great acclaim promulgated his Fourteen Points, which called for the self-determination of nations. That would seem to have included Vietnam, which was then a French colony. Rebuffed by Wilson, Ho joined the French communist party, later explaining: "It was patriotism, not communism, that inspired me." Apparently, Wilson was more focused on European than Asian self-determination. I hope that some of our talk struck home but, I fear, probably not much of it.

I traveled to my class at the Heidelberg base a couple times a week for about four months. What struck me most about the place was that it was a totally self-contained unit, almost hermetically sealed. The military personnel who lived there had no contact with German society and seemingly no interest in learning about the country, its culture, or the language. The Americans had no curiosity to explore Heidelberg, a charming medieval city. As a person who felt such strong mental and intellectual deprivation early on in Iowa, and who was so eager to broaden his universe, it was difficult to understand them. I wished that their children's generation would be more open to learning about things beyond America.

My interactions with Germans, coupled with teaching American soldiers at Heidelberg, added up to a fabulous self-learning experience. All people, but Americans especially, would benefit enormously from living in a foreign land for a period of time. They would learn more about themselves and their own culture. For one thing, seeming differences between cultures prompt one to think about taken-for-granted aspects of one's culture more closely. Frequently, universal dimensions can be seen in the *differences*. I was puzzled and delighted to learn that an alien culture could bring me closer to home. It opened my eyes to see what I had not before seen about my own upbringing.

Germany Still with Me

AFTER THREE YEARS OF HARD WORK, often accompanied by extreme loneliness, I came back to the States, exhausted and with my research findings stored in countless boxes. Those boxes sat unopened for years, while I engaged in a variety of jobs to make a living. Only when Dai Sil and I moved to New Paltz, New York, in 1997 after my retirement, did I make some serious effort to revive those notecards. I was becoming increasingly convinced that I could write something of importance, perhaps not so much to add to the scholarly record, as to shed light on the mystery of how such a horrendous regime could come to power among quite decent people. The project was far from coming into focus, but I had a definite start. Alas, it was destroyed by the flames that burned our house.

After so many years, it still puzzles and saddens me deeply that Hitler grabbed an unfortunate time in German history and made it into a monstrous period in human history. Sometimes, in a pensive mood, I compare the case of the Nazi voters with U.S. voters who supported George Wallace, a Democrat from Alabama, in his run for president in 1968 as an independent and in his presidential primary races as a Democrat in 1972 and 1976. His campaigns fed upon the resentment of poor, working-class whites against blacks, who the whites felt were protected, favored, and coddled by civil rights legislation, including affirmative action laws. Wallace extended this resentment beyond the South into the blue-collar regions of the North and into the Democratic party's New Deal coalition. His was an appeal to the prejudices and fears of the insecure middle class.

The insecure middle class was also one of the groups to which the Nazis appealed in the 1930s in Germany. This group in Germany feared change in general and many specific threats—including modernism, the unusual, the unexpected, homosexuality, sexual freedom, and others—to their fixed sense of normality and morality. Or should I say normalcy?

Looking back at my life, one of the few things I regret deeply is my failure to write my dissertation and thus complete my PhD. I had more research than necessary for several dissertations.

Perhaps, I can still try to write something—if not from note-cards, from my memories—that might bring some insight into one of the most horrendous historical events. Now I live in northern Manhattan. One day in July 2004, riding the elevator to our apartment, I felt the impact of Hitler's monstrosity. An elderly woman suddenly burst into tears. She recovered herself and then said, "I apologize, but sixty years ago today, my husband was taken to Auschwitz. I never saw him again."

Back in our apartment, sitting at my desk, I renewed my determination that I would try to write something coherent about my findings for people like that elderly woman, if only my health leaves me a long enough time on earth.

Don, the hard work you did in Germany is beyond my wildest imagination. I thought I was diligent, but reading what you did takes my breath away. Why does true realization always come too late? I thought I understood your sadness when all those cards, along with your actual writings, were consumed by our fire in 2001. But I didn't, not nearly. That a man of such discernment could be put off his purpose is something I thought I understood, but I never fathomed the extent of your suffering for not finishing your dissertation. No wonder you had trouble writing this chapter.

Your dissertation advisor David Schoenbaum wrote me after your passing with his apologies. Paraphrased, he said: "I was a young advisor. I realize in retrospect that I was asking him to climb Everest in a four-minute mile."

You, Don, lived to be a man of strength, wisdom, and imagination. No dissertation could equal that.

~ *D S K-G*

Don's official NEH portrait

PART VI

National Endowment for the Humanities

⚬

Humanities and Democracy

HARKING BACK TO 1977, my life was largely defined by Dai Sil and a small, independent federal agency, the National Endowment for the Humanities.

When I landed the job at NEH, I thought it was just a happy accident, a temporary berth with a regular paycheck, until I could find something more directly related to politics. I figured it would buy me some time, maybe a couple of years, and allow me to catch my breath and regroup. I could not have imagined that I would stay there for twenty years until I retired. Dai Sil would say it was destiny. If not that, it was at least good luck.

It didn't take long for me to discover that at NEH I could actually combine my scholarly background with my political passion and experiences in a most serendipitous way. I also discovered my ability to flourish within a bureaucracy. I remembered reading Montesquieu, the French Enlightenment political commentator, who wrote that institutions are fundamentally important not only for the maintenance of a society, but also for its progress. I agreed, and at NEH my conviction only deepened. Crucially, my work there gave me the sense that I was contributing something meaningful for the good of society. Yes, for the good of society beyond my personal ambition, whatever that was.

NEH was created in 1965 by the 89th Congress and the Johnson Administration. It sprang from deep-seated beliefs regarding the importance of a public understanding and application of the humanities—history, literature, philosophy, religion. The creation of NEH wasn't pie-in-the-sky intellectual idealism. Rather, Congress believed that a democracy requires citizens who are well-informed, knowledgeable, and thoughtful; and, therefore, that the humanities are critical to the proper functioning of a democratic society. Congress believed that the critical application of the humanities could inject wisdom and vision (in the form of educated citizens) into a democratic society.

I was in complete sync with the NEH founding principles. To my mind, both pessimistic and optimistic views about the workings of democratic society played a role in the establishment of NEH. The pessimistic view was well expressed by Walter Lippmann in his *The Public Philosophy*—"The people have acquired power which they are incapable of exercising." That profoundly pessimistic assessment had a deep impact on me and remains disturbing to me today.

In contrast, the optimistic view was expressed by Thomas Jefferson when asked if mass opinion could be trusted: Thomas Jefferson said: "I know of no safe depository of the ultimate powers of the society but the people themselves; and if we think them not enlightened enough to exercise their control with a wholesome discretion, the remedy is not to take it from them but to inform their discretion by education."

As I worked at NEH, I became aware that the humanities are most decidedly not idle luxuries for the intelligentsia. They are, first and foremost, bodies of knowledge, knowledge about people (great people and ordinary people), belief systems, historical events, cultural achievements, and cultural conflict. The humanities are also a set of intellectual disciplines and powerful methods of inquiry, analysis, and interpretation. It is through the humanities, that is through the study of history, literature, philosophy, language, and religion, that we confront the most fundamental questions of who we are, what we wish to be, where we have come from, how we relate to our fellow human beings, and how we can mold a society that honors our common aspirations as well as our differing beliefs and cultures.

I started out as a GS-12 program officer in the Division of State Programs. The way it works is that each state council around the country has its own staff and office. The Division of State Programs serves as a national headquarters supervising the state councils. Each program officer is assigned to several state councils.

When we got married in 1979, I was still a GS-12 and Dai Sil was a GS-13. But that was to change on our wedding day. Immediately after we had exchanged our vows in front of Dr. Muelder, a phone rang. Mrs. Muelder answered it and gave the phone to me.

"Don, it is for you, a call from your office in Washington." I put the phone to my ear, still struggling with the tears in my eyes. The conversation was brief, ending with my polite thanks. Returning calmly to the waiting ears and eyes of Dr. and Mrs. Muelder and of course, my new wife, I informed this eager audience, "I received my first wedding gift. That was from my director, B. J. Stiles, my boss. He said I was just made deputy director of the Division of State Programs." I was not only promoted, but skipped a couple of ranks to be made deputy director!

How did that happen? I was pleased, but I wasn't totally surprised. I knew—well, I will say it, at the risk of sounding pompous and conceited—I knew that I was doing a good job, especially with the representatives of the state councils. The political and managerial skills that I had been cultivating, knowingly and unknowingly, from my 4-H days in rural Iowa and all through my involvement in political campaigns and civil rights activism came in handy at NEH. Further, I had solid academic training, which equipped me with knowledge and insight into the humanities disciplines. Unlike most of the other professional staff at NEH, though, I felt comfortable enough to jettison the constipated academic jargon and speak freely, frequently with a self-deprecating sense of humor. My outspokenness was probably refreshing and even fun to many people in the state councils and to some of my NEH colleagues.

Before leaving for our wedding and honeymoon, I had had a feeling that there might be a surprise waiting for me when I returned. B.J. Stiles, however, didn't want to wait. He preferred to make my unusual promotion a wedding gift. From that time onward, my journey at NEH was upward. And I knew NEH had become more than a job to fill until a better one came along.

While I believed in the importance of all divisions of NEH, I was glad that I worked in the divisions of State Programs and then Public Programs (where I was made division director in 1984), because those divisions supported out-of-school education initiatives. I've always believed that education is a lifelong process. And from my days at Simpson College, I also believed that all a student really needs is one good, inspiring teacher who can transmit the magnificence and the excitement of intellectual life. In combination, those two convictions explain my passion for public humanities programs. Though sporadic in terms of the exposure they provide, individual museum exhibitions, television and radio broadcasts, library discussions, and the like can spark that love of learning.

Culture Wars

NOW, ONTO SOMETHING I BECAME HEAVILY INVOLVED IN at NEH: culture wars. Henry Luce, founder and long-time publisher of *Time* magazine, as well as a staunch right-wing Republican, once proclaimed that the 20th century was the American Century. In contrast, Henry Wallace, the Progressive Party candidate for president in 1948, declared it the "century of the common man." Their positions proved prophetic. Over the past few decades, America has been, and in many ways continues to be, divided between those two schools of thought and has engaged in three contemporary civil wars—the Civil Rights movement, the antiwar movement, and the culture wars. And as it turned out at NEH, I was to be an active participant in the third.

By the time I joined the staff of NEH in February 1977, the agency had already been involved in a variety of culture wars for the past decade. The agency could not remain on the sidelines, unaffected by the winds of change sweeping the land. Nor should it have been sidelined. In taking a leading role, NEH did what it had to do.

The culture wars arrived in force during the sixties, an era not restricted to a literal decade. In fact, the sixties was extended by former NEH chair Sheldon Hackney (who taught a course on the sixties at the University of Pennsylvania) to last from 1954 (the date of the landmark case of *Brown* v. *Board of Education*) to 1974 (when Nixon resigned in the wake of Watergate). That definition seems reasonable to me. Crucially, it encompasses both the Civil Rights movement and the antiwar movement. Other observers have assigned differing dates, but they all speak in common to an age of widespread revolt against any authority perceived as repressive.

The sixties were important to me personally. Among other things, that was when I achieved a degree of political maturation. Without that period, I would probably never have become politically active, that is, organizing demonstrations and managing electoral campaigns. Nor would I, most likely, have ever become a successful federal manager.

The crises of the sixties brought the culture wars not only to the mainstream power elite, but also to minority and underserved communities. Those marginalized populations that lacked full recognition, representation, and access had internal as well as external struggles with which to contend. As Franz Fanon wrote in *The Wretched of the Earth*: "The major weapon of the colonizers was the imposition of their image of the colonized on the subjugated people." In other words, many colonized people internalized the images that their colonizers had of them into wretched self-images that, in some cases, devastated their souls.

But during the upheavals of the sixties, long-subjugated or -marginalized ethnic groups began to recognize an urgent need to reclaim their own cultural and historical heritage. And so it was that the demand for ethnic studies—such as African American studies, Asian American studies, Native American studies, and Hispanic studies—were on their way to revolutionizing American academia. The arrival of the women's movement and the creation of gender studies added to the stew.

So the culture wars invaded NEH and I was thrilled to take up arms to correct what I saw as the shameful history of my own country. I recently found an opening statement I made before the Congressional Reauthorizing Committee on June 17, 1993, when I was acting chair of NEH:

> We have immense diversity in this country. It is vital that we comprehend and appreciate that diversity and the varying

truths that are represented. But we need also to seek the common good. Through the disciplines of the humanities we can come to terms with our common heritage and our diversity. For the humanities are more than a body of knowledge. They entail critical thinking, intellectual discipline, reflection, and vigorous debates about ethical choices and value judgments. This is fundamental for a democracy.

Not long ago, I reread Ralph Ellison's *Invisible Man*, a magnificent presentation about the plight of black Americans as invisible. As an undergraduate, I was chastened and saddened by the book, but I focused then almost exclusively on the particular. This time around, I understood that Ellison was using the particular to speak more broadly to human universals. We should be respectful and tolerant of the widest range of views, not losing sight of the particular or, perhaps even more important, the underlying universals among different men and cultures. The humanities examine and honor the particular, while at the same time they seek to identify and explicate the universal.

In my first nine years at NEH, I worked under two chairs, first Joseph Duffey, a Carter appointee and a liberal democrat, and then Bill Bennett, a Reagan appointee and former Democrat turned neoconservative. To be sure, Bennett and I locked horns on numerous occasions around a variety of thorny issues. But as it turned out, those skirmishes were lightweight in comparison to what was to come. In 1986, as multicultural debates still raged, in came Lynne Cheney, the wife of conservative Dick Cheney, newly appointed by Bush 41 as NEH's chair. And it was with Lynne Cheney that I had the most direct and by far the most conflicted dealings of my career.

I had met Lynne at a restaurant in Washington for lunch not long before she became my boss. We were meeting to discuss an application she wished to submit to NEH for a film based on the book she had cowritten with her husband, *Kings of the Hill*, a history of various speakers of the House of Representatives. Actually, she was thinking about resubmitting a proposal that she had already submitted. (Dai Sil had been the program officer on Lynne's proposal, and she prepared me to deal with the film application before she left for the Big Apple to direct the media program of the New York State Council on the Arts.) At the time of our lunch, I was the director of the Division of Public Programs, which included the agency's Media Program.

It was a pleasant lunch. Clearly Lynne was smart and quick minded, often throwing in witty remarks mixed with laughter. She was enjoying herself and perhaps was glad that she was now dealing with none other than the director of the program, not a demanding program officer (Dai Sil). She felt comfortable conversing with a politically savvy person (I learned that this was her view about me when she became my boss), with someone who understood power play. Well, if she thought she was equally savvy, she didn't quite know me well enough. There is an awful lot behind my casual *façade*.

The next time I met Lynne, she was being sworn in as chair of NEH by John Agresto, then acting chair (and formerly Bill Bennett's chief aide with a variety of titles). It was, in retrospect, a striking ceremony. Present were the agency's division directors and about fifteen or so others, all gathered in the chair's office. After she was sworn in, she read a passage from a novel. (God, I wish I could remember the author and title.) The essence was that a leader shouldn't—or doesn't need to—dictate; that a leader sets the tone for things. It was better than that sounds, quite moving and touching actually. After reading that, she moved from behind the chair's desk, walked toward me, put her hand in my arm, and said, "I know one person here. He rejected my application for a grant," her eyes full of tease. It was a gracious moment. Dai Sil also wrote her a heartfelt note from New York expressing how pleased she was that NEH now had a woman as a chairperson.

After that, there was one time in which I saw a personal side of Lynne Cheney. For Christmas 1986, she gave a party for NEH staff. The senior members were invited to her townhouse in McLean, Virginia. Dick Cheney in his light-brown wool jacket greeted us at the door. Dai Sil and I went in, eager to learn about the private side of their lives. Well, we were led to a room with a large table where catered food was on display, the usual fare of turkey and ham. The food was tasteless. We lost interest, and walked around a bit. We did not find one original piece of art on the wall. In the bookshelves were some paperback thrillers by Dick Francis, Dai Sil's favorite reading for the train rides during her weekend commutes between New York and Washington. Lynne mixed with the staff, but she appeared ill at ease and uncomfortable. That was the last time I saw a vulnerable side of her.

For the first several months of her chairship, she tapped me as someone she could rely on and who could protect and guide her in a new environment with so many former professors. I guess she was somewhat unsure about the highly trained, professional staff. Granted, she had a PhD in literature from the University of Wisconsin, but in terms of experience she would stand at the very back of the staff at NEH. Apparently, she felt comfortable with me and also thought that she would do well with me on her side with my background in the world of politics.

All that soon changed. She transformed, became a different person. Soon she began confidently proclaiming that she wanted projects that would appeal to Joe Six-Pack. And she would carry on about what she called elitist projects. I wasn't fully aware then how much of a mantra anti-elitism would become for the Republican right during the coming years, right up to today.

Lynne set out to lead a countermovement against the era of the sixties. She launched a right-wing fight against the era's struggle to remove puritanical and authoritative restraints upon personal behavior and on democratic action. She did not blink as she redefined the values fought for in the sixties as moral permissiveness, moral relativism, and irresponsible behavior, not to mention elitist.

The charge of elitism, I presume, results from the fact that some people believe the better educated tend to lean a tad farther left. To Lynne, all liberals were elitists. And Joe Six-Pack could not care less about civilizations other than his own. To Lynne, speaking for Joe Six-Pack, the only civilization worthy to be called civilized was western civilization. This woman with a PhD in literature and married to a (then) member of Congress considered herself to represent the somewhat conflicting interests of corporate America and fundamentalist Christians. And millions of Americans who were neither corporate or fundamentalist would be attracted to Lynne's campaign to evoke the demons of elitism and moral relativism. Furthermore, subliminal messages that awoke ingrained racism against minorities would be sent as the consequence of favoring the dominant culture.

Much of the conservative assault dealt with what the conservative critics derisively called historical revisionism. By this, they meant that left-wing historians—particularly in the fields of social, ethnic, and gender history—were forcing their political viewpoints into straightforward, factual history. Did they really think history as it used to be taught was straightforward, unvarnished, factual? Was it not simply political, as opposed to social, history taught by privileged white men who selected the facts recorded, provided interpretation, and presented it all as objective truth? Did they not know that historical study since Thucydides and Herodotus has been a matter of interpretation? Even the act of selecting which facts to record is an act of interpretation.

Lynne Cheney represented to me what distressed me most about American culture—the materialism, the insistence on what she regarded as the superiority of our way of life and philosophy, the anti-intellectual posturing in political life. I believe the basic educational mission of NEH was impeded by Lynne's focus on fundamentalist and anti-elitist values, by her view that certain puritanical certitudes should restrict openness in the society and influence our foreign policy.

Review Process

BILL BENNETT HAS BEEN BLAMED FOR POLITICIZING THE AGENCY. Lynne Cheney carried politicization to a drastically enhanced degree, using what I thought to be deception and duplicity. My direct confrontation with Lynne started over the review process, the center of NEH. She never wanted to overturn a staff recommendation on a grant application on her own, though the chairperson clearly had the authority. The staff was upset to find their chair circulating lists of preferred panelists and lobbying members of the National Council (the board appointed by the U.S. president to advise the chair of NEH). She never failed to say that the panelist lists she sent around simply included persons encountered by members of the senior staff—meaning her office—and found to be most qualified. Finally, I was not surprised to find that she left no paper trail about her political and ideological concerns.

The stories of certain grant proposals under the Cheney chairship provide some telling examples of the culture wars. For example, a proposal for a multipart documentary on "the other" Americas, with Carlos Fuentes as narrator, was submitted to the Media Program of the Division of Public Programs, where I was the director. Everyone—all the panelists, reviewers, and NEH staff—thought it was a compelling project and a wonderful opportunity for NEH.

However, Lynne objected, apparently not so much to the content of the project as to the participation of Fuentes in it. Fuentes, a Mexican born in Mexico—who had spent most of his formative years in Washington as the son of a diplomat—was an author and a political figure who expressed some mild criticisms of the United States. Well, mild to any reasonable, objective person. To Lynne, any criticism of the United States was unacceptable and unpatriotic. The case for the excellence of this series was so strong that its supporters managed to win the fight, but the price was high.

The Columbus quincentenary occurred on Lynne's watch. In meetings of the National Council and with staff members, she outlined her vision of this 500th anniversary as an opportunity to celebrate the magnificent spread of European culture and American democracy across the continent. A true triumph. Alas, a surprise was in store for her. Under its Columbus quincentenary initiative, NEH received quite a few grant applications. But most of them, consistent with the standards of scholarly balance demanded by NEH and the historians' quest for new insights and perspectives, did not accentuate the positive. Many grant applications proposed to treat the atrocities committed by Europeans and Americans against Native Americans. Cheney was appalled and did all she could to renounce and escape from the initiative that she had supported.

A grant application for a documentary film on Diego Rivera, the Mexican artist, which many reviewers, including myself, thought to be a well-balanced proposal that showed strong potential to be a powerful film, failed to gain approval. I will always believe that Lynne found a way to undermine the application through communications with panelists and National Council members. Rivera was a Marxist, after all, and Trotsky had been staying at his house in Mexico when Stalin had him killed.

If she was extra sensitive about nonwestern projects, she was also incapable of seeing the value of studying potentially controversial subjects as part of complex human phenomena. The endowment's Museum Program included a project called Arts of Voudon, which focused on the religious practice of Voudon (Voodoo). Lynne was fearful that support for this project might send out the message that NEH was approving the practice.

Yet another application involved a film proposal about George Wallace. The applicant was a historian from Emory University, and the proposed a film would be based on a book he had written. A thesis of that book is that it was Wallace who had demonstrated to the Republican Party—and particularly to Richard Nixon—that Republicans could get the votes of blue-collar Democrats in the North by appeals to race; and that the party's ultimate and vigorous adoption of a race policy—one that was more subtle than it was blatant—helped Nixon win and elected Ronald Reagan.

I read the professor's book while we were reviewing the film application and I thought it was sound scholarship. Furthermore, the thesis had stood the test of time. George Wallace was a Democrat from Alabama who, when he ran for governor and lost, said: "I'll never be outniggered again." And, true to his word, he wasn't. He won the governorship four times and ran for president four times.

Richard Nixon, as he pondered how he could return to national politics after losing the presidency in 1960 to Kennedy and the governorship of California to Pat Brown, endorsed what became known as the southern strategy, that is, an appeal to those white, poor folks in the South and the North who felt abused by the federal government's civil rights actions. Reagan and his successors expanded upon this effort, by characterizing all liberals as elitists, intellectuals, and wine-and-cheese folks who attempt to impose their unrepresentative views upon common folk.

Apparently, the George Wallace proposal enraged Lynne. She never personally confronted me on the topic, but she commissioned her deputy, Jerry Martin, to administer the bludgeon. During one of our regular meetings, Jerry raised the topic and said he considered the thesis absurd. Having both read the book and participated in the elections under consideration, I was able to swiftly demonstrate that the thesis was indeed valid. My input was to no avail, of course. As I had anticipated, the National Council recommended against the project.

So Lynne Cheney became the warrior chieftain in the American cultural wars at a federal funding agency, openly criticizing the elitism of liberals, the left-wing control of universities, and political correctness. What I found most difficult in fighting the war with her were her absolute moral and intellectual certitude, her prejudice, and her insistence on categorizing everything and putting it in a box either labeled TRUTH or labeled RELATIVISM.

Frustrated and angry, Lynne instructed Jerry Martin to hold a weekly meeting with me under the guise of a performance appraisal. Those sessions were bad, so bad that I could have felt humiliated or hopeless. But I tried to turn them into bad jokes. Occasionally, however, I began to feel mentally tortured. To make some sense of this turn of events, allow me to provide some background about Jerry and myself.

Jerry was hired as the director of the Education Program. Previously he had been a professor of philosophy at the University of Colorado and a staff aide to Senator Hank Brown of Colorado. He struck me, initially, as an amiable sort who didn't know the first thing about management and this impression was confirmed time and time again. In addition, I soon learned, he was a hard-right ideologue.

Shortly after he was hired, Jerry would wander up from his third-floor office to talk with me. He told me once that he had mentioned to Lynne when he was offered the job that he didn't know much about management. She told him that her ablest director was Don Gibson and that he (Jerry) should talk with him (Don). We had pleasant talks sitting in the hallway—so that I could smoke—and he asked good, if frightfully *naïve*, questions about management, which I attempted to answer and believe that I did pretty well.

My relationship with Jerry changed radically when Lynne appointed him assistant chair for programs, which made him my immediate supervisor. By then my relationship with Lynne had also changed. I was no longer her best director, though I know until the end she thought I had the best managerial and political skills. I was just on the wrong side of political thinking.

Soon I paid for not being an obedient employee. As just mentioned, Lynne ordered Jerry to meet with me once a week and go over my performance. Those meetings were scheduled on Wednesdays at 4:45. I would arrive promptly in his outer office and his secretary would invariably greet me and inform me that Jerry was busy and that he would see me shortly. On average, he made me wait fifteen to thirty minutes.

Jerry would finally invite me in. I would enter, and sit in the designated chair. A few more minutes would pass in silence. Simply to break the silence, I would start informing him about some stuff that was going on in my division. He rarely had much to say. Within several weeks, it became clear to me that he was ordered to bring me in line. But the poor guy had no idea how to accomplish that.

I often wondered if Lynne's certitude resulted from conviction or opportunism. Both during and after her tenure at NEH, she clearly had her eyes on national political attention. While at NEH she cultivated a coterie of journalists—nationally syndicated columnists—to promote her ideas and her persona. George Will and Charles Krauthammer were prominent among them. The editorial page of the *Wall Street Journal* became a significant promoter of her ideas and programs. After leaving NEH, she was a regular participant in the television program *Crossfire*. It was the antithesis of reasoned debate.

A Party at Our House

BECAUSE LYNNE CHENEY WAS SO PROBLEMATIC, both Dai Sil and I thought her husband Dick Cheney a nice person by comparison. When we first met him at a Christmas party at their home in Virginia, he appeared unassuming, down-to-earth, and polite. The second time we saw him was at our 17th Street house in DC, a historic house, which used to be included in the list of Dupont Circle historic houses open for tour. We were able to buy that house because it was at the outer edge of the Dupont Circle neighborhood, still not gentrified enough for rich folks to venture to live.

Anyway, Dai Sil and I decided to give a party for Charles Burnett, a much loved African American film director/writer who was then a rising star, with a MacArthur genius award and a just completed film starring Danny Glover, *To Sleep with Anger*. He directed the ninety-minute feature documentary, *America Becoming*, which Dai Sil cowrote with Virginia Kassel (a creator of the 1976 PBS miniseries, *The Adams Chronicles*) and produced. He was in town from Los Angeles and we wanted to welcome him to our home.

Many of the PBS and the Corporation for Public Broadcasting (CPB) people, including the presidents from both organizations and a good-size film crowd from the African American community were invited. We didn't think it would be something the Cheneys would show up for, but I had sent an invitation.

Well, the day before the party, Lynne's secretary called and told us to start cleaning the house. She was a friend and our relationship was casual. She informed me that Lynne and her husband, the secretary of defense, were going to come. We were truly surprised. On the day of the party, the Secret Service people appeared about two hours ahead and combed through the house. Just for fun, I offered them drinks, but they refused.

By the time the Cheneys appeared, the party was in full swing. Nearly everyone who had been invited showed up, including the presidents of PBS and CPB. Drinks in hand, everyone seemed to be enjoying themselves. When Lynne and Dick entered, for a few minutes the gaiety turned into stunned silence. After all, not many people there would have had a chance to meet the secretary of defense in person. To their credit, the Cheneys were pleasant and polite, encouraging everyone to return to the party.

Lynne asked me to introduce our guests, especially those from NEH. So I took her around, starting downstairs and moving up to the second floor. Suddenly, I felt a force on my shoulder. Lynne had grabbed me, her eyes focusing on an African American man.

"Tell me, Don, who is that tall, black man?"

"He is a former employee of NEH who now works at the Smithsonian Institution. His name is James Early."

"I thought so. That's the one who attacked me in the *Boston Globe*. Introduce him to me!"

Now, her voice turned into that of a general's ordering his troops. Not a sign of politeness. Even before I completed my introduction, Lynne shot out verbal attacks that made my face red. They were embarrassingly crude. Jim stood there with a sarcastic grin.

As the host, I felt nervous about the unfolding scene. Then I noticed Dick Cheney right behind his wife, facing me. His face was that of a father who felt ashamed by the bad behavior of his child.

He didn't say a word, but wanted to communicate with me with his rolling eyes. At that moment, I had lots of sympathy for Dick and saw an image of a good human being.

Actually, there was a third occasion to experience Dick Cheney. It was, however, just Dai Sil's. About a week after our party, a huge dinner was held at the Willard Hotel to celebrate the Ken Burns *Civil War* series. By the way, if it were up to Lynne Cheney, I wouldn't have been surprised if she had given all the Media Program's money at NEH to him. She was crazy about the series, because it was quintessential Americana and safe.

So at one point during this Willard Hotel dinner, Dai Sil got up to take a break. Later that evening, she told me her Willard lobby story: "I went out just to get away from all those congratulations and praises. Enough was enough. Standing awkwardly in that huge lobby, I looked to the other end. There was Dick Cheney. I debated if I should walk over to him and say hi, but decided against it. I thought he would not care to be greeted by me. Then I noticed that he was walking toward me and before I knew it, he was standing in front of me. 'Hi, Good to see you. Remember me? I was at your house not long ago.' Don, I could not believe it. The person I saw in that encounter was actually nice, so unlike his wife!"

Well, history proved otherwise. We were made humble, yes terribly humble, about our ability to judge people. We had been proud that we were good at entering into the hearts of people and understanding their essence.

When I think back about my struggles with Lynne Cheney, I am amazed and yet proud of how resilient I was. At that time, I already had Crohn's disease and my health was not in top shape, but I still did not give in. I am glad that I survived without compromising to save myself.

Disasters Turned into Blessings

IS NOT LIFE FULL OF SURPRISES? Do not disasters often prove to be blessings in disguise? Who would have guessed that Lynne Cheney pushed me to prepare, if unknowingly, to clean up the mess of her making and to do whatever I could do for the agency I loved? After Lynne, I was interim chair of NEH for five months, from April to August of 1993. It was exhilarating. Never have I felt so confident and comfortable in what I was doing. It was as if I had been studying and preparing for the position for years. Indeed I had been. I had patiently—or sometimes impatiently—observed Joseph Duffey (1977-1981), William Bennett (1981-1985), and Lynne Cheney (1986-1993). Increasingly critical of their actions, I was always observant, constantly making mental notes about what I would do differently.

The appointment by President Clinton was long in coming. My extreme discomfort with life under Lynne Cheney made me eager for change in political leadership in the country and at the endowment. Was the agency so politicized that its reputation was damaged? Perhaps so. But it also made me attentive to how the agency operated. As I saw Lynne manipulate her authority to work her will, I mastered the policies of the agency, the legislation governing it, and the intricate rules of the federal bureaucracy, including the personnel rules. What I had done years ago with 4-H and *Robert's Rules* came back like roaring waves.

On the morning after the presidential election, I appeared in my NEH office on time, teary about the victory of Clinton. Candace Katz, whom I had promoted to be my deputy when I became the director of Public Programs, greeted me and gave me a simple congratulations. We did not need many words between us. We understood what trials we had gone through together.

Still, I had the wish that Lynne would serve out her term. NEH was created by Congress as an independent agency, not as part of any cabinet department. The agency's chair, though a political appointee at the pleasure of the president, serves for term appointments. I firmly believed that NEH should be apolitical in concert with the authorizing legislation. Were Lynne not to serve out her appointed term, it would send the signal that the agency is political, hence it can be politicized. But was that the message she wished to send?

In early December, I received a notice of a division directors meeting with the chair in ten minutes. As I walked out of the division offices, my assistant handed me a memo from the chair, the first of a large package intended for the entire staff. Lynne was resigning, effective January 18, 1993—Inauguration Day. The decision I feared and lusted after.

She held her head completely still for several moments and then in a shaky voice announced her intention to resign. All the other directors spoke fondly and supportively. I remained silent. She never looked at me, never acknowledged my presence. I just stared at her. It was quite possible that she had already heard that the Clinton transition team had tagged me as her interim successor, as I had.

I had wanted to tell her, and to this day wish that I had, that I deeply regretted her resignation because it would reinforce the impression that NEH was a politicized agency. (It is a vital point!) Why didn't I? Probably because I was so relieved, but also because I didn't think I could control my emotions. Congress clearly intended that independent agencies operate outside the policy preferences of any presidential administration.

The next several weeks continued to be fraught with uncertainty, gossip, and guessing. But the long-awaited call did come and I was asked if I would serve as the interim chair of the endowment. When I said yes, my voice was controlled and calm but never was my mind filled with so many ideas and my heart with so much passion.

*I keep thinking of what Don's boss in the Division of State
Programs, Carole Huxley would later say in a speech about him
at his retirement party:* "[You embody the] *belief that excel-
lent management is an honorable and desirable goal of a public
servant* . . . [then, said with a smile] . . . *Your work has gone
a long way to undermine the important concept that government is ineffectual, bureaucratic, and wasteful. Just for one
example, making Public Programs mission driven, rigorous, and
consistent in its reviews; generous with help to applicants; and
resistant to political manipulation makes it extremely difficult
for some of your former bosses to succeed. I think they may even
believe that your loyalty to NEH was allowed to exceed your
personal loyalty* . . . [now in all seriousness] . . . *You genuinely
believe in NEH's importance to this country. You are, in fact,
passionate, even zealous, in this view, and no one has been able
to get you to keep your mouth shut about it. You have displayed a
stubbornness on this point that is monumental.*

~ D S K-G

Finally, Chairman

A FEW DAYS LATER, OUR PHONE RANG AGAIN. It was Deborah Sale,
the chair of the transition team for arts and humanities. She informed me quietly that there had been a glitch and that my appointment was postponed. Another call later in the week informed
me that the deal was off. As it turned out, Lynne Cheney had argued persuasively to the Clinton team that a standing order of authority memorandum took legal precedence and that Jerry Martin
would serve as acting chair. Lynne was wrong and the Clinton team
was wrong to accept the argument.

The associate general counsel of NEH had worked on transitions in the past and was fully informed about such matters. He assured me that the president had the authority in such situations, one that had been established by the Vacancy Act of 1866. The White House staff was just too busy with other things to research it thoroughly.

The whole thing meant that I had to wait three more months to claim what was coming to me and for which I had been prepared. (I still grind my teeth thinking about those wasted months and how much I could have achieved.) Finally, one early morning in April, one of the transition team members, Bill Gilcher, called and asked me to show up on time and wait.

On April 14, 1993, I arrived at my office at 8:30. Bill Gilcher arrived shortly after and explained that they had figured out how to resolve the issue. President Clinton had appointed Michael Shapiro as chair of NEH, with an explicit instruction that he would write a memorandum delegating all responsibilities of the chair to Donald Gibson. Bill took me to Jerry Martin's office and informed him that, as of that moment, I was the interim chair.

Finally, the time I had been preparing for all my life from the days of rural Iowa materialized right in front of me. I did not waste a minute in starting my new job. My first actions were quick and decisive. Within two hours of my appointment, I had sent a memo to all staff and all members of the National Council simply stating that I did not intend to be a caretaker and that I needed their help. The response was quiet, respectful, and accepting, an understandable reaction. Some might have worried that I wouldn't be any different than Lynne, in that I would try to bring my own (liberal) ideologies into play, only with more skill and knowledge.

My first meeting with the entire staff went extremely well. A majority of staffers were pleased that I was acting chair. At that meeting, I made it clear that I wanted NEH to be nonideological. Every proposed topic and every scholarly approach would receive a fair hearing through the proper review process. I told the staff that NEH should be open to ideas, and that it should relish the clash of perspectives and the pluralism of cultures. I told them that I wanted the agency to reach out to underserved communities with new dedication and vigor. I wanted the endowment to be inclusive, open, and responsive, ever mindful of the highest standards of scholarship. I would have none of Lynne's politicization of the agency. I made it abundantly clear that the humanities are about questioning, about uncertainty, about the search for varying truths, and about the search for the common good.

The first weekend after I was made acting chair, Dai Sil marched into my third-floor study and announced, "Don, we are going shopping."

"For what?" I didn't even lift my head from the papers I was reviewing.

"We are going to buy you a couple of suits!"

I was about to protest, then thought better of it. I was stubborn but not stupid. I knew she was right. I needed to look halfway decent as acting chair in appearances before Congress and as the NEH representative at meetings all around the country.

We got lucky that day. On Connecticut Avenue, Dai Sil saw a big Going out of Business sign in front of a well-known men's store. She went in and I followed. She chose three suits. I had to admit that she did a superb job selecting them, all of them less than half the regular price. As we got out of the store, Dai Sil said, "I saw a tailor shop close by as we walked here. Let's find it. I bet it is run by a Korean!" Well, sure enough, she was right on both counts.

The jackets were fine, but the pants needed to be fixed. By that time, I'd had Crohn's for several years, which took away my appetite. Further, all my hard work made me so thin that most of my pants rolled around my waist. A nice young Korean man came with a measuring tape. I stood meekly, even though I was somewhat impatient to get out and back to my work.

"When would you get them done?" asked Dai Sil in her sweet, negotiating voice. "The sooner, the better. Can I collect them in a couple of days?"

"Well, I will do my best. The trouble is, though, it will be more work than just fixing the waist. You see, your husband has no ass!"

He said it in such a matter of fact, no-nonsense way, in a bright voice. I don't know if I ever laughed so hard.

"A man of no arse!" Saying this, Dai Sil laughed so much that I thought she might end up rolling on the floor. Those pants were the best fit I'd had in a long time. I admitted that more than a few times to Dai Sil.

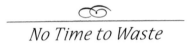

No Time to Waste

WHEN I TOOK OVER THE ENDOWMENT, the structure and general atmosphere of the agency were at their worst. Lynne Cheney had created an elaborate structure at the top, with a deputy chair, two assistant chairs, and five assistants. Plus, she had the Budget and Public Affairs officials reporting directly to her. A number of these people held career appointments. She created career positions and then filled them with people politically loyal to her, calling them senior staff, while excluding division directors and other office heads who had traditionally been considered senior. That senior staff (unaffectionately known to most of us as the SS) met every afternoon at 4:00 and made decisions, with no advice or information from the rest of the staff. We were only informed of the decisions. The message was clear: there were two camps at NEH—the *we* and the *they*. There was no collegial sharing of information, no open discussion of options, just decisions from the top with no rationale attached.

All that had to be changed fast. Jerry Martin, who had gone back to being one of the assistant chairs, asked if I wanted to hold the senior staff meeting at 4:00 p.m. I said yes, and instructed him to invite all of the division directors and office heads. When 4:00 arrived, I walked into the room and said that I would need a lot of help and advice from them and that I would listen. Then, I said: "I invited division directors and office heads to this senior staff meeting because I have always considered directors to be senior staff, and that term will not be used again unless you are included. And this is the last daily 4:00 p.m. meeting; we will all meet once a week on Wednesdays and I will be meeting with all of you individually." The two assistant chairs, Lynne's people, had nothing to say.

I had no time to waste. I had too many things I had been itching to put my hands on the minute an opportunity came. First and foremost, I wanted to restore the integrity of the review process. I wanted to lift the morale of the staff. And, I wanted to restore the perception of NEH in the academic and public communities as an agency that leads the nation in expanding and elevating the world of ideas and stands firm in its mission no matter how the political wind blows.

I made one major staff appointment in my capacity as acting chair: Candace Katz became my deputy chair. A Harvard PhD in literature and a Georgetown JD, Candace had a sharp mind and a positive disposition. She was able to get things moving and to read my mind without much explanation. She was exactly the person I needed as my right arm to help me achieve urgent and compelling goals in a limited period of time.

For a morale boost and to share a true sense of solidarity, I invited all the staff to a post-Council party in the chair's office after a National Council meeting. I spent my own money and Dai Sil agreed with it wholeheartedly. It was a huge hit. They came in mobs with looks of awe on their faces. I also met separately with the staff of each division. Thus my first priority—to let the staff know that I respected their work and cared for them—got off to a good start.

Raising the morale of the staff had to be accompanied by steps to increase the agency's efficiency. As is typical for many government agencies in Washington, it wasn't difficult to see the first task at hand. NEH needed to upgrade its computer system. NEH had a well meaning but not so competent person in charge of the computer system, which was hopelessly out of date. No chair before me had thought a computer-system upgrade to be a priority. When it came to crucial management aspects, management had been as antiquated as the computer system.

First, I retained a consultant, Michael Lim, a young computer geek with an AB in physics from the University of Chicago, who would work within our limited money constraints. The real hurdle was the budget. Could we afford the necessary investment in new equipment and training? I had to assume that money was there for me to find. I asked Budget and Planning to provide me with all expenditure and planning documents for the year, which I took home. I spent three days in my third-floor study with a small calculator in hand, playing with figures. Time and time again, I would start with an assumption, toy with the figures, reach a conclusion, question my assumption, and then start all over again.

By Monday evening I was comfortable. The next morning, I called a meeting of senior staff. I walked them through my assumptions about past and projected expenditures. Some were surprised by my questions and my detailed knowledge, but all provided the answers I had expected. The meeting lasted forty-five minutes and ended with my announcement that we were going to buy a new computer system. They looked stunned, but also pleased and impressed. No other chair with whom they had worked had shown an interest in mastering the agency's budget, especially in relation to questions of management.

What I did that day was actually remarkably similar to a scene in the movie *Dave*, which Dai Sil and I had seen the previous weekend. I wasn't aware of the similarity until I was in the middle of the meeting. In *Dave*, the title character (Kevin Kline)—a double of the dying U.S. president whom his chief of staff wants to keep alive until it becomes safe to announce his own candidacy for president—learns that the first lady (Sigourney Weaver) is terribly upset with him (Dave) because he had cancelled a program for the homeless, the first lady's treasured program. Deeply distressed, Dave invites a friend, a budget officer from his real-life office, to the White House and explains the situation. Once his friend gets over the incredible, stunning situation Dave is in, he sits with Dave, munching fat sandwiches and chips, and goes through each budget item. The two of them go through "all expenditure and planning documents" of that year and the friend is safely smuggled out before the White House wakes up.

The next day, Dave calls for a special meeting and reviews each item, saving enough money to reinstall the program for the homeless. I could not get over how similar that scenario was to what I had done to buy NEH's new computer system.

Management and Bureaucracy

I KNEW THAT MANY STAFFERS THOUGHT that I was too bureaucratic, too concerned about management. But I believed firmly that without efficient procedures and means, no agency could carry out its mission and vision, however lofty and important. If I may say so, my unique contribution at NEH, especially as acting chair, came from my political and managerial skills as well as from my hunger and respect for intellectual undertakings. I do not mind saying that I was more successful than my colleagues at NEH because I viewed matters through a political lens and also understood how to use and move the bureaucracy.

The terms *politics* and *bureaucracy* are grossly abused and misused. Politics, in popular parlance, means the absence of merit and the dominance of personal interest. Bureaucracy has come to mean a system concerned primarily or exclusively with its own survival and the survival of the people in it, that is, the bureaucrats. There is some truth in both definitions, but I consider them to be basically simpleminded and dismissive. The ancient Athenians, notably Aristotle, defined politics as the process of dealing with human beings in a community, and all humans live in a community. Bureaucracy, in my judgment, is the mechanism of the institutions we establish to ensure that the decisions made by the authorities (hopefully through a democratic political process) are instituted thoroughly and fairly.

represent NEH at that opening inauguration, and to be sitting as a featured guest in the front rows beside people with concentration camp tattoos on their arms. Eli Wiesel and Bill Clinton spoke. Their speeches were good, but not nearly as powerful as those tattoos.

I believe I achieved a few essential things during my acting chair days: I restored the review process and removed the image of NEH as a politicized agency, restored order to a chaotic agency devoid of management leadership, and improved efficiency through the acquisition of a new computer system.

I did, however, have some disappointments. The greatest was the failure of my plans to promote NEH grant applications from minority and underserved populations. I became too painfully aware that past directives to reach out to minorities and underserved areas had been cynically appraised by Bennett and Cheney and that both of them took actions that were simply perfunctory. Bennett hired one minority outreach person, who spent virtually all of his time on the road, visiting historically black colleges, Indian reservations, barrio communities, and the like. He was unfamiliar with NEH programs and his energetic travel harvested no real results.

NEH had no coordinated, systematic approach to promote its activities to minority communities in a helpful way. Institutions with ample resources applied to NEH with sophisticated grant proposals and got funding. In reality, though, it didn't take a sophisticated proposal to get NEH funds. I had long thought that it was only fear and lack of knowledge about NEH that disadvantaged these small communities. All three chairs under whom I worked failed to develop a systematic approach to provide NEH programs in these communities. Duffey, a Carter appointee, fared no better than the two conservative chairs. He practiced his own form of affirmative action by appointing minorities to a number of senior positions. However, their work was, at best, piecemeal.

My plan was to take a fully integrated approach—involving all divisions, the Office of Public Affairs, and the Office of Planning and Budget—under the direction of the deputy chair. I thought the only way to attract competitive applications from underserved audiences and areas was to firmly embed the goal in the agency's ongoing promotional activities. The applications submitted in response to invitations or to the haphazard interests and initiatives of program officers had not historically fared well. My idea would involve long-range planning. I simply did not have the time to implement it while I was acting chair.

A New Chairman

DURING THIS SHORT PERIOD, I was also eager to prepare the endowment for the new chair, Sheldon Hackney, who had been appointed by President Clinton. I designed a format for the division directors and administrative office to prepare briefing books for the incoming team. The agency was prepared for Hackney when he arrived in August 1993, but I fear that he was not prepared for the agency.

Hackney immediately appointed me interim deputy chair, that is, chief operating officer. Within a few weeks, he also announced at a division directors meeting that he was going to open the search for a deputy chair. He told us the reason by turning around to look at me: "Don looks too much like me." As a liberal, he wanted to be politically correct and hire a minority.

I found being deputy chair under Hackney more time consuming than being chair. The burden of running the agency fell largely on my shoulders, while I was also busy teaching him about agency policies and its history. He also had me write some speeches. While the Cheney folks had treated me badly, Hackney was a gentleman and treated me with respect. That is not to deny that I was overworked by this former academic, eager to carry out his liberal views. To be sure, I was on Hackney's side when it came to political ideologies. But the job of the chief executive officer of NEH is not to push his or her political preferences.

When Hackney hired Juan Mestas as his deputy chair, making me chief of staff, things didn't improve much. Mestas was a Cuban American, whom I liked a lot. But he, like Hackney, was a former academic—and also like Hackney, he was not that keen about managing. I know they both respected me, and even liked me, but it was frustrating to work under them, especially after I had tasted how fast and efficiently I could move things along.

Hackney dropped the most difficult work that Mestas should have done into my lap: to plan and implement a major downsizing of the agency. In 1994, the Republicans, under the leadership of Newt Gingrich, managed an electoral victory that put them in charge of both houses of Congress. Gingrich, as speaker of the House, was the acknowledged leader of efforts to downsize the government. It was stunning and frightening. Government agencies were instructed to downsize.

Mestas was too new for the task and I was the only senior official with sufficient knowledge of the agency, its programs, and its people to plan a downsizing. I was given the task of cutting the entire staff of NEH by 25 percent. This meant letting go some people whom I respected and liked. After the task was accomplished, I heard no complaints against me—officially or in person. I like to believe that the general acceptability of my downsizing plan might have had something to do with my professional attitude. Perhaps because I grew up on rented farms and worked as a manual laborer and machine operator to pay my way through college, I gained great respect for professionalism in all sectors of work.

I deeply respect the skilled factory worker, skilled gardener, skilled maintenance man, skilled cleaning woman, skilled lawyer and, yes, skilled politician. I carried that attitude with me into the managerial portion of my career and, to be perhaps a tad self-centered about that, it served me extremely well. I respected and treated with respect the people who cleaned my office, who dealt with personnel matters, who fixed my telephone or my computer. I talked with them, asked their opinions, and listened attentively. In return, they taught me a lot.

In the end, though, performing the downsizing put me beyond exhaustion. If you can imagine the hard work it would take to hire

25 percent more people on the staff, try to imagine cutting by 25 percent! If it was physically exhausting, it was also emotionally devastating to shrink the staff you knew so well! Yes, Hackney had assigned me an impossible task. What frustrated me most about Sheldon Hackney, however, was not the hard work. It was mostly his lack of toughness and decisiveness.

I confess I was frustrated working under Hackney. Surely part of that was because I had been in charge and simply wanted to make the decisions myself. But, I am confident in retrospect that it was because I thought we should be bolder, make more changes, be more assertive. He took the right-wing criticisms, including the views of National Council members, far more seriously than did I.

Hackney's principal initiative at the endowment was the launching of a multiyear "conversation" on who Americans are as a nation. It was called the National Conversation on American Pluralism and Identity. In one sense, this initiative had begun with a small plan of mine (made while I was acting chair) to establish a program on pluralism, which I had not intended to be restricted to the United States. Hackney's program was restricted to the United States and it emphasized conversations, thus minimizing some of the needed scholarly underpinnings. The National Conversation was a good notion with good intentions, but it was a failure. In part, it was effectively aborted by the 1994 elections that created a wave of conservatism that overwhelmed efforts to carry out an effective, open national conversation.

It also failed because Hackney had put me in charge and I was too exhausted to deliver. I remember one evening—and there were many others like it—when I returned home and promptly threw myself on the sofa. I was too tired to eat dinner or even to go to bed. Dai Sil sat on the couch beside me and begged me to get up and eat something. I couldn't move. Only after a couple of hours could I drag myself up the stairs and go to bed. By this time, my body had already been invaded by multiple illnesses (Crohn's disease, defective heart valve, and so forth) that I had tried to ignore in the name of work.

As a human being and a scholar, Sheldon Hackney had my respect. I was moved to read what he had to write about me in his 2002 book, *The Politics of Presidential Appointment: A Memoir of the Culture War*:

> He [Don] was a career civil servant who had been at the NEH since Joe Duffey's chairmanship in the late 1970s. He was trusted by the staff, and I came to trust and rely on him as well. He was not only a historian with good intellectual taste across a broad front of humanities fields, he was a master of getting things to happen without running afoul of the civil service regulations and without being defeated by bureaucratic behavior. We became close allies and good friends.

Farewell, NEH

I KNOW THAT I COULD HAVE STAYED AT NEH, getting regular paychecks without doing much work. There are countless career bureaucrats in DC who have no problem collecting checks without working in return. In the end, however, that was not me. I had to work to deserve the pay. And I had to have a sense that I was doing good for the agency, and for people and society. For whatever it's worth, I have never been comfortable with easy money. More important, I had to believe in my work, feel worthy of my salary, and feel valuable. I am my father's son.

For my own integrity and perhaps peace of mind, I made a decision to take early retirement and leave NEH in January of 1997. NEH gave me a farewell party. People came from all over the country, and it seemed like everyone in the agency attended. Speaking on behalf NEH's State Programs was Ev Albers, the founding and longtime executive director of the North Dakota Humanities Council. In many ways, he was the soul of the State Programs. He fervently believed in, preached, and practiced two key aspects of the program—public education and scholarly integrity—and he never indulged in parochial, state-specific antics as did so many of his colleagues. He came from North Dakota to attend my farewell party, and I was immensely proud that it was he who spoke. (And I was deeply saddened to hear in April 2004 that Ev Albers had passed away.)

Dai Sil was standing in a corner; I saw her eyes becoming teary. Even Hackney stated that the farewell was "the greatest expression of love and loss that he had ever experienced."

In all candor, I could not deny the depth and breadth of people's approval, love, and admiration for my work at NEH. I would like to think that at the top of the list of my admirers was Dai Sil, though she had not been on the NEH staff since 1985.

Dai Sil made two comments about NEH and me that come to my mind. First, when Joe Duffey took Dai Sil and me to lunch once, Dai Sil said: "I did not care for many of the American missionaries. I left Korea to get away from them, but alas I ended up marrying one!" (Dai Sil often teased me that I was a humanities missionary.)

The second Dai Sil comment is one that I cherish as the best compliment I ever received about my work at NEH. Dai Sil said to me: "As you know, I had a snobbish (alas, sometimes even contemptuous) attitude toward administrators and managers, especially when I was striving to be a true scholar—whatever BS that was. However, you changed that, Don. You showed me how there is a creative dimension in management, a truly profound creative dimension."

Don with Joan Mondale and other NEH staff members

Don with Henry Hampton, director of the documentary series Eyes on the Prize

Don at the peak of his career

With a colleague at an NEH function

Don working in Washington

At our new house on 17th Street

A party at the Northampton house

Dinner party at home

At home on 17th Street in DC

PART VII

More in Life than NEH

∽

My Spiral Notebook

THIS IS A STORY ABOUT MY PIG NAMED GERTRUDE. But it is also a story about the married life of a farm boy and a city girl with imagination who loved me.

After living in my bachelor apartment on Capitol Hill for about a year, early in 1981 Dai Sil and I bought a house on Northampton Street in Chevy Chase DC, a neighborhood in northwest DC. Shortly after we moved into that lovely, white-brick colonial on a tree-lined block, Dai Sil came to me one day with a small spiral notebook.

"I was cleaning the basement and found this. It looks like somebody's accounting. Do you have any idea what this is?"

I took one glance at the yellow-stained pad in her hand and knew instantly. "Oh, that's my bookkeeping for Gert. You might call it my college funds." (See photo on page 40.)

"What are you talking about?"

And that's how I came to tell Dai Sil the story of Gert, the pig I raised to earn the money to go to college and escape the Iowa farm.

Since then I have had to retell Gert's story in many versions. Dai Sil would not leave it alone, asking question after question, consumed with curiosity about Gert, until my boyhood pig assumed a kind of totemic status in our lives. In no time at all, Gert became famous to all our friends and visitors. Porcine objects of all shapes, sizes, and materials began to appear in our house—ceramic pigs, bronze pigs, glass pigs. As I write this, I am drinking coffee from a mug that our niece Stella brought from England, a mug covered with images of every conceivable kind of pig.

In truth, I had affection for pigs even before my wife made Gert into a living legend. I gave Dai Sil a Steuben pig for our first Christmas together. Now that I want to write about Gert, it's hard to separate fact from fantasy, so contaminated have I been by Dai Sil's curious obsession with her. But I remember vividly how she came into my life.

When I was eleven years old, my father gave me the gift of a litter with eight piglets and told me to take good care of them. They
were about three weeks old, just ready to try some solid food after
being weaned. I fed those piglets diligently every morning and evening and, with pride and affection, often watched them eat.

But when Dai Sil asked me how I picked out one pig in particular from the litter and bestowed on her a name like Gert, I stumbled, because to my great chagrin, I could not remember exactly.

"Well, I know," said Dai Sil. "Gert told me."

And with that, she disappeared to her desk and returned a while
later with a typewritten sheet that read:

> My name is Gertrude, but the boy who gave me this name
> called me Gert for short. With a name like this, you might
> think I am a German girl or an American girl with Ger-
> man ancestry. But actually I am an Iowa pig, a pig who grew
> up on an Iowa farm. I am not, though, just an ordinary pig.
> After all, I grew up under the tender loving care of a special
> boy. Oh boy, did I love him, but maybe he loved me even
> more, if that is possible. His name is Donald, but his father's
> name is also Donald. So his parents called him Donnie. He
> hated to be called Donnie; he preferred just plain Don. So it
> was always Don between the two of us.
>
> One morning when Don came to feed us, I wandered to the
> fence away from my siblings. Don came up close, gave me
> food, and watched me eat it. Then the most amazing thing
> happened. He talked to me as if I were his friend. "I am go-
> ing to tell you a secret," he said. "Most people think you are
> all ignorant oinkers. But I know pigs are beautiful, clever,
> and pure of heart. I have been observing you very closely.
> Sometimes I watched you when you were in deep sleep. I
> felt you snort and dream while you slept, and imagined you
> smiling. I think you have lots of wisdom in you and I know
> that you are going to help me to go to college!" I stared at
> him. His eyes did not blink, but they were moist, moist with
> what I could only call hope. Then his eyes were gazing as

if at something far away, and he was still. Something was clearly stirring inside him. Of course, I did not know what it was, but I was moved by it anyway and quietly swore to myself: Boy, I do not know what you want from me, but I am all yours.

I stopped reading and looked up at Dai Sil. She sat across from me at the kitchen table, her face brimming with mischief.

One night, Don came just to see me. It was not feeding time. He was crying. I wanted to hug that boy in the worst way and wipe his tears. He said nothing, and he did not even touch me. Darkness fell and he was still there watching the clouds move. Then a lone star appeared through the drifting cloud. His eyes twinkled, and he said, "That star can see what's out there. I want to travel with that star and see the world. You see, I have this unquenchable sense of wonder and curiosity." Slowly, he turned to me and said, "I love my mom and dad and even my brother, who beats me up once in a while. And I love the sky, the stars, the cornfields, and you. I love everything around here. But Gertrude, I want to see more." My ears perked up. I didn't know who he was talking to. With a bright grin, he said, "From now on, your name is Gertrude. It is a German name. I've never been to Germany, but I read that there are lots of accomplished German composers, philosophers, writers. If you are going to help me learn about them, you should at least have a proper German name. So your name is Gertrude, but I will call you Gert."

It was vintage Dai Sil. She had told me that in her youth she thought about writing children's stories. Now I could see why she had that urge and how wonderful her tales would be.

As charming as Dai Sil's story was—and also emotionally resonant—I cannot vouch for its factual accuracy. It is true that Gert is short for Gertrude and I did name the piglet Gertrude. But I still don't know why—and it had nothing to do with the fact that I went on to become a student of German history. For some reason, probably perverse, I gave most of my farm animals strange names. For instance, there was baby cow I named Satan, much to the chagrin of my mother.

By the time Gert matured from piglet to full Hampshire, she was mostly black with a white band around her shoulders and front legs. Much later in my life, I learned that the black Hampshire was a hardy old English favorite—known as a lard pig—that had been imported by the Americans. Had I known this when I first met Gert, I might well have given her a British name.

We fed our pigs well with lots of corn and oats mixed with skim milk. We were very keen on making sure they had well-balanced diets. As enamored as Dai Sil is with my farm stories, she wrinkles her nose and her face and becomes a tad gloomy whenever I talk about what our animals ate. I know what goes through her mind, that animals in this country are being fed so much better than so many people around the world.

Despite Dai Sil's fictional embellishments, Gert was not my favorite among the litter. I tried to treat all of them with care and affection. If I had special feelings for Gert, it was because she and I went to the county fair together. I remember, like it was yesterday, how I prepared her for that outing. First I set out to make her look nice. I rubbed hair oil on the black parts of her body so they were shiny and clean. On the white band, I applied talcum powder. I spent lots of time brushing Gert's hair with a stiff brush. Then I devoted hours to building a roughly two-square-foot wooden panel. Using the panel to guide Gert, I would walk her around to practice for the fair. The judges claimed that they didn't take points off for poorly behaved pigs or incompetent trainers, but I didn't believe them. In any case, I figured it wouldn't hurt if I could demonstrate just how much I was in harmony with my pig.

Well, finally it arrived—opening day of the 1954 Shelby County Fair. I guided Gert around the judging pen with that wooden panel. We were an impressive pair, she and I. And we won a purple ribbon. Gert was the grand champion. I felt enormously proud. Proud of Gert, of course, but even more than that, I tasted what it was like to accomplish something and be publicly recognized. A social recognition! That day I had an important lesson—if I could help a pig to win a purple ribbon, I could work with people, even lead people, and win whatever I pursued in life. I also realized that the joy of winning did not come for free. One needed to work hard. My parents were there and, as usual, they didn't say much. But their bright smile said volumes. By that time, I was used to their wordless approval and pride. That was a happy day for Gert and me.

Gertrude and Her Piglets

EVENTUALLY, GERT GAVE BIRTH TO HER OWN PIGLETS, and it was those piglets who saved me from the destiny mapped out for the majority of Iowa farm boys of that era—graduation from high school and then on to a life on the farm like their fathers before them. Of course, I am exaggerating a bit. There were other piglets that helped me, too. I was responsible for several litters during my teenage years, which meant lots of pigs to take care of. My parents let me save some of the money from the sale of those pigs, which eventually became my college funds.

Birthing time for the pigs was both exciting and traumatic. The delivery was called farrowing. Farmers tried to control the breeding so that the piglets would arrive in the spring, a mellow season when their chances of survival were enhanced. One could anticipate an average litter of seven to nine. Sows—mother hogs—are loving creatures and ferociously protective of their young. I can still see a pink roiling litter of piglets at their mother's teats. But sows can also be quite clumsy. So the farmer always tried to ensure that the sows gave birth in special pens, which were small, fenced areas that featured heating lamps for the new arrivals and spaces where they could retreat to protect themselves from being crushed when the sow decided to lie down.

But sometimes sows refused to cooperate. I can recall occasions when our sows gave birth in unanticipated places of their own liking, far from the barn in areas where they could gather brush for nests. When that happened, I had to scurry to fetch the new mother and her brood back to a farrowing pen. I would carry a wicker basket to the birth site, grab a stick, and hit the sow on her nose, which would make her back off a bit so I could gather the piglets into the basket and run like crazy. Sometimes the relocation process went without a hitch, but other times it gave me a lot of grief. The sow could run faster than I could, and when she was about to catch me, I would drop the basket on the ground, find another stick, and land another whale on her nose. She would retreat, I would advance. This could be repeated several times for one litter. Eventually, I would make it to the farrowing pen with the piglets in tow.

Feeding the nursing sow was another challenge. I had to be extremely careful entering the pen. If a piglet squealed, the sow would lunge with huge open jaws. I knew that a sow could take a man's leg off in one gulp. I confronted that gaping orifice on more than one occasion myself. Luckily, I was able to leap out of the pen quickly enough. Having great respect for a sow's speed and strength, I was scared.

Gert was mated when she was about nine months old. Sows carry their young for a little less than four months before farrowing. I remember the day when Gert had her babies, a pretty decent litter of thirteen. She didn't break the record—some sows deliver as many as twenty-seven piglets—but I was happy with thirteen.

I tried to take fine care of Gert during her farrowing. Sadly there were two runts. Farmers usually kill runts since they rarely live long enough to go to market. To try to raise them was considered a waste of time and money. I would not and could not kill runts—Gert's or any others. I just couldn't bring myself to do it. Gert's two runts eventually died, but the other eleven made it to market when they were six months old.

Gert herself was pretty easy to take care of, but one of her piglets hurt me. Every spring, we had to vaccinate the newborns. Actually, it was a simple, two-person operation. One would grab the piglet by its front legs and hoist it up to waist level, while the other jabbed a needle into an armpit. I was supposed to grab the legs and immediately tuck my thumb underneath. Well, I forgot to protect my thumb with one of Gert's babies. The piglet threw his head sideways and clamped his sharp teeth right into my digit. The pain was so intense that I dropped him. Realizing what I had done, I decided to ignore the small puncture in my thumb, picked up the piglet, and kept working.

A week later, my thumb was still throbbing. So late one afternoon after milking the cows, I sat down on the concrete foundation and, after a bit of investigation, cut away the part of my thumbnail that had been bent downward and was by now quite literally growing directly into my flesh. There is still a scar on my left thumb to commemorate the experience.

Sadly, not long after she gave birth, Gert contracted a terrible parasitic disease. The distress of seeing that sweet sow lying on her side in the throes of death remains with me. Gert's life was cut terribly short. Hogs can live nine to fifteen years, but she was only a year and a half old when she died. This also meant, of course, that she farrowed only once. Hence, many other sows delivered many more piglets that contributed to my college nest egg. So it wasn't due to the money that Gert held a special place in my heart. Dai Sil holds the firm view that although Gert died, her spirit has always followed and watched over me.

Indeed, Dai Sil believes that Gert literally lives within me. In the summer of 1998, we learned that my heart's aortic valve was in trouble. It couldn't snap shut properly and blood kept regurgitating back into my heart's lower chamber. I needed surgery to replace the defective valve, and like many others who have had the procedure, had to choose between a pig's valve and a man-made one. Dai Sil and I opted for the porcine version, and she is convinced that it was Gert's valve that the surgeon implanted in my chest.

We can only imagine the day-to-day life Don had on the farm, but that life instilled in him something that cannot be described. Let me say this: Each time I see Good in the world I think of him—Don, who could not and would not kill a single runt.

~ D S K-G

What Do the Doctors Know?

DURING THE EARLY YEARS OF MY LIFE, I enjoyed perfectly good health. I didn't even get my first cavity until I was in my twenties. I had my share of childhood diseases, of course, like chicken pox and mumps. And when I was ten, I had my tonsils removed, only to be rushed back to the hospital three days later to have my appendix out. But that was all routine maintenance, if you will, and pretty much the extent of my ailments.

Then in middle age, I became frightfully weak, unable to stand for any extended period, repulsed by food, afflicted by bouts of diarrhea. I went to my regular internist, who subjected me to test after test and couldn't figure it out. I recall one spring weekend, Dai Sil and I were invited to a party at the home of our friends Jed and Sydney Johnson, but I was too sick to go. I insisted that Dai Sil go without me. I was lying inert on the couch in our Northampton Street house when the doctor called. I dragged myself to the kitchen to answer the phone, and he reported that all the tests had come back negative. That was supposed to be good news. I hung up the phone and cried, so ill that I thought I was going to die. I could barely make my way back to the couch.

A few weeks later, in mid-June, I was so depleted that they rushed me to George Washington University Hospital. Over the course of the next week, the doctors conducted a series of tests, one after another. Finally, a young resident appeared at my bedside with a smile on his face. I even remember the date, June 26, 1986.

"Well, at least we know now what you are suffering from! You have Crohn's disease."

"What the hell is Crohn's disease?" Dai Sil and I asked in unison.

"Well," the young doctor began, "it's a chronic disorder that causes inflammation of the gastrointestinal tract. Crohn's is the general name we use for diseases that cause swelling in the intestines. Because the symptoms of Crohn's are similar to other disorders, like irritable bowel syndrome and ulcerative colitis, it can be difficult to diagnose."

"Could it become cancer?" I questioned.

"Not likely," explained the resident. "Ulcerative colitis can indeed turn into cancer. But what you have is ileitis, which is much less prone to become malignant, but also, unfortunately almost impossible to fix with surgery."

"What does the word Crohn stand for?" Dai Sil asked.

The patient resident gave us a crash course in my new disorder. We learned that Crohn was the name of the doctor who first identified the disease, and that its cause remained unknown.

"Well, if they don't know the cause, that sounds bad," I said. "Are you basically saying it's incurable?"

"That is correct," he replied. "We can treat it but we can't cure it."

He went on to explain that it seems to run in some families and about 20 percent of people with Crohn's have a blood relative with some form of inflammatory bowel disease.

Not only is Crohn's incurable, but also, as the doctor informed me, I would never again have as much energy as I once did—loss of energy being a permanent side effect of living with the disease. But I dismissed his negative news with joy, delighted just to know at last what was wrong and thinking to myself that I had always had more energy than I really needed anyway. Little did I know.

They put me on massive amounts of steroids and my appetite immediately returned, for the first time in a long while. Within a day or two, I felt much better and was discharged from the hospital.

I was ecstatic to come home. As soon as we entered the house, I rushed to our screened-in porch, my favorite spot. I was happy to sit at the round wooden table and look out at the backyard.

Dai Sil instantly made her way to the kitchen and cooked up two T-bone steaks, giving me the larger one. She had barely made a dent in hers, and I had already devoured mine. She looked at me and commented drolly, "You are panting like a dog, eyeing my steak." She plopped it on my plate, and I gobbled it down. That was the first time we both understood the power of steroids, double-edged though they were.

My primary care doctor said my diet would have to be severely restricted—no fresh fruit or vegetables, no milk products, no nuts, no alcohol. Basically, I thought, I couldn't eat anything that was part of a normal healthy diet. Even with bread, he told me to stay away from varieties with lots of fiber. Blindly obeying him, we bought Wonder Bread.

I know that Dai Sil was glad that liquor was on the list of no-nos for my new diet. I was aware that she was secretly worried that my drinking habit was too regular and that it might lead me to become addicted. Then came Crohn's and, obeying my doctor's orders, I did not touch a drop of alcohol for a year. So her secret worries were gone.

As luck would have it, we found a specialist at Johns Hopkins Hospital, a university hospital in Baltimore. For several years, I traveled to Johns Hopkins periodically to have my Crohn's monitored. Thanks to their help, the disease was often in remission, and I gained back most of the weight I had lost, always hovering close to 155 pounds. But I never regained that pure glee at the sight of good food, and my once enormous appetite was a thing of the past. Prior to my diagnosis, I'd never even heard of Crohn's. But afterwards, it was amazing to learn how common it was, afflicting all kinds of people from all walks of life, including President Dwight D. Eisenhower. That one comforted me: "If one can be president of the United States with Crohn's, I can surely work as a federal bureaucrat," I proclaimed, and never slowed the pace of my professional exertions.

⚭

What's Happening to My Body?

BUT AS IT TURNED OUT, CROHN'S WAS ONLY THE FIRST of many illnesses that I put Dai Sil through. It represented the beginning of an increasingly difficult life that I unwillingly imposed on her. I wanted us to go on living normally as if there were no health problems. And much of the time, she went along with that wish in a determined and graceful fashion. But I knew how difficult it was for her, in reality.

In January 1988, Dai Sil resigned from her job in New York and came home to me. I was happy that we were no longer a commuting couple. It was wonderful to have her back full time. By then, my Crohn's was being carefully monitored by Dr. B——, and I went on with my work, perhaps harder than ever before, almost as if that would help me forget the Crohn's. Of course, I often felt exhausted, but I ignored it. Meanwhile, Dai Sil was trying to find the rhythm of her new life, that of a freelancer.

Then in 1996, after we had moved to a townhouse near Dupont Circle, my health failed once again. I was plagued by extreme exhaustion and lack of energy. I became easily fatigued beyond what could be attributed to hard work, and started losing weight again. I also suffered from shortness of breath, had muscle aches and pains, and my feet were always swollen.

More seriously, after taking repeated blood cultures, giving me an EKG and an echocardiogram, and heaven knows what else, on June 4, 1996, the doctors told us that I had acute bacterial endocarditis. In addition to the Crohn's, I now had an inflammation—a bad infection—of the lining of my heart chambers and valves. The doctors immediately began to administer intravenous antibiotics and, once those had kicked in, I was discharged, allowed to go home with detailed instructions for long-term outpatient therapy.

I was placed on a regimen of antibiotics, to be taken intravenously three times a day, which was to last for six weeks. Dai Sil had told me many times that her parents had hoped to see her become either a doctor or a lawyer. I know she could have pulled off a legal career, but medicine was out of the question. The simple sight of blood, or even a needle, freaked her out. And nursing a sick person was not her forte. So I felt doubly sorry that she had to administer my intravenous antibiotic infusion. I knew that the strain of concentration literally hurt her, but as she got the hang of it, I could tell that she had relaxed into the task.

We set up the IV system in our TV room on the second floor. There Dai Sil and I sat looking out at the world from big windows that overlooked 17th Street. The street was full of drama—a flamboyant gay couple passing by, a homeless person pushing a cart, a young child prancing with her mother. We didn't talk much, but we were together. It relaxed me to be there with her, and I felt happy. We even watched Oprah Winfrey, which we had certainly never done before.

I was impressed by how careful and proficient Dai Sil had become. But then, something totally stupid and unexpected happened. My medical supplies were delivered in packages that came with detailed instructions, which Dai Sil always read carefully. One of the antibiotics was gentamicin and the orders for its use clearly specified that it should not be administered beyond the expiration date. So when that precise day arrived, Dai Sil—interpreting the expiration literally—declared that we were done with the gentamicin and that the prescribed treatment for my endocarditis was over.

The next day, Dr. S——, my primary care provider, telephoned to see how I was doing. I heard Dai Sil carrying on an excited conversation, and then she handed me the receiver. Dr. S—— was indignant that Dai Sil had stopped administering the gentamicin without consulting him. He ordered me to continue with it. What a fool I was not to be more careful. We, or rather I, decided to follow his instructions, and Dai Sil went along with it.

By the end of that week, I became dizzy and had difficulty navigating the stairs. We had a three-story house, and our bedroom, along with my study, were on the third floor. We called Dr. S—— and reported my symptoms. He told me to come see him right away. After he examined me, he prescribed some medicine. While I was waiting in line at the local pharmacy, I happened to pick up a paperback book on drugs that was on display. Leafing through the pages, I learned that gentamicin—the very antibiotic I was taking—could cause dizziness and vertigo. That's why it came with such careful instructions about when to stop taking it. Dai Sil had followed that instruction, but Dr. S—— knew nothing about it. And not surprisingly, the medication he prescribed for my vertigo did absolutely nothing to help me.

Still dizzy and off balance, I consulted an ear specialist and a neurologist. They confirmed that the gentamicin was the cause of my symptoms. As a result of Dr. S——'s ignorance, I suffered permanent damage to my inner ear and my vision was also severely affected. I learned from experts that the inner ear controls the movement of the eye. My eyes now functioned like a primitive camera in that images would jerk as I turned my head. As a result, for more than a year I couldn't drive because I couldn't turn my head to check the mirrors. Ultimately, my brain compensated and took over those eye-movement functions from my inner ear. The doctors also warned me not to have even a single glass of wine before driving. My now unbalanced gait would make me appear drunk, and a policeman who smelled even a whiff of alcohol might not believe me.

The dizziness persisted for quite a while and really made walking difficult. Nothing was automatic anymore; I had to think before I took each step and carefully move my foot forwards, backwards, or sideways. I briefly considered filing a malpractice suit. Indeed, both of the specialists I'd seen said that it was malpractice. Dai Sil was inclined to go forward, but ultimately, I decided I didn't want the mess and complication of extended litigation. Dai Sil didn't protest. Shortly after that, Dr. S—— retired and disappeared. I am sure he realized his carelessness or ignorance—or a combination of the two, we never knew for sure.

Italy

EVER SINCE WE GOT MARRIED, I NOTICED A CERTAIN RESTLESSNESS IN DAI SIL which signaled a change in her life. She was far more creative than many of the people who received creative grants under her auspices. Here's a woman who in 1962 crossed the Pacific with $25 of borrowed money in her pocket to make something of herself. And it was not becoming a grant maker of which she dreamed. But she was still afraid to quit her job. She told me more than a few times that once she were jobless, her identity as Dai Sil Kim-Gibson would mean nothing to most people: "I would rapidly fall into the category of a nobody."

Finally she marshaled her courage, prompted by my ill health, and took that gigantic leap. She resigned from her job as director of the Media Program at the New York State Council on the Arts. In January of 1988, we rented a U-Haul and dragged her New York belongings back to our DC house on Northampton Street.

It did not take me long to see that all of Dai Sil's fears were for nothing. She was perfectly happy alone at home, reading, painting, and writing. She clearly didn't need the structure of an office or co-workers. She was there in the mornings to say goodbye to me and there in the evenings to greet me with laughter and food.

It became clear that the house was too small for Dai Sil to spread out the growing body of her work. Her papers were piled up and the number of canvases increased. We began to explore the possibility of adding on a room or, alternatively, buying a larger place. One Sunday, Dai Sil found an ad in the *Washington Post* for an open house at a historic property on 17th and S Streets NW close to downtown. We both liked old houses. We liked our home on Northampton Street but it was in a section of DC that felt suburban, and we really weren't suburban types. We preferred to be either right in the city or really in the country. So off we went to see this historic house near Dupont Circle.

It was a corner house with the front facing 17th Street, a splendid red-brick structure with huge, irregular size windows. We entered through a large front yard and climbed a few steps, which passed under an impressive arch leading to a spacious stone porch.

The house was 109 years old. The owners were a young couple who had done some renovations while maintaining the property's integrity. I watched Dai Sil looking at a huge modernized kitchen with an island in the middle. It had the feel of a country kitchen, but was thoroughly outfitted for a contemporary cook. "Oh my, Don. Can you believe this kitchen? I've never had a kitchen like this." I knew we were going to buy the house, no matter what.

The asking price was beyond our means, but there was a finished basement, and we figured if we could rent that out, we might be able to swing it. So we made an offer, which to our delight was accepted, and thus we became the proud owners of a century-old house! Having such a home in our life together was beyond our wildest dreams.

We took residence in late September 1989. October 1 was our tenth anniversary. Honestly, I had forgotten about it with all the excitement of the move. One day with boxes still piled up on our first floor, Dai Sil marched to the kitchen table where I was working on memos with a glass of scotch. She sat down and waited for me to lift my head, as if she had all the time in the world. When I finally looked at her, I could not help but notice her dancing eyes. I knew that any minute some unexpected words would be coming out of her lips. "What?" I said.

"We are going to Italy for our tenth anniversary!" She announced with perfect composure that she had booked first-class tickets to Rome with her frequent flier mileage accumulated on TWA. (Because she was working on *America Becoming*, her first major film project with the Ford Foundation, she had been flying a lot.)

Neither of us had ever flown first class before. The minute we were settled in our seats, the flight attendant came around to offer champagne. The whole flight felt like a fitting first-decade celebration!

Because Dai Sil had put together the trip in such a hurry, she had managed to reserve a hotel in Rome for only two nights, and a car rental in Florence. We agreed that Rome alone merited at least a month of exploration, but this trip was primarily for us to enjoy Florence and Tuscany.

October 4 found us on the train to Florence. We located the car rental place with relative ease, but then quickly managed to get hopelessly lost—although the concept of *lost* was more or less meaningless, since we didn't have a destination. No hotel had been booked. We thought we could just pull in somewhere outside of Florence and find a nice place to stay. Wrong. But none of it mattered. Bouncing along inside our little Fiat, whose wheels did not know which way to roll in a totally foreign land, we were two kids, giddy and relentlessly cheerful. If we didn't know where we were or where we were headed, it was of no consequence. Neither one of us was irritable or the slightest bit inclined to cast blame. We were just happy to be together on an adventure.

As luck would have it, we literally bumped into a travel agency. The director told us they only booked hotels in Firenze, but seeing our lost faces, he said, "Wait a moment. I have an idea." He made a call, talked for a moment, then put down the receiver and told us, "You're in luck. I found a room for you nearby in a small town called Galluzzo." He sent us on our way with elaborate directions, which seemed quite specific. We still managed to drive around for a couple of hours before we found the place. Clearly, neither of us was noted for a strong sense of direction.

When we finally pulled into the large yard of what looked like a modern farmhouse, it was as if we'd hit pay dirt. A huge woman with a loud voice and a small man with a friendly smile greeted us effusively in Italian. We didn't understand the content of their words but the warm welcome was unmistakable. They led us to an ample room equipped with modern conveniences—a clean and spacious bathroom, queen bed and comfortable sofa, desk and chairs. We could not believe our good fortune.

In the evening, more pleasant surprises awaited us in the dining room. We shared a table with two young Germans who spoke perfect English. From them, we learned that our inn had been a fortress—hence its name, La Forteressa—and had been renovated by the husband and wife owners who had greeted us earlier in the day, Amelio and Angiolina. The inn catered to regular recurring guests from Germany and Switzerland who generally booked far in advance, often a year ahead. We were able to procure our room only because one couple's arrival had been delayed by a few days.

Angiolina served as the chef and Amelio was the server. From antipasti through dessert, the meal was a masterpiece. I can't remember the entire menu, but what I shall never forget were the fried zucchini flowers, served as an appetizer, along with a smooth, delicious jug wine. This delicacy was presented on a large platter, so beautifully arranged that I hated to disturb it. The German kids dug in without hesitation. I placed one in my mouth, and the taste was literally out of this world! No word could describe that crisp feel and exquisite flavor.

After a restful night at La Forteressa, we ventured out the next day to Florence. We took the #37 bus for free, which got us to the train station in fifteen minutes (the same distance it had taken us two hours to drive the previous night, given our navigational disability). From there, we walked to the famous Uffizi. Starting with the magnificent stairs leading to the galleries, the Tuscan and Florentine art displayed within its forty rooms was overwhelming.

The couple who had reserved our room was due to arrive and we needed to vacate. We hoped to find another congenial lodging in nearby San Gimignano or elsewhere in Tuscany, but all the hotels we called were full. Amelio and Angiolina spoke little or no English and we were useless in Italian. So here's what happened! Dai Sil lay down on their kitchen floor to convey that we needed a place to sleep. What do you know? They cleaned up their family guest room and offered it to us! The dinner that night was especially memorable. Angiolina's steak and pasta were cooked to perfection, the red wine was superb, and there were those divine fried zucchini flowers!

*But we both knew what Italy had given us—a stretch of
our relationship that knew no boundary in time and space.
We felt our love deepened and fortified as we walked shoulder-
to-shoulder, hand-in-hand, through the narrow streets of
Siena and San Gimignano, up and down the Tuscany hills,
meandering through the timeless works of art in Florence,
and savoring those delicate fried flowers of zucchini that came
wrapped in the affection of a large Italian woman.*

~ D S K-G

My Parents at Apache Junction

MY PARENTS BEGAN TO TRAVEL TO APACHE JUNCTION, Arizona, in
the 1970s to escape fierce winters in Iowa. Eventually, in the mid-
1980s, they made it their full-time home.

A couple of years after our marriage, while we were still living in
our Northampton Street house, my parents came to DC to visit us.
I think the high point of the whole trip for Mom was dinner theater
at a fancy restaurant in Virginia. The play was *Fiddler on the Roof*.
She raved about it. I had never seen her face glow with such pleasure.
Dad had a good time, too, even though he was a skeptic on the front
end. One weekend, we gave a back-yard party and invited a bunch
of our friends, including Don and Sue Kaul. Don was something of
an Iowa folk hero, a popular columnist for the *Des Moines Register*.
My parents could not believe that they were at the same party with
midwestern royalty.

What my father enjoyed most of all was establishing a secret
bond with Dai Sil. Every evening, she would bring him tonic wa-

ter with a splash of gin. He clearly loved it—and her! I know that my dad drank before he got married, but he stopped to follow my mother's wishes.

For me, it was a real revelation how quickly, naturally, and completely my parents accepted their new daughter-in-law during that visit. Right now I am reading a card my mother sent Dai Sil a long time ago. She wrote to Dai Sil, "I don't like that in-law part of the card, because you are like a daughter to us. If we really had one, I would like her to be just like you, so caring and loving."

There was also a letter to me: "That dear little Dai Sil wrote such nice letters to us . . . Your letters sound so happy and we are so happy for you. You waited so long that we knew it would be someone extra special when you did make a choice. She seemed to fit right in as one of us. We hope this feeling is mutual." I know it was mutual. In fact, I observed Dai Sil's affection for my parents grow with the years.

Dai Sil and I would visit them in Arizona at least every other year for Christmas. If truth be told, we found their trailer home a bit tacky, but their warm welcome more than made up for what the venue lacked. As soon as we arrived, Dai Sil would take over the kitchen, preparing tasty meals beyond their usual fare. I was thrilled to see how much they enjoyed our company and how much they admired Dai Sil. Nor did they attribute Dai Sil's domestic prowess to her being Asian.

During those visits, I learned a lot more about my own mom. Yes, she certainly still fretted over "what the neighbors would think," but I also came to grudgingly admire how much she wanted to expand her horizons and sample life beyond the narrow confines of our Iowa farm.

Then in December 1994, we got a call from my dad with the distressing news that Mom's colon cancer had advanced. We went as soon as we could, but by the time we arrived, Mom was already in a residential hospice and fading fast, barely responsive. We sat with her for about an hour and then Dad wanted to go home for a bit. We had just walked in the door when the phone rang, and a nurse informed us that my mother had passed away. I was the one who had to tell Dad.

We drove back to the hospice in stunned silence. Dad sat in the waiting room. He couldn't bear to see her. I watched as they took the rings off her hands, loaded her onto a gurney, and rolled her out. That image of her being rolled out of the building is the one that stays with me all these years later, far more than the sight of her embalmed body in the casket at the funeral home. Seeing my mother lifeless on that gurney, I was deeply shaken. Sadness swept over me, but I found some consolation in the knowledge that at least I had gotten to know her better, and like her more, during our desert visits. That same evening, we brought the clothes in which she was to be buried—her beautiful green velvet wedding gown from more than six decades earlier—to the funeral home.

Dad Alone

DAD WAS IN A DAZE FOR THE NEXT SEVERAL DAYS, almost like sleepwalking. Dai Sil packed his underwear and his one good suit, a blue three-piece. We flew together to Iowa and were inseparable throughout the next several days. Surprisingly, he seemed to awaken after the funeral and burial. He went out and bought a new car, insisting that he was going to live alone in Arizona. He went about his life. We knew he was mourning his wife and coming to terms with a life alone. But he suppressed his loneliness, sorrow, and fear as an act of independence. He did not wish to burden his sons. And he never did. He and my mother had paid for their own funerals and arranged everything with a local funeral home twenty-five years before.

Dad thought he could live alone in Arizona with the memories of his wife. And he did for four years. But age was catching up with him, and in 1998 David and I suggested—insisted, really— that he move near one of us. Dai Sil and I offered that he move in with us, but the thought of living in or near a big city appalled him, even though New Paltz was some ninety miles removed from Manhattan. We had a perfect room for him, with its own bathroom, almost like an independent-living unit. But Dad chose Iowa and moved to an assisted-living facility in Harlan near my brother, where he maintained as much independence as he could.

In the summer of 1999, Dad came and stayed with us for a month. He was about to turn ninety and we wanted to give him a birthday party to remember. An Italian restaurant called La Stazione had just opened at the town's old railroad depot. The owner/chef was glad to cater a private party, so we took over the whole place and he cooked up a storm for us. Friends came from all over, old and new.

My tenant farmer father, who generally shunned the limelight, often characterizing our friends as too intellectual for him, had no problem at all being the center of attention. Indeed, he seemed to love it. Our neighbor David Mesches, a medical doctor, commented more than a few times on how enviably alert and smart my father still was at age ninety.

It brought me great joy that Dai Sil and I were able to fête my father this way to mark his ninth decade of life. Everything was perfect but for the absence of my mother. I could see how radiant she would have been at that party. I missed her and wished that we could have celebrated her own noteworthy birthday with the same elegance and festivity.

A couple of years after that visit, my dad started to deteriorate. As his health worsened, David, who rarely calls me, started ringing me up more regularly to report on Dad's condition. It got to the point where every time the phone rang, I jumped. In April 2006, he fell and broke his hip. I knew he lived for our nightly phone calls and it pained me that I could no longer talk to him regularly, as he was often either in no condition to talk or in the hospital.

Despite my own fragile health, we decided it was time to go see him. Since he was last with us in New Paltz, our house had burned down and our lives had become so entangled in fixing disasters that we had let many years pass by without seeing him. My emphysema was so severe that we thought driving was a better option than flying and we made the 1,250-mile trip in three days, arriving in Harlan in early afternoon.

We immediately went to see Dad and found him lying flat on his stomach, his legs dangling off the end of the bed. He was apparently struggling to pull his upper body to the pillow, but couldn't summon the strength. Dai Sil rushed to help him, while I stood helpless, trying to hide my own shortness of breath.

We were there for three days and two nights. When it was time to leave and we went to say goodbye, we found him sitting in his recliner, small and frail, but considerably more vibrant than a few days earlier, and clearly disappointed that our visit was at an end.

"So soon," he gazed at us. Then he asked me to bring his checkbook from the bedside table drawer.

"What do you need money for?" I asked.

"Well, I want to give you some money for gas. I am sure you spent a fortune driving out here."

We almost had a shouting match, but I finally had to give in. He wrote out a check for $200, the last check he wrote with his own hand. Dai Sil went over to him, gently touched his thin leg, squeezed his shoulders, and said, "Take care," in a voice that expressed how much she loved him.

Dad said, "I love you."

"I love you, too," replied Dai Sil, her lips brushing his forehead.

He looked up at her, "I mean every word of it." Dad knew it was the last time he would see us.

Shortly after, Dai Sil and I flew to Iowa for the funeral, arriving in Harlan on Sunday afternoon a couple of hours before the visitation at the funeral home. My breathing was even worse than usual, no doubt aggravated by the emotional strain of Dad's death. His funeral was particularly difficult for me. I felt so ill that I could barely walk even three steps at a time.

After the service, I had to sit down rather than standing and greeting people with David. A stream of folks came over to me, some of whom I had not seen or even thought of in fifty years. Later Dai Sil asked, "How did you manage to remember all those people?" In truth, I didn't recall most of them, but my years of political campaign work and my life at NEH came in handy that day. It wasn't acting, though. I was deeply touched that so many mourners turned out to bid Dad farewell. He was the last one to go among his peers.

I didn't think I could make it to the cemetery, but I did. As I stood by the gravestone for both my parents, the deep sadness of what we were doing—lowering my father into the ground forever—stirred inside me. I reflected back on the day of my mother's burial. I knew that Dad was happy to rejoin his wife, but for me it meant I was now an orphan.

When my father, an immigrant who carried the sweet smell of Korean soil mixed with sweat in his soul, made the transition from life to death, Don and I stood on either side of his bed. The night my father died, my brother Daeil brought my mother to the hospital shortly after Don called him. Mother looked so tiny and fragile as she held the hand of her husband of sixty-two years, quietly crying, my mother who had married the dashing young sportsman with the good brain, courageous heart, and a baseball always in his hand. I will never forget that day, the last image of my dying father and my mother. But what comes back more and more is how Don was with me at my father's deathbed, how he took care of my mother. How blessed I was to have such a husband.

~ D S K-G

Don with his parents at Apache Junction

Above, on a trip to Maine, around 2002

Below, in Prague celebrating our 25th anniversary

Don with our nephew Paul leaving the hospital in Berchtesgaden, Germany

27th wedding anniversary at the Wayside Inn, Sudbury MA

After the fire in New Paltz

PART VIII

Life in Retirement

⌢

Home of Dead Heroes, Valhalla

THERE IS MORE ABOUT MY ILL HEALTH. After I took early retirement in 1997, we moved to New Paltz with plans for both of us to do freelance work. Dai Sil wanted to pursue her filmmaking and writing, and I wanted to write and do consulting. But during 1998, I found myself once again in a state of constant fatigue and frequent shortness of breath. I went to see our primary care doctor at the local medical center. They told me that my heart was in trouble.

Back when I'd been in George Washington Hospital for the endocarditis, I learned that my heart had a leak. Apparently I was born with a defective aortic heart valve. A normal valve has three little flaps, whereas mine had only two. I remember the day they told me about the leak. I was so confused and ignorant that I couldn't stop pondering what leaking meant. Did it mean that blood was leaking into other parts of my body? No, as I learned subsequently, it meant that blood was seeping back into my heart. As a result, I wasn't getting sufficient blood flow into the rest of my body to provide adequate energy. I was confounded by how doctors never told me anything directly. They all seemed to speak in a roundabout fashion. Finally, one told me straight out that the defective valve could and probably should be replaced, but it wasn't urgent.

But it caught up with me in New Paltz. The doctors there urged me to see a specialist, Dr. Howard Axelrod. We met him, a boyish man, on the short side but with an aura of confidence, at Westchester Country Hospital on July 10.

The thought of someone carving through my breastbone and inserting a new object in my chest scared me. But Dr. Axelrod assured me that I would regain great energy, so we scheduled the surgery for two weeks hence. At the outset, Dr. Axelrod told us to make a choice between a pig valve and a man-made valve. Asked for his recommendation, he said the pig valve.

"There is only one disadvantage to the pig valve," he explained. "It lasts only about ten years. That means you have to replace it again. But a pig valve, because it is so much like a human valve, usually works fabulously well. There tend to be many fewer side effects."

Dai Sil and I looked at each other and opted for a pig valve right away. I knew that she wouldn't have it any other way. With the legend of Gertrude, how could we do anything else?

I found it intriguing that Westchester Medical Center was in Valhalla, New York. I joked with a couple of the doctors about that name—Valhalla, a name that dates from medieval Germany, is the home of dead heroes—but none of them understood or appreciated the humor.

According to the doctors, my surgery went well. But I did not regain my energy. I guess my other maladies redoubled their efforts.

A few months later, I went back to my primary care doctor, Dr. Davis Sprague. He asked me a bunch of questions and then ordered a few tests. When the results came back, I was told that I had chronic obstructive pulmonary disease (COPD).

At least when I needed heart surgery, I didn't feel guilty about it. But COPD was a different thing entirely, especially when Dr. Sprague cautiously informed me that my smoking was a contributing factor. I felt terribly guilty. To make matters worse, even with my shortness of breath and fatigue—primary symptoms of COPD—I still craved to inhale nicotine deeply into my ailing lungs. It was time to do something drastic.

Before we got married, I had told Dai Sil that I knew how bad my heavy smoking was and that I wanted to stop. I told her that I would do everything possible toward that end, but I made her promise not to nag me about it. It would only make it worse. I must say, she kept her part of the bargain pretty well all through the years of our married life. Even though I continued to smoke heavily, I also kept trying to quit. Sometimes she tried to help. She found an acupuncturist, and then a doctor who could hypnotize me. None of this worked. It was no fun to struggle so much without success.

Now, as I fought with my smoking addiction, I came across a letter from my dad, dated July 18, 1990.

How is your battle with cigarettes coming? I am going to give you a bit of advice. You are never going to whip it unless you just quit cold. You can't smoke a few every day and really kick it. I know that it won't work. I also know that quitting cold turkey won't be easy. But I know you can do it and you will have better health if you do.

Now that I'd been diagnosed with COPD and told that I must stop smoking, I made up my mind to try cold turkey while Dai Sil was gone. The first such opportunity came in June 1999, when she went off to Portland, Oregon, to screen one of her films. While she was away, I stayed in bed almost the entire time. I believe she was gone three days. In the past, I had smoked everywhere except in bed. So that was the only place that didn't act as a smoking cue. I got through those three days without a cigarette and even a few days more after that, which made me feel positive. But the simple truth of the matter is that I never stopped. I just couldn't do it.

I feel so badly that I have put Dai Sil through so much with my ill health. I was both blessed with and plagued by exceptionally good health until I was well into my forties. Then it all caught up with me. When I say plagued, I mean only that I never felt compelled to take any measures to preserve my health.

In the hospital waiting for Don to get out of valve-replacement surgery, I am looking at two wedding bands—one mine, the other his. Actually, these two were once one, and mine. After Don's original band slipped off his thin finger when he was ill, I suggested that we divide my wide band into two narrow ones. At this moment, they are both on my finger, as I wait to put his back on his hand when he is rolled into recovery.

~ D S K-G

The Night of the Fire

On December 29, 2001, the brightest light threw us into the darkest pit. A fire devoured our house in New Paltz, New York, in less than an hour. We stood shoeless in our front yard, our hands shaky and legs wobbly, aghast as the flames spread with astonishing speed. The entire house was ablaze, a roar of sounds coming from everything that was burning and melting, from shingles flying up and rafters dropping.

The day started out much as any other day, though, with our planning a dinner for our friend Yongjin, a sculptor and the husband of Dai Sil's best friend Miae. They had been married since 1963, but were having some marital problems and Miae had asked us to talk with him. We invited him to join us for dinner at our home that evening. He readily agreed to drive the eighty miles. As sunset approached, we became anxious and wondered if Yongjin was going to show up. Then we found him in front of our hearth, building a fire.

"Oh, my. I didn't even see you come in. Did you just arrive?" said Dai Sil.

"Yes," said he, continuing to play with the logs in the fireplace. With that, Dai Sil headed off to the kitchen to put our meal in motion.

She baked a luscious fillet of Chilean sea bass, flaky biscuits, and acorn squash. She also made mashed potatoes, smothered with butter, clearly to fatten me up—and also Yongjin. We sat around the kitchen table, washing down tasty food with good and lively dialogue.

Dai Sil and I were trying to lead the conversation around to Miae's concerns, when my eyes caught the most fantastic glow of light on the majestic spruce trees in our backyard. The light was both glorious and mysterious.

"Look, how beautiful!" exclaimed I.

"Oh my," both Yongjin and Dai Sil simultaneously raised their voices in admiration.

"It must have snowed while we were talking," Dai Sil said. Then all of a sudden, the kitchen light went dead, followed by Yongjin's voice in the darkness. "Look, the electricity is out," he said, "but then where is that light coming from?" Panic-stricken and bewildered, I turned my head to look out at our front yard.

"It looks like it might have snowed, but I can't be sure."

"But look, where is that light coming from?" Yongjin repeated the question.

Then we heard a pop, a low but distinct sound coming from the direction of our laundry room. Deciding to step outside and investigate, I opened the door to our mudroom, which led to the garage and outside, with Dai Sil and Yongjin right behind me. We saw flames.

"Oh, my God, look, the house is on fire!"

I don't remember who yelled first. Yongjin asked where the fire extinguisher was and I yelled, "Call 911!"

I handed Yongjin a small fire extinguisher and he struggled to figure out how to use it. When he did, whatever came out of it was like piss in a storm.

Dai Sil reached the kitchen phone, but apparently there was no dial tone. By that time, I disappeared upstairs to see if my office phone might work. Then I heard Dai Sil yelling at the top of her lungs, "Don, come down now. Come out wherever you are. I called 911. They are on the way!"

Outside, I heard my own voice, a voice like a wail. "We are losing everything. My life is over."

The Morning After

I KNOW I TURNED OVER IN BED what felt like a million times, unable to sleep, but I must have dozed off toward dawn. When I opened my eyes, I felt groggy and empty. Then I saw Dai Sil curled up beside me. She was in black corduroy pants and a blouse, with her legs folded up close to her chest. She looked small and sad.

"Oh my God," I sprang up, slowly realizing that we had spent the night at our neighbor's house. Careful not to wake up Dai Sil, I tiptoed downstairs and slipped out the back door.

The yard where our elegant house had stood just hours before was filled with debris, charred wood, and steel beams that looked like bones minus flesh. I noticed smoke drifting up in the cold morning air from some piles of half burnt logs, all blackened. My legs went weak. As I struggled to stand firm and not fall down, I heard a voice. A middle-aged man came around and extended his hand, a man whom I had never seen before.

"I am so sorry," said he, eying our once beautiful home, now reduced to ashes.

I just stood there, concentrating on my legs and on not falling down. He handed me a card, and told me that he was a public adjuster, a title I had not heard before. On that morning, several more of these people knocked at our neighbor's door, or grabbed me outside, and offered their services.

I knew about ambulance chasers, but not about fire chasers. They would handle all our dealings with the insurance company, they proclaimed forcefully, and make sure that we received the maximum benefits. In exchange, they would receive 10 percent of the proceeds. Numb, but with perfect composure, I calmly told each and every one of them that we didn't need or want their services.

Alone with the full view of our fire-ravaged house, I relived the night before. The shock wave I felt when I first saw the flames through the mudroom door must have paralyzed my mind. After

Dai Sil grabbed the kitchen phone and found it dead, I ran upstairs to my study to try my phone. What was I thinking? Moreover, I didn't even feel stupid to find it dead, too. I just stood there motionless for a full minute, until I heard Dai Sil's voice in a blend of despair and sorrow.

"Don, where are you? I called 911 on my cell phone."

I needed to go down, but I could not inhale. My shortness of breath became worse with every step. Damn my breathing! It took me forever to make my way down the short flight of stairs. By then, the smoke was everywhere and flames had engulfed the kitchen. Dai Sil and Yongjin were nowhere to be seen. They must have left the house. I went outside, stepping shoeless through the front door.

I found Dai Sil standing in the front yard, also shoeless. I went to her and we stood together briefly. Neither of us said anything. I think she held my hand for a moment and then let go. By that time, a number of cars had driven into our yard. People were gathering to witness our house being swept up in flames. Smoke rose and formed black clouds that hung like doom in the frigid night sky. I felt that my life was over. I felt as if a big hole were opening up under my feet, pulling me down to bury me beneath the black earth.

Our good neighbor, David Lent, walked over holding a pair of shoes and urging me to put them on. His kindness made my eyes tear. But Dai Sil was gone. I felt panicky.

"Where is Dai Sil?"

As I looked around, someone—I think it was Yongjin—told me that she'd been taken next door, to the house of other good neighbors, David and Betty Mesches. Thank God, she is safe.

I stayed rooted to the spot, unable to turn away as I watched our cedar-shake roof burning swiftly. The firefighters didn't arrive for fifteen to twenty minutes, which felt like hours. By the time they came, the entire roof was in flames and the flames were moving downwards, from the garage toward the master bedroom 100 feet or so away. I envisioned all that was being consumed, destroyed. I later recalled that cedar-shake roofing had been banned a few years earlier in California, after the Oakland fires, because it burned with amazing speed.

It was a huge fire. Later I learned that units from four different towns converged in our yard, with another on standby downtown. It was the event of the holiday season in New Paltz. For several days, I encountered people who claimed they had seen the blaze from miles away. One fire department official reported that the flames leaped 100 feet in the air. A construction engineer who witnessed the conflagration from afar told me the flames were so high that he thought it must be the multistory apartment complex not far from us.

The 911 dispatch must not have worked. Later, as Dai Sil and I thought back, it was also clear that the firefighters were not professionals. They were well-meaning, hard-working volunteers.

That night, I watched it all. I couldn't do anything else. David Mesches, our neighbor who offered us a bed that night, is a doctor. As the fire raged, he urged me—especially because of my already severe lung damage—to go to his house and stay inside. I finally acquiesced and went in, but I went out again and again, until it was all over and exhaustion claimed me.

A Sack of Charcoal Briquettes

THE HORROR OF THE NIGHT BEFORE STILL WITH ME, I slipped back into the Mesches' house, and found Dai Sil sitting at their kitchen table with a cup of coffee in hand. She was glad to see me. Her face momentarily brightened. Then she asked in a voice almost inaudible, but distinctly clear, "Don, do you still feel blessed?" We used to tell each other how blessed we felt to live in such a beautiful house.

"Yes," I replied. I didn't and don't yet know how and why I said yes, but the response was unreflected, spontaneous, confident. Her eyes glistened with tears. At that moment, even in my despair, I felt the hope of redemption from the dark hole I thought would swallow me up when I was outside, standing alone. Now I had Dai Sil beside me.

The next morning, I called our insurance company and was told we should stay at a hotel until—in consultation with them—we found something more substantive.

Someone drove me to Rent-A-Wreck where I rented a car. We drove around in it and settled on a hotel on a major road leading to Poughkeepsie. I believe it was a Marriott. Our room was an impersonal one with a bed where we could lay our heads after we had been driven out of our own place on Old Mill Street, for reasons we still did not understand.

I spent most of the last day of 2001 speaking with the insurance people, trying to figure out how much we might be entitled to. At the very top of the list of things to do in 2002 that I had started in my little spiral notebook was: "increase insurance coverage for our house." Well, the fire got to us before I could get to that. Thus, our insurance coverage will be based on the $235,000 we paid for the house in 1997.

December 31 was also the day when we learned about the cause of our fire—an unopened sack of charcoal briquettes!

Two inspectors, one from our insurance company and another from the town of New Paltz arson squad, went to work in earnest to establish the cause of the fire and determine if it was an accident. Our insurance people wrapped the burnt Volvo in plastic so they could cart it away, and then take it apart somewhere in Connecticut. The inspectors went through everything they could think of. Finally, they agreed that the spontaneous combustion of an unopened sack of charcoal briquettes, which had been tucked into a corner on the floor of our garage, was the culprit.

Dai Sil told me that she had bought the charcoal at ShopRite. "They were on sale," she said, "and I thought, why not throw a couple sacks in the car trunk? They'll be handy if we want to have a barbecue one day. They were in the car trunk for a long time, and then when I needed to empty it, I just threw them in the corner of the garage."

I remembered Dai Sil mentioning them on the night of the fire to an inspector, but I thought her statement went unnoticed. But apparently, it was duly recorded and those fumed-up sacks were subject to the sharp eyes of the inspectors.

When we both rolled our eyes and asked them to explain what the hell they were talking about, one of the two inspectors said, "If the sack was exposed to different temperatures, plus wet and dry conditions, and left for a long time, it is definitely possible that spontaneous combustion could have happened inside the sack and ignited the fire. Clearly, the briquettes were in the garage and when you parked your cars after driving in the snow, they must have became wet, and then dried out, etc."

"Oh my!" A feeble sound of despair came out of Dai Sil's mouth. No more words. She just stood there as still as a log. It was long after that day that I wondered if the spontaneous combustion happened in one sack, or both sacks.

We had arranged a meeting with the insurance adjuster on January 3 at noon at the skeletal remains of our house. We arrived before he did and stood in eerie silence. Soon a pleasant looking man in his late forties or early fifties appeared.

He gave a sweeping look over the ruins of our life, the heaps of ash, charcoal, and debris where our house had stood. "I am going to label it as total destruction and proceed with my paperwork. We will pay you for the house and for the contents. But you will have to itemize everything that was inside. And you did not have a separate rider for valuable jewelry, antiques, or paintings, so we won't cover those." Dai Sil asked him about her films and tapes and was told that they belonged to her business, so that she could not claim those either. He advised us to look for a house to rent until we could rebuild ours or buy another one.

"Do you have any questions?" To this, we shook our heads and sighed, our faces ashen with dismay. "Look, shit happens in life. You must go on." With that, he instructed us to call him with questions any time.

Collapsing into our rented car, I said to Dai Sil, "Shit happens in life. That's the perspective we should use for the fire and move on."

"It is not as simple as that for me," she said and looked away. We pulled out of the driveway and I asked, "You are not taking this personally, are you?"

"Well, I am the one who bought those ridiculous sacks of charcoal, wasn't I?"

"That is absurd. It was a fluke." But Dai Sil was not buying it.

"If the senseless wars and divisions of the country do not bring flames, I buy charcoal to do the job! You didn't know that you married a disaster carrier, did you?"

I put up a brave front and went on dealing with a million details involved in the aftermath of the fire.

Early on in January, Andre, the real estate agent who had helped us to buy the Old Mill Street house, and his wife Eleanor invited us to stay with them until we could find something more permanent. I worked out an arrangement to report their home as our bed-and-breakfast to the insurance company, so we could pay them a bit for their gracious hospitality. It turned out to be the best arrangement we could have had.

Looking for Gertrude

WE PURCHASED A USED BUICK, and every day I would drive from our B&B to our burnt-down house and spend hours at a time looking for small things, big things, anything at all, digging with my bare hands beneath the ashes. Other times, I would just stand and contemplate the magnitude of our loss.

One of the objects I kept searching for was the Steuben glass pig. The first Christmas Dai Sil and I were married, living on East Capitol Street in DC, I ordered that Steuben pig. It had cost $500, a princely amount to us, even now. I had taken so much time and care to choose it. It was neither shiny nor refined. Dai Sil frequently described it as "unassuming and lovely, like a tiny baby grinning up at her mother." I knew that Dai Sil fell in love with it the moment I gave it to her and she had prominently displayed it everywhere we lived. Of course, the pig was named Gertrude and she had survived all our moves—to Northampton Street, 17th Street, and Old Mill Street.

After our house burned down, even though it was frigid January, I kept returning to the scene of the crime almost every day for weeks, hoping against hope to find Gertrude. I knew where she had stood, or sat, on the top of a small stand in the living room. Where the stand had been a tall heap of frozen ashes towered. In my weakened state, I couldn't make my way through the ice. One day I even took along a thermos bottle of hot water and tried to smash through it.

But one day a few weeks later, when the relentless cold had eased up a bit, Dai Sil—who had resisted returning to the house—came along with me. Feeling quite weak, I remained standing by the car in the front yard. After a few minutes, Dai Sil returned with Gertrude in her hands! The Steuben piece was riddled with cracks, and as I tried to carefully remove the accumulated soot and grime, her head came off. Distressed, I collected all the pieces and wrapped them in a cloth. Bob Walsh, a friend of ours in New Paltz, an expert in antique furniture and restoration, took the glass and managed to put Gertrude back together again magnificently—except for her left ear. The heat of the fire was so intense that her left ear had melted and fused into the side of her head.

I knew that Dai Sil felt sad about finding Gertrude herself, instead of me, but whoever made the find, I was just happy to have Gertrude back. The pig was a symbol for me of my love for Dai Sil, but also a symbol of our survival and continuing life of renewal.

In the midst of our tragedy, there was one more happy bit of story about my treasure hunting. Two weeks after the fire, I was standing in my study, where three of the four walls were gone, and I could look out over the countryside. After a while, I looked down and there, right in the middle of the floor, lay a small white envelope. I picked it up, opened it, and discovered my parents wedding announcement from 1932. Now, I don't believe in the supernatural, but that was pretty spooky.

*In the forefront of my mind is always my father's portrait.
We hung it on the kitchen wall right by the table. I always
felt that he was watching over us. After we buried him, I
was unable to mourn. Then, one day, I just went to my easel
and started painting. My soul is in that painting. That's why
everyone said it was museum quality. It was my spirit and my
heart. How I wish I'd rescued my father from the flames.*

~ *D S K-G*

We Were Not Alone

THE REACTION OF OTHER PEOPLE to the news of our fire ranged
from a marvelous outpouring of love and support from friends
and neighbors to indifference to noncomprehension. For days after the conflagration, I was busy on the phone canceling accounts
or trying to reestablish them. Talking with one customer service
agent about altering our E-ZPass account, I initially began by
saying that our house and car had been destroyed and I wished to
cancel the tag.

She said, "Certainly, sir, all we will need is your PIN and account
number."

I replied that I didn't have them.

She then said, rather sternly, "Just go to your files and get it."

I said, "I must not be communicating very well; our house was
destroyed and I have no files."

"Sir, we must have those numbers."

This went on a while. I finally had to ask to speak to a supervisor, who resolved the issue, but not before my frustration level

soared. So many people simply didn't hear or if they did, it went in one ear and out through the other. It was as if their ears could not absorb the full import of those awful words. They just heard what they wanted to hear. I would say, "The entire house burned down," and many listeners would hear, "small fire in the kitchen." It was bizarre.

On the other hand, one of the more endearing reactions came from the Shelby County (Iowa) treasurer. I needed some documents related to the farmland we own there. I explained what I wanted and why I didn't have them (the fire). The treasurer said she could provide the help, but the statements would cost 25 cents a page for two pages. That was okay, but I wondered in my mind how one made out a check for 50 cents. The documents arrived a few days later with a handwritten note, "Due to your loss, we will waive the 50-cent charge."

Clearly, in our suffering, we were not alone.

So many friends and relatives came bearing home-cooked food from far and near. Countless e-mails poured in and packages and letters of support arrived in the mailbox of our rented house. No way that we can list them all. But nothing touched us more deeply than Igor's simple white-line drawing on black paper. He wrote, "Dear Dai Sil and Don, I was horrified by your disaster. Part of me went in flames!"

Igor, the only son of a brilliant philosopher and art critic, Ileana Marculesco, Dai Sil's friend, had been disabled ever since he had a stroke in the early 1970s. His drawing was and is the compassionate meditation of an artist who knows what it is to suffer.

Then there were Val and Manny, a sweet and caring couple who used to clean our house. Val had seen the flames and when she realized that they were coming from our house, she went home and cried her heart out. Later when they learned that we were both alive, they shed tears of joy. As Manny relayed the story, Dai Sil and I sobbed together, blowing our noses like little kids. They knew how to be grateful for what counted, that we were alive.

February 11, 2002, was moving day. With Andre's help, we rented a house on Climbing Ridge Road not far from Andre's, but farther into a quiet country lane that was ideal for long walks. The house had a view that was not spectacular but pleasant of the Shawangunk Mountains and the road was quiet. As agreeable as it had been to stay with Eleanor and Andre, we both felt liberated to have a place of our own.

We ordered two single beds and put them next to each other in the master bedroom upstairs. But the very next day, I had to propose that I sleep in a small study attached to the living room downstairs. It was just too hard for me to climb to the second floor. My lungs were getting worse. While a couple of friends helped us move one of the beds, I was worried that my bottled-up sadness might explode. I managed to hold back the tears, wanting to stay strong for Dai Sil. She was scheduled to leave for Los Angeles to continue with her film editing, a long overdue trip, and I didn't want her fretting over me.

It didn't take long to realize that it was impossible to find anything in New Paltz that we could afford comparable to our old house. Dai Sil pushed the idea of packing a couple suitcases and moving overseas, to somewhere like Portugal perhaps, to start a new life. She wanted to disappear to a place where we would be total strangers. However, I could not see myself starting over in a strange land at age sixty-four (we were both approaching sixty-four, come summer), especially with my health problems. So instead, we agreed on Manhattan, where we had always hoped to end up in our older years.

In late February, we spent a day in the city looking at a couple of apartments. We saw three places in Harlem, which by then was already an up-and-coming residential area. But compared to downtown, we thought it would be affordable. How wrong we were! Every place we looked at was beyond our means. Feeling deflated, we let the real estate agent lead us farther north to a prewar co-op complex of five buildings at the top of a hill on a street called Cabrini Boulevard. It was in a neighborhood known as Old Washington Heights, which earlier in its history had been home to generations of retired Jews. More recently, the realtors had renamed it Hudson Heights, to create the impression of a more inclusive neighborhood. By the time we arrived at the bottom of the hill and found parking, I was exhausted and could barely breathe. I urged Dai Sil to go on ahead. Slowly, I trudged up the hill.

When I reached 200 Cabrini, I was pretty much gasping for air. I stayed in the lobby while Dai Sil went upstairs to see a three-bedroom apartment. On the drive home, I could feel her excitement. At home, Dai Sil told me more:

"When I first walked in, I encountered a typical New York apartment: the first room I saw was the kitchen, nothing unusual about it, small and compact. Then my eyes caught sight of a big window in the living room that directly overlooked the Hudson River! Every window in the whole apartment looks out over the river, Don! I almost felt healing taking place by that window as I gazed out. It was as if all that vast flow of the river were wiping out the flames, and all the hurt in our hearts."

"Let's make an offer immediately," I said.

"Are you sure?" she asked, "You haven't even seen the place!"

"But I trust your judgment and taste. Let's do it."

But alone in my bed that night, I lay awake fretting about the prospect of a move to the city. It seemed like a huge step to relocate to Manhattan. My confidence in myself, once considerable, had dwindled in the face of retirement, the fire, and most of all, my failing health. As much as I trusted Dai Sil's taste, I hadn't set foot in the apartment. My anxiety spiked. In the morning, Dai Sil came downstairs to find me sitting in my study. I had been up since 5:00 a.m. But in the quiet of dawn, my worry had been replaced by a flash of positive intuition. When Dai Sil asked me what I was doing, I told her that I'd had something like an epiphany about the apartment and I now felt emotionally prepared, as well as intellectually, to make the move.

We made an offer the next morning and I went to work on buying that co-op, which took lots of time and effort.

During July, I accomplished two things. The first was appearing with Dai Sil in front of the co-op board to be interviewed. We had been quite nervous, but contrary to what we were told, it almost felt like a formality. In less than twenty minutes, we were welcomed into Castle Village.

Then, a couple of days later, Dai Sil and I went to Poughkeepsie to close the deal on the sale of our 27 Old Mill Street land. The transaction was swift. We were done in no time at all. On the way, Dai Sil made a rare request, that we stop by the burnt-down house. I think she wanted to have one last look at the homestead before we moved on to a new life in the Big Apple. I didn't want to get out of the car that day. Sitting and waiting, I watched her walking through the carcass of our brutally destroyed house, then disappearing into the back yard. I was sure that she wanted to peek down into the basement office where she used to work. I waited for my shoulder friend who would surely appear and get back in the car for our drive to wherever life would next take us.

For a moment I was alone with a distant view of Mohonk Mountain. I had the road all to myself, accompanied only by the bird songs and a deer or two who ran into the woods at the sounds of my footsteps. Then I turned away.

~ D S K-G

Now What?

THOSE FIRST FEW DAYS AFTER THE FIRE remain a blur. But I do recall clearly that I began to reorganize my life with a three-by-five notebook, a cheap ballpoint pen, and a cell phone. I'd stand in the New Paltz post office to sort mail, write notes, assemble my thoughts, and then go outside and place phone calls. Following that, I would go to the college library and use their computers to check our e-mail and respond.

The fire devastated me emotionally as well as physically, far more than I could have anticipated. My past, present, and future were destroyed. I can't say I had a premonition exactly, but with every house we ever owned, I recall coming home after trips—I traveled often at NEH—and wondering each time as the taxi or my car approached the house whether it would still be standing. I always felt a physical sense of relief when it loomed into view.

I never imagined that I would be sitting inside my own home when the flames snarled and that I would watch it burn to the ground! The core of my being was invested in that dwelling and what was housed within. Still, for the first six months after the fire, I handled life reasonably well. I went to the burnt-down site almost every day and was focused, almost obsessively, upon all the minutiae as well as the major tasks—settling the insurance, rescuing a handful of precious items from the remains of the house, settling all our accounts, exploring the best way to sell our now vacant land, and much else.

My immersion in details allowed me to deny the full impact of the fire and to believe that I was handling it. That was a lie, a lie to myself most of all. For, after all the immediate needs had been addressed, culminating in the purchase of our New York City co-op, there was *nothing*. Or at least that's how it seemed to me. I thought—and I felt—nothing. Dai Sil had given up her Fulbright fellowship to Korea, yet she still had her current film project which she had started before the fire and she went back to resume editing on it. In any case, it is probably true that Dai Sil is stronger than I.

I was retired, and struggling to come to terms with that and trying to fashion a meaningful life. I was beginning to write and do some consulting. I was writing about the Germans and their 1932 election, the subject of my dissertation research, with a book in mind. But the fire destroyed my computer, my dissertation notes, my previous writing, and all the random notes I had taken. Everything was destroyed.

One day upon returning home, I collapsed on the living room floor. When my cell phone rang some time later, I answered. Thank God, it was Dai Sil calling from Los Angeles. I could hardly talk, but she had the uncanny ability to know my condition, near or far, and immediately grasped that I was in serious trouble. From her edit suite, she arranged for help.

In the hospitalization that resulted, I often felt as if I were stranded alone on a battlefield. When I first saw Dai Sil walk in, enormous joy swelled inside me. She touched my hand, and I knew I was no longer alone. She was there with me. She would always be there, fighting any and all battles right by my side.

Yes, I know we are blessed. We now live in a beautiful apartment with fantastic views of the river and park. I am trying to create a new life for us, but the fire remains with me. I miss the days when I was alone in my second-floor office with my glass desk, gazing over the yard and trees toward Mohonk Mountain. I miss smoking the occasional cigarette, leaning out of the window. Dai Sil wouldn't scold me. I miss walking in the woods near the house. Though we actually owned only two acres, our back yard abutted a large parcel of undeveloped woodland, which felt like it was ours.

Besides the portrait of Dai Sil's father, I miss looking at the Abraham Lincoln print that Phil Lasansky gave us. It was done by his father, Maricio Lasansky, an internationally known printmaker. Hanging on the center wall of our living room, Honest Abe watched us as we entered, as if challenging us with a critical question of the day or the century. As much as I valued the Lincoln print, perhaps my favorite piece was a painting by Lu Bro, an Iowa artist, of a boy peering through chicken wire. I identified with that boy. Our original Frank Miller political cartoon also gave me much joy.

We also had some fantastic paintings by Korean artists, such as Whanki Kim, Changyeul Kim, and Miae Moon Han (Dai Sil's, and eventually our, best friend). I miss them all, but what saddens me most is the loss of Dai Sil's own paintings. She had over fifty oil paintings of all sizes, most of them impressionistic and some leaning toward abstract.

Oh, then there was the Korean antique chest that Miae and Yongjin brought us in Washington as a wedding gift. Dai Sil had long admired that chest at Miae's house, and Miae had said flippantly, "If you ever get married, it will be yours!" At that point, they had given up on the idea of Dai Sil ever getting married. But Miae kept her word and parted with that chest.

I miss our kitchen table, which Dai Sil had bought at This End Up. We played an awful lot of Yahtzee on that table, looking out at our back yard. Speaking of Yahtzee, after hearing about the fire, Andrea Anderson, a former colleague at NEH and a friend, sent us a leather Yahtzee cup that had belonged to her father. It is a beautiful cup. Can't find one like that any more. That was so thoughtful.

When I think of the calendar clock my maternal grandfather bought in 1898, which sat on top of our mantel above the fireplace, I feel as if I lost a cherished link to my ancestors. Grandpa got it for $1.25 at an auction in Iowa. I also miss—not so much for me but for Dai Sil—our tire-rim footstools. When she first visited my apartment on Capitol Hill, she immediately noticed them. I had made them in 1965, when I was at graduate school, welding two tire rims together and attaching a specially sawn round piece of plywood for the top. The rims were painted black. Dai Sil complimented my ingenuity. When we got married, one of the first things she did was to paint the tops with cadmium yellow over black.

And yet, despite all we have lost and the accompanying pain, the fire was also a catalyst—first sending me into despair and drinking, and then opening me up for renewal. Fueled by the trauma of the fire and abetted by the move to the New York City, I discovered an urgent need for discipline, and a reinforced appreciation for the value of rituals, by which I mean regular times set aside routinely for writing, reading, walking. With those fixtures in my life, I have tried to adjust. And crucially, I have confined my drinking to one glass of wine with Dai Sil at dinner.

All of this progress notwithstanding, there is still the irreducible reality of my ever-worsening health. I consistently experience lack of energy and shortness of breath. I live in constant fear of falling (how could I ever get myself back up?). And I experience extreme anxiety about any proposed outings, be it to a restaurant, a museum, the theater, or simply going for a walk. Going any place where I might be required to climb a flight of stairs or trek down a long hallway is especially worrisome. A significant part of my apprehension is that I don't want to be embarrassed in front of others. I know I can manage it eventually. That is, I can climb the stairs or walk into the theater or whatever, as long as I can proceed slowly and pause frequently. It just takes me a long time and I look so enfeebled as I attempt it. It's mortifying. Or it can be as I walk around Hudson Heights. My health remains problematic. But I have life, Dai Sil, and hope.

Don collapsed. His COPD worsened, and his energy was at rock bottom. We had to hospitalize him. On my way home alone from there, around 2:00 a.m., I got lost in the rain and wandered around Poughkeepsie for what felt like hours before I finally found my way to the Mid-Hudson bridge and back to our house. When I opened the door, weak with exhaustion, the house felt so empty without Don there, but not as empty as my heart. I sat on the sofa and sobbed quietly. At that moment, I knew that nothing mattered, not the fire, not anything but Don's health.

~ D S K-G

PART IX

From the Bavarian Alps to the Hudson River

Silver Anniversary in Berlin

FOR OUR TWENTY-FIFTH ANNIVERSARY in October 2004, we thought it would be a good idea to get away from familiar surroundings and inject some new energy into our lives. We chose Germany. To be honest, Dai Sil decided and I went along. She chose Germany, I know, to help me rekindle my long-dormant book project.

Dai Sil had saved her earnings from translating a book from Korean into English. She wanted to use that money to allow us to stay in Germany for an entire month, thinking it would give us a fresh start. I knew she really wanted that and I appreciated the generosity of her gesture. If only she knew how scared I was. A long flight to Europe and a month away from home with all my health problems? Perhaps I should have said no, but I did not have the heart. If that's what she wanted for our twenty-fifth anniversary, I wanted her to have it. And, of course, I was excited at the prospect of showing her *my* Germany. If only my health were better. The night before our departure, I was so worried that I couldn't sleep.

In the morning, my cell phone alarm went off at 5:00 a.m. I sprang up saying, "Oh, shit," and saw Dai Sil doing the same thing.

I started to calm down. After all, we were going to Germany!

As we checked in, an airline attendant arrived with a wheelchair. Despite a bit of embarrassment, I felt a huge relief. I sat down, and Dai Sil followed me and my chair with the carry-on luggage. We finally boarded and settled into our seats! For the first time that morning, I felt safe.

The first leg of our trip took us to London Heathrow. We spent a night at an airport hotel and got up at 5:00 a.m. for an early morning flight to Berlin. But no sooner had the taxi dropped us off than we realized we were at the wrong terminal. It was out of question for me to walk and the cabbie we hailed demanded £15, while we had only £11. We literally begged, but the taxi driver nastily refused. A skycap told us to take a shuttle train. It was a long walk to the platform, and with every labored step it felt like a thousand miles.

By the time we reached the right terminal, we had only about fifteen minutes left to get to our gate.

"I can't make it," I declared.

Dai Sil yelled at me, "Don't say we can't make it. Try."

We kept going. Breathing became ever more difficult. Dai Sil spotted a luggage cart, grabbed it, and told me to sit down. Then she literally ran, pushing me on the cart.

There was a long line at the security checkpoint. By now, we had five minutes. For the first time, I read resignation on Dai Sil's face. In a strikingly calm voice, she said, "Don, just wait here or walk as slowly as you need to. I am going to go ahead of you and tell the people at the gate that you are coming." Then she strode away. I knew she would come back to me. With my cane, I slowly started, putting one foot at a time in front of the other, in the direction she had run.

Before I knew it, I saw Dai Sil walking toward me. She had talked with British Airways attendants at the gate and they are waiting for us. As she informed me of this, an agent behind me called out, "Stop right there!" and came forward with an abandoned wheelchair, a child's wheelchair. My ass was so small I could fit in, no problem.

We were on board! I was elated when we finally touched down in Berlin. Instead of Dai Sil constantly ministering to me, I hoped to take the lead on this trip, to be strong and sure and in charge, my emphysema notwithstanding. To do so would meant the world to me. As Dai Sil had predicted so many times, I felt a surge of confidence. We took a cab to the Hotel Kempenski, where we planned to spend a leisurely ten days. We told ourselves that we deserved some luxury and pampering after all we had gone through.

At the hotel registration, everyone spoke English, but I was happy to use my German. The staff didn't seem all that impressed that I spoke the language, but Dai Sil was. That's all that mattered. Our room was impeccably clean with a simple ambience. That first night, I was happy to use my nebulizer and literally breathe a sigh of relief. We stayed in the room and watched some CNN newscast about the Kerry v. Bush presidential campaign.

The next morning was October 1, our twenty-fifth anniversary. We went to the dining room to have breakfast. Dai Sil seemed less than thrilled with the fare, but I was happy to eat hard rolls with honey and hard-boiled eggs, which had often comprised my breakfast during my research sojourn. I felt somewhat nostalgic for those days. They might have been lonely and difficult years in certain respects, but I brimmed with physical energy. If only I could get back that vigor, even half of it, with lungs that didn't struggle for every breath.

I made some inquiries about a restaurant that served good German food, nothing pretentious but elegant enough for our anniversary. I wish I could remember the name of the place, but all I recall is how long it took us to walk there. We had been advised it was a short stroll and there was no need for a cab. With numerous stops to rest along the way, we made it. The food was mediocre, but I was pleased that we were able to share our twenty-fifth anniversary dinner in Berlin, just as Dai Sil had wished.

The following day, we toured Berlin by bus, getting on and off whenever something caught our eye. At Dom zu Berlin (the cathedral), I told Dai Sil to go off and explore by herself while I sat at a sidewalk cafe and read. There was no way that I could climb up all those stairs to the top of the Dom, but Dai Sil was thrilled with the view of the city from the top.

It was clear that I could not possibly accompany Dai Sil everywhere she wanted to go. We talked about it at dinner and she readily agreed that we should each do as much or as little touring as we chose and meet for meals. I spent a lot of time at an Internet cafe where I wrote e-mails. "Hi, I am in Berlin. How are you?" That was fun.

There were a few things I wanted to do with Dai Sil for sentimental reasons while we were in Berlin. Visiting the Brandenburg Gate, for instance. I don't know how many times I had told her about hearing JFK speak there during my visit in 1962. And I wanted us to see together how the German people had put the Berlin Wall behind them and how they were coping with unification. As we slowly walked around the gate, she sighed. I knew that she was thinking about how Korea was still divided.

I wanted to take Dai Sil to Potsdam to show her where the historic 1945 conference had taken place when the World War II allies—the United States, the Soviet Union, and the United Kingdom—discussed how to deal with the aftermath of the war. I also wanted her to see Sanssouci, the rococo summer palace built by Frederick the Great in the mid-18th century.

Perhaps the most memorable thing we did in Berlin was attend a concert at the Berliner Philharmoniker. We took a taxi and arrived at the concert hall way early. We were all dressed up in our elegant concert attire, but we strolled across the big lawn and came upon a small outdoor food cart. The man looked at us quizzically, as if to say, "Why are you here? You look way too formal to be eating at my stand." I told him that we were headed to the concert but wanted a little snack, and I ordered us each a beer and sausage. We sat there outside and enjoyed our food. It was delicious.

The entire evening was magical. The program was gorgeous, even to my tone deaf-ears. I had to walk quite a lot before we collapsed happily in a taxi, but I felt energy flowing and could manage my breathing a little better than usual. Back at the hotel bar, we lingered for a bit, as I sipped Scotch neat and Dai Sil downed a glass of champagne.

Prague to the Bavarian Alps

WE HAD TEN WONDERFUL DAYS IN BERLIN. We had arranged from the States to rent a car and drive on to Prague. When we went to pick up the vehicle, it was a VW stick shift, which meant that only I could drive. That worried me, but I tried not to show it and we made it to Prague without incident, to my happy surprise.

Prague is a magnificent city, and Dai Sil had reserved us a room at the Hotel Uraka, reported to be one of the most romantic spots in the world. As it turned out, it wasn't actually a hotel at all, but an old mansion with just a few rooms. The owner had a background in architecture and had renovated the place with exquisite taste. It was stunning. Our room was simple but elegant, and we loved it.

Once again, I couldn't do much walking around with Dai Sil, which was a little sad for both of us, in this city built for ambling. But we made the best of it and found a congenial cafe where I could sit and amuse myself, while Dai Sil walked alone, knowing I waited happily for her return.

After two nights in Prague at the fairy tale Uraka, we left for Lake Chiemsee and the Bavarian Alps. Driving on a major road with fantastic views on both sides, we passed through a succession of Czech villages, which looked rundown and poor, kind of shabby. But once we reentered Germany, everything looked instantly different—clean, orderly, and well maintained. In the car, Dai Sil asked, "Don, tell me. How could those compulsively clean people be the ones who committed the horrific mass murders of the Holocaust?" I said nothing. She continued, "Perhaps it was that very obsession with orderliness and cleanliness that contributed to the urge to eliminate all non-Aryans."

By the time we reached Passau, a fairly large city that is home to a university, an opera house, and a number of museums, I was exhausted. So there, where the Danube and Inn Rivers merge, we decided to spend the night. We checked into the first hotel we found, Jesuits Little Castle. What a name!

The next morning, after a leisurely breakfast, I felt refreshed and we set out to explore. We made our way to Lake Chiemsee, which Bavarians call their sea. Facing it, I understood why. It is vast. Right by the lake was a cafe, where we enjoyed a delicious lunch of soup, cappuccino, and strudel.

After a couple of days, we ventured on into the Bavarian Alps. We were both in complete awe as we drove along the winding mountain roads. The spectacular peaks and green pastures, interspersed with tidy Alpine villages beckoned us with their beauty. I can well imagine how Dai Sil felt but I know I felt cleansed, refreshed, exhilarated, even inspired.

Of nature's many splendors there in the Bavarian Alps, Dai Sil's favorite were the streams that flowed down from the mountainsides right through the middle of the villages. She exclaimed, "Look, the water is so clean and clear. I wish I could drink it, bathe in it, and hear the songs of flowing water."

Soon enough, we found ourselves in a storybook town called Ramsau, where we decided to stay put for a few days. Dai Sil was enchanted by the white hilltop church with its onion spire, the pristine stream that ran through the middle of town, and the wooden bridges that crossed it. We registered in a comfortable guest house with a restaurant. The view was lovely, and most important of all, it had a small elevator, which helped me. By that time, my breathing was becoming rougher, and it struck us that perhaps the high altitude could be an aggravating factor.

Actually, I had thought about the possible effects of high altitudes on my health, but said nothing. I did not want to spoil Dai Sil's enthusiasm to see the Bavarian Alps. If Dai Sil did not say it aloud, I knew that she went over it in her mind so many times, "What was I thinking when I suggested the mountains as our destination! Was it shortsightedness, ignorance, carelessness? Maybe all of it and more. In fact, Don probably *had* thought about it, but said nothing. He wanted to go along with my wishes and acquiesced to his thick-headed wife. How could I have been be so hopelessly dumb and insensitive?"

In Ambulance to Berchtesgaden

ON THE 22ND OF OCTOBER, SIX DAYS BEFORE we were scheduled to fly home from Berlin, I woke up gasping for air, barely able to breathe, far worse than usual. As always, I told myself that given a couple of hours, I would improve. I stepped into the little elevator to go downstairs for breakfast. At the dining room threshold, I collapsed.

How can I possibly describe the desperate state Dai Sil was in, trying to find a doctor. All I could do was to continue to pant, uttering "Oh my God," the words that always slipped through my lips when I was in unbearable pain.

Finally, I saw the ambulance arrive. Two sturdy young men came in, lifted me onto the stretcher, and transported me gently to the vehicle. Dai Sil wanted to ride in the back with me, but the driver insisted that she sit in front. A paramedic watched over me and gave me oxygen. The ambulance screeched along the mountain road and then pulled into a depressing gray cement building, Kreiskrankenhaus Berchtesgaden.

I was rushed into a room where a couple of male doctors were waiting. After a brief examination, they conferred with each other and signaled for an attendant to move me to the intensive care unit. In the ICU, a team of nurses, one male and one female, got me situated in a room, stripped off my clothes and put on a clean hospital gown. They checked my vital signs, gave me a nebulizer, and tried to make me comfortable. I remember muttering a few German words in response to their questions, but soon pain dominated me and made me almost delirious. The last thing I saw was Dai Sil sitting in the corner of the room, apparently praying.

I later learned that, after their shift, the two nurses drove Dai Sil in the female nurse's car to our hotel in Ramsau and waited for her to pack up. Then the male nurse drove our rented VW to her new digs, which they had found for her across the street from the hospital. Dai Sil added, "You know, Don, he even came up to the room to make sure it was okay."

The next morning, I was still alive but in accelerating pain. With every labored breath, came a deep groan. I was gravely ill. A series of tests were conducted, but the results did not reveal the cause of my unbearable pain.

Toward evening, a female doctor, Dr. Kornelia Zenker-Wendlinger, came in and she pored over the test results, examined me thoroughly, and listened intently to my lungs and heart. After a couple of hours, I noticed that she invited Dai Sil to exit the room with her.

I was too sick to worry about what was happening outside of my room. All I could manage was to wrestle with my pain, often thinking that I would rather die than bear that pain. It was only after my pain diminished enough for me to recover my senses that Dai Sil told me, "The doctor sat me in a little anteroom, politely pointed me to a chair, looked into my eyes, and spoke in English, not fluent but clear enough for me to understand every word."

What Dr. Zenker-Wendlinger said to Dai Sil is: "It is with great sorrow that I have to inform you that his condition is extremely critical. I do not think I can save him. His lungs are weak, as you know. I have to determine what is causing him this extreme pain in order to treat him, and so far we just don't know."

During that night, I began to feel a bit better. My breathing became less labored. Dai Sil was still sitting in the corner. Around 10:00 a.m. the next morning, Dr. Zenker-Wendlinger appeared: "I am more hopeful today than yesterday. You are improving."

Dai Sil and I both had tears in our eyes. I gripped her hand in mine with all the strength I could muster. She later told me that my grip was astonishingly strong.

The doctor started treating me with antibiotics for some bacteria common in that area, coupled with massive IV nutrition. After four days in ICU, I was transferred to a regular room. On October 27, the hospital-room door opened and in came Paul, our nephew whom Dai Sil had e-mailed to ask him to fly over as soon as possible. He wore a backwards turned baseball cap on his head and a radiant smile. Paul drove us in our rented car to Berlin, where we got on the flight to New York. On November 6, we landed at JFK and found Yongjin waiting for us. It felt like a miracle. We were home. We were alive. We were together. We had missed the presidential election, but John Kerry didn't need our two votes to carry New York.

I Am Your Weapon!

I STILL FEEL TERRIBLE whenever I think about that grey, cement hospital in the Bavarian Alps. I was in terrible pain, the worst I had experienced since I was first diagnosed with COPD. But in many ways, I think it was even worse for Dai Sil. She felt totally responsible that we had roamed around the high-altitude mountains. As for me, though my doctor and I talked about death directly and concretely, in my heart I did not feel that I was going to die. But Dai Sil had to live with what the doctor had told her, that she might not be able to save my life.

By the time we got home to New York, I had progressed enough to take short walks, often stopping by a local bar to chat with a congenial group of neighborhood buddies. But in late autumn, I came down with the flu and, shortly before Christmas, I was once again rushed to the emergency room. They declared that I had the influenza, and I was put in isolation.

I remember that on Christmas morning Dai Sil came into the room looking like she hadn't slept all night. I was in terrible pain. Even the slightest movement took my meager breath away.

Dai Sil looked at me with steely determination and said, "Listen, Don, if we triumphed over a bacteria in Hitler's vacation town, we can certainly fight this influenza with the army of doctors at Columbia Presbyterian!"

"But I no longer have any reserves to fight with!" I said. "I am weaponless."

"I am your weapon," she responded.

And indeed, ever so slowly, I once again prevailed. But a few months later, something totally unexpected happened. On May 13, 2005, an ambulance once more had to be summoned, only this time not for me but for Dai Sil.

She had spent the entire day before in bed with severe abdominal pain, plus extreme dizziness. I called her primary care doctor and described her symptoms. The doctor thought that internal bleeding was likely. That's how it all began, a new threatening chapter in our lives.

Dai Sil went straight from the emergency room to the intensive care unit. The doctors discovered a large lump in her stomach, which turned out to be malignant. Then came a series of tests to stage the cancer. For several days, Dai Sil and I lived in a state of simultaneous shock and terror, with the strong suggestion that her cancer might be quite advanced, even stage 3 or 4. All of the doctors recommended surgery, followed by radiation and chemotherapy.

Looking back, although Dai Sil had always seemed healthy and functioned normally, over the years she had also complained somewhat regularly of stomach pain. More than a few times, I found her in the middle of the day lying flat on her stomach and writhing in discomfort. I urged her to consult a doctor and she did—three different doctors, in fact, in New Paltz and in Manhattan. One of them had sent her for a colonoscopy, but all basically opined that her pain was likely constipation. Dai Sil diagnosed herself as having an ulcer. None of the doctors sent her for an endoscopy, even though stomach cancer is well known to be relatively common in Asians.

Now I truly understood everything Dai Sil had felt in the Bavarian Alps. There, she was terrified that I would die. Now the tables were turned. The thought of her death seemed utterly unreal, yet here it was staring me in the face. I felt helpless and petrified. Life was impossible without her.

We met with a surgeon on June 9. The doctors were afraid that the cancer might already have metastasized to her pancreas, liver, and lymph nodes. Dai Sil and I stood in the hospital room that day, each of us struggling to suppress our innermost terror. A small man in a white gown entered the room. I eyed him calmly.

"John Chabot," he stuck out his hand. "And you are Dai Sil Kim-Gibson. Am I saying your name correctly?" He addressed Dai Sil directly.

I studied his face. His eyes were alert and intelligent, and he had a kind mouth. His whole demeanor was gentle, but he carried an aura of confidence and competence. I liked him right away and knew that I could trust him to cut Dai Sil's stomach open. On the day of the operation, when Dai Sil's dear friend Tae Hee met Dr. Chabot, she commented, "He looks like a royal seamstress whose each stitch has to be perfect!"

Before we even met him, I had checked out Dr. Chabot and determined that he was one of the best gastro surgeons in the country. So I wasn't totally relying on my intuitive impressions. But I was surprised to hear Dai Sil asking him if he could immediately squeeze her into his overbooked surgical schedule. No point waiting around, Dai Sil apparently thought, and trusted that I would agree with her. In half an hour, Dr. Chabot returned and asked if she was prepared to go under the knife the very next day.

On the night of June 9, we lay on our bed, fully clothed. I heard the words coming out of Dai Sil's mouth: "I believe that everything will go okay, but if anything happens to me, please be strong. I do not want you to be a pitiful old man. Be strong," she said. I did not say a word. It was impossible to say anything. She turned her head toward me and looked into my eyes, and I gazed right back at her.

Early the next morning, I took her to Columbia Presbyterian and up to the third floor of the Milstein Building. I filled out the paperwork, and then we were sent to the pre-op. Dai Sil went into booth #6, where she changed into a hospital gown. Soon her sister's family and her friend Tae Hee arrived. After a succession of nurses, doctors, and medical students had stopped by, Dr. Chabot and his team showed up. It was real. It was going to happen. He was going to cut her stomach open. I was terrified, but I tried to stay calm as I pecked her cheek and said, "I love you."

I do not know how I got through the rest of that day. All I remember is Dr. Chabot coming to find us and report on the surgery. He told us it went well, even though he had to remove her entire stomach. But he saw no signs of cancer in her pancreas or liver, which was a huge relief. He couldn't be sure about the lymph nodes.

"We have to wait a week or so for definitive results on the lymph cells I took out. But I'm optimistic." With that, the good doctor left.

We were able to see Dai Sil in the recovery station. Only a brief moment, but she was alive and safe.

When I got back to our apartment, there was a white envelope by the lamp on my desk. Dai Sil had made sure that I could not miss it by scrawling DON in capital letters across it. I opened it, my eyes filling with tears as I tried to read.

June 10, 2005

My dearest Don, I know I will beat this thing with your love. You know that you are my life. I've loved you and I will continue to love you in body and spirit.

It is a fact of life that one of us has to go first. If I am the first, be strong. You have physical problems, but I know that your spirit is strong. Be strong. Knowing that you will remain strong for both of us will help me wherever I am. Of course, I will always be with you. You can't get rid of me either in life or in death.

I took the letter to bed with me that night, but I could not sleep.

Dai Sil was discharged from the hospital five days later. When she climbed into our king-size bed, I felt alive again. She was home! I stood by the bed for a while, but I felt like I might collapse.

"I'll just lie down beside you for a bit." I lay on top of the bedspread next to Dai Sil. Then I had to say, "I hate to do this to you, but I need to go to the emergency room. I can't breathe." Two young men appeared within ten minutes, put me on a stretcher, gave me oxygen, and rolled me out.

It was clear what had happened. For almost a week while Dai Sil was in the hospital, I had summoned all of my energy to visit her every day and stay strong. But the minute Dai Sil was back home, I collapsed. Fortunately, the doctors sent me home after relieving me from pain. At the sound of the door click, Dai Sil emerged from the bedroom to find me coming through the door. We sat at the dining room table.

"What is going on, Don?"

There was a packet of ginger cookies on the table. I started eating them. I heard an ode of joy in the sounds of those ginger snaps going down my throat. Not only could I breathe, but I could also eat!

But there was still ample cause for anxiety. I was waiting to hear from my pulmonary doctor whether the white spot the CT scan had revealed on my lung was cancer. Dai Sil was waiting for the results of the pathology test on her lymph cells.

June 20 is a date I will always remember. I learned that I didn't have lung cancer, *just* a touch of pneumonia that could be treated with antibiotics. And Dai Sil got a call from her doctor reporting that her nymph nodes were cancer free. June 20 was a day of liberation for both of us, at least for a while.

I am still thinking of January 3, 2009. I walked to my bathroom, trying to steady my shaky legs, and dressed quickly to be ready to take you to the hospital again, which seemed likely.
In half an hour, you sat up, but your head was down and your shoulders drooped. I grabbed you, shivering with terror. You were clearly in terrible shape, your face ashen.

"Emergency 911?"

"Not yet," you said.

Well, we lost ten precious minutes before you let me call 911. By then, you were turning into an image of what might come. A shadow of death. In all the years of ambulance rides and life-and-death crises, you never said "I'm dying," not even in the Bavarian Alps when a German doctor told me to prepare for the worst. But that morning, with your head on my chest, you whispered, "I am dying. Let me die." Don, I am struggling with the memory of that moment, still so vivid. Remember what I did? I begged you, "Not yet, not yet. Don, please. It is not time yet for you to go. Please stay alive a bit longer, please, please, for me."

~ D S K-G

PART X

Life Goes On

A Time To Confess

DURING THE LAST DECADE, my ailments plus my retirement have deprived me of my confidence, which in turn has made me feel less competent, if not in actuality, at least in my own mind.

Dai Sil repeatedly tells me that what initially drew her to me was my confidence and my strength. She struggles greatly with my loss of confidence and my growing inability to feel competent.

My lack of confidence has reached a point where I reflexively say, "I am sorry," or "It's my fault," or "I am wrong once again." Ordinarily, these remarks might have soothed Dai Sil, but now they make her furious. She believes my apologies are reflections of my fear that my mental abilities have been reduced in proportion to my diminished physical capabilities. She becomes especially indignant whenever I say, "You are right again." She says she is not interested in being right or wrong and that I am making her out to be a self-righteous bitch who insists on being morally right. So I have started using the word correct instead of right, and incorrect in place of wrong. Not that that has fixed the problem.

I know there is a lot of anger in me. A lot of my anger stems from my heavy dependency on others, especially Dai Sil. I feel impotent and useless when she does the heavy work—does the laundry, goes grocery shopping alone, totes all the heavy bags, gets the car inspected, cleans my desk and computer table, or takes me to physical therapy. Or a dozen other things, large and small. I feel especially bad when I cannot eat her carefully prepared meals.

She has told me many times that I would do the same for her, were the situation reversed, and that as long as she is healthy enough to take care of things, we should be grateful.

I am not trying to blame myself totally and declare her faultless. She can sometimes be pig-headed and judgmental. And sometimes my ire erupts in response, and I find myself threatening that she will not see me alive the next morning or that our marriage is over.

And she responds with equal vehemence, "Okay, how many times do you have to threaten that you will die? If you really mean that death would be better than life, just die!" Then, she'll often go on, "If you want, I will move out. I can always find a job and survive on my own. I do not want anything from you."

Those awful moments do not usually last long. One of us simply puts a hand on the other's shoulder and the battle is over and we are reconciled. One time, after a screaming fight, I walked over to our master bedroom where Dai Sil had retreated and shut the door. I had to stop a few times just to catch my breath. I knocked at the door, opened it, and put my head in, gasping.

"What just happened? What was that all about?"

"Oh, Don, I was going to come to you in a minute. Nothing happened. None of it matters."

There was no trace of anger on her face and in her voice.

I know it is hard for her to believe from the way I behave, but I really am trying to gain back my confidence and strength. I know that I will never be as healthy as I once was. After all, I am not just ill, but also getting old! But I am trying.

I have told Dai Sil numerous times that I am not really mad at her but at myself—for having smoked so heavily, and for being unable, even now, to quit completely. I remember the time just last year when Dai Sil caught me smoking early in the morning at my desk. At the sight of her, I hurriedly put my lit cigarette into the top drawer. Without a word, she just walked out of the room. As she banged the apartment door, she yelled that she wouldn't be back. And she was gone all day. I am not sure if she has any idea how scared I was that day.

I can't begin to express how relieved I was when I finally heard her voice on my cell phone many hours later. I told her to come home. I said I had reserved a room in a hotel and that she could be alone in the apartment. She ignored what I said and proposed that we meet at Bleu (my favorite neighborhood restaurant) and have supper together. I remember her plea that evening, and it was not the first such plea. She wished I could stop smoking completely, of course, but if I had to smoke, she wanted me to smoke openly. She said she could not tolerate my sneaking a cigarette like a criminal. I agreed with her, but I was never able to smoke openly in my room or use the big ashtray she had placed on my desk. Not only that. To this day, I still sneak a cigarette here and there. Sometimes I loathe myself more than she can imagine. Still, I am trying to somehow replace my anger with peace and confidence, for her as much as for myself.

So as sick as I feel so much of the time, I am trying to continue to wake up in the morning (to the sound of Dai Sil pounding on the keyboard in her little study next to mine) and call out a hearty good morning! As long as she is there, my resilience will be strong, and my anger eventually will be supplanted by gratitude for being alive.

Believe it or not, as strong and seemingly tough as Dai Sil can be, at the core, she is soft, tender, and insecure. She has told me countless times that even if ill health has taken away my sense of self-worth, I should know that in sickness as in health, I am her quiet fortitude, the one who sustains both of us through good times and bad. That I am her husband, shoulder friend, and hero. I confess it has not always been easy to believe those words, but had I not believed in their truth, I would have been dead a long time ago.

I fear I will always fluctuate between hope and despair, but I will do my best—even better than my best, as Dai Sil likes to say—and I will apply a lesson that I learned growing up in Iowa: I will not be defeated by bitterness. In 1941, Winston Churchill said in a speech,

> Never give in, never give in, never, never, never—in nothing, great or small, large or petty—never give in except to convictions of honour and good sense.

Well I don't know about the honour part, but the 4-H taught me a lot of good sense.

In ICU, a few days before you left me, you noticed that your wedding ring was missing and were concerned. I told you that I had it. The expression of relief on your face was something no one could miss. I wanted to put it back on your finger, but your hand was too swollen. I assured you that I would keep it safe. Now I am wearing both rings on my finger.

~ D S K-G

Baseball

BASEBALL WAS CENTRAL TO MY LIFE AS A CHILD. It was the game of choice among all of us neighbor kids, principally because it needed no special equipment or playing fields. There are no playgrounds on farms, and we had no suburban garages with paved driveways for basketball hoops. All baseball required was a bat, a ball, and gloves—and gloves weren't mandatory. An old balled-up shirt or a cap or the odd tree branch worked just fine as a base. A diamond could be set up in a cow pasture, pig lot, or corn field. And whenever more than four of us could gather, we would do precisely that.

I also spent hours playing catch, mostly with my brother, although occasionally I would rope my father into the act, even if he didn't much care for it. In fact, I often organized baseball games right in the farmyard, consisting of me, my brother, my parents, and the hired man.

The more satisfying games took place at school during recess or whenever a few of us farm boys were together at a picnic or family reunion. We didn't have organized teams. Ordinarily, we would just pick two boys as captains, and they, in turn, would pick their players. That's how it had been done for decades in small towns and rural areas throughout America. There was no Little League back then. Adults rarely coached, supervised, or participated in any way. Nor did we have any umpires, so there were countless arguments and, once in a while, fist fights, which actually added excitement.

One of my boyhood heroes—Bob Feller—had a lot to do with my love for baseball. Feller broke into the major leagues with the Cleveland Indians in 1936 at age seventeen. He was a farm boy from Van Meter, Iowa, and he came home right in the middle of the season in his first year to graduate from high school. He was elected to the Baseball Hall of Fame, even though he lost three and a half years in mid-career to his military service during World War II. Many years later, I learned that he was hard right-wing politically. That diminished my ardor, but by then, my playing days were far behind me anyway.

In retrospect, my principal motivation for playing baseball was the desire to fit in. My primary interests—in reading and *big ideas*— were shared by none of my childhood friends. Basketball was the really big sport in rural Iowa, but I was an utterly untalented basketball player, and besides, the game involved only five starters. In baseball, on the other hand, there are nine starters, and with just twelve boys in my high school, even I could make the team.

Long after I'd left Iowa, I still enjoyed watching occasional baseball games, whether live or on television. But my ardent love for the sport had waned by the time I married Dai Sil. Before Dai Sil, I had thought baseball was a thoroughly American enterprise. Europeans considered it staid and slow. During an exhibition game played in the 1936 Olympics in Berlin, several hundred German spectators left the stadium en masse after just a few innings. In the 1950s, during my high school years, I learned that the Japanese were fanatic players, and I blithely assumed that their enthusiasm was just a result of the U.S. occupation following World War II. So I was stunned when Dai Sil told me that her father had been a star player for a Japanese college in the 1920s. After that, I learned that the first baseball game in Japan took place way back in 1873, and that it rapidly became the most popular sport in the nation. Baseball was also introduced to Korea in the late 19th century by a missionary, Phillip Gillett.

Early in our relationship, I took Dai Sil on a date to a softball game I was playing in. I was keen to impress her with my athletic prowess, but alas, I fell down no fewer than three separate times. Then when I ran up to her between innings to say hi, she drolly noted, without even a smile, "Please do not boast to my father when you meet him that you play softball. He will think of it as a chicken shit offspring of baseball."

Later, I was amazed to learn that Dai Sil had never set foot in Fenway Park despite having lived within walking distance of the stadium for seven years. I remember once calling her from a public phone at Fenway just to needle her: "Dai Sil, I am standing in Fenway Park, where you never once came to watch a game." I'd bug her like that periodically. Finally, one afternoon many years later, she explained.

> In Boston, I didn't live. I studied. My only toy was my typewriter. If my nose was not poked in a book, I was sitting in front of that typewriter staring at the keys. So many goddamn term papers to write! Every grade was also my meal ticket. I was on a scholarship, $60 a month in addition to tuition and room. I sent $15 home every month out of that $60 to help my mother buy rice for the family while my father was hustling to find some kind of business venture. It wasn't just Fenway Park that I skipped. I went nowhere—except to classes.
>
> I never looked around; my eyes were always on the prize— receiving my PhD and returning home where my family waited. I went to bed alone when others made noise with their boyfriends and then I got up at ungodly hours like 2:00 a.m. to study. At first I drank my coffee with milk and sugar, but whenever my eyes drooped, I gulped strong black brew, desperately trying to stay awake. It looked and tasted like the Chinese medicine that my grandmother

had forced me to drink at the slightest sign of sickness.
Who had time or spare cash for Fenway Park or any other
amusement?

I had never imagined that teasing Dai Sil about Fenway Park
would result in such an emotional revelation. She sat before me
brooding and sad. It brought to mind a boyhood story of my own
that had stayed with me all these years. I shared it with Dai Sil.

There weren't many opportunities to play organized baseball
in my childhood hamlet of ninety-five people. The only organized
youth baseball was Junior Legion, for boys twelve to seventeen, and
it required the sponsorship of an American Legion post. Tennant
didn't have an American Legion post, which struck me as grossly
unfair. So I shot off a written appeal to the Legion authorities in
Harlan, the county seat, which had all of 3,000 inhabitants. To my
surprise, they sent me back a thick packet of forms.

My father and mother thought this was all rather silly when
I first broached the idea. So I proceeded in secrecy. During study
hall and history class (not because I disliked history, but because I
liked it and mastered the materials fast), I filled out the forms and
composed an impassioned justification.

I mailed in the application without telling a soul. Weeks later I
received a letter of authorization to organize a Junior Legion Baseball team in Tennant. I was exhilarated, of course, but I still faced a
few challenges. For one thing, the Legion required that we have an
adult manager. Remarkably and wonderfully, there were no require-
ments about equipment or uniforms. Violating my self-imposed
vow of secrecy, I had gotten permission from my principal to use
the high school's field and catcher's gear, so there was no problem
there. The players could provide their own gloves and bats, and I
had saved a little money to buy balls. But what to do about a manager? I summoned the courage to ask Dad. Without a moment's
hesitation, he said, "No, I know nothing about baseball." I didn't
consider that a necessity, but decided not to press the point. Instead,
for the next several weekends, I drove our rickety pickup truck to
the homes of a number of local farmers, and pleaded with each of

them to serve as manager. "You won't actually have to do anything," I said, "other than show up for the games. I'll handle the practices. I just need this to satisfy the Legion." Finally, one man took pity on me and agreed.

Success was within reach. Three weeks before the opening of the season, I had a manager and three team members—including myself and two other Tennant High players. I needed at least nine players to make a team. My parents knew I had Legion approval, but I led them to believe that I also had a team lined up. So the secrecy continued. Late at night, after everyone else had gone to bed, I would roll the pickup down the farm lane and onto the road until I got to the bridge, far enough away from the house that nobody could hear the engine jump to life. Then I would start it up, drive to town, and cajole the owner of the general store into letting me use the phone. And I called and called and called, reaching out to every possible player I could think of from other nearby towns that didn't have Junior Legion teams. By opening day, I had managed to corral nine players, and over the next few days, a few more came aboard.

I desperately wanted to play catcher, and for one game I did. The pitcher I'd recruited from a neighboring town was superb, but he had a wicked sidearm delivery. He sized up the situation quickly and accurately and did some recruitment himself, nabbing the catcher from his own high school team. By the third game of the season, I was no longer playing. And by that time as well, my manager had decided that he knew enough to make decisions about coaching the team. That marked the end of the playing season for me, although I went to all the remaining games and sat on the bench. It took me years to understand that this turn of events was a success, not a defeat.

When I got to this point in my story, Dai Sil was quiet, her eyebrows drawing up. Then, I related the climax.

Well into the season, long after my brief stint as catcher, my father walked into the barn where I was milking the cows one day around 6:00 a.m. He said, "I'm proud of you." He was a man of few words. But those few words I've carried with me all my life.

Decades later in the 1990s, he wrote in a letter, "I remember how hard you worked to get that baseball team started. I am very proud of you yet for that. I should have given you more help." I admit it, I cried reading those lines.

"Now Don, don't cry," she chided me. "If you do, I'm going to cry too. Knowing your father, that just about sums up everything. And even before you knew it yourself, he recognized your exceptional skill at organization and management, not to mention persistence and resilience."

"You know he was one smart man. The only trouble is—he didn't think he was," I noted softly.

"And you do not know how smart and wonderful you are and how much I love you," said Dai Sil. To which I had no response but to put my arm around my shoulder friend.

Don, always in my heart

DONALD D. GIBSON

Donald D. Gibson grew up a son of tenant farmers in Iowa. He left life on Iowa farms to become a scholar in German history—a teacher, political activist, and senior government official. His studies took him to Simpson College, the University of Iowa, and then to Germany, where he conducted his doctoral research, and pursued advanced studies at the University of Mannheim and Free University of Berlin. His studies in Germany centered on how Hitler got elected, with essential research on how and why individuals voted for Hitler. A Fulbright awardee and a devoted teacher, he taught German and history at Indianola High School, Simpson College, the University of Iowa, and the U.S. military bases in Mannheim and Heidelberg, Germany.

Gibson's political concerns led him to involvement in the electoral campaigns of Eugene McCarthy (running for the Democratic presidential nomination in 1968) and Harold Hughes (running for U.S. Senate from Iowa in 1968); to involvement in the establishment of political caucuses in Iowa; and to involvement in the civil rights and Vietnam War protest movements in the 1960s. He served from 1977 to 1997 in various high-level managerial positions at the National Endowment for the Humanities. The climax of his career at NEH was serving as interim chairman under President Clinton.

CHRONOLOGY

1930   –town of Tennant reaches its peak population: 118

1938   –Don born in Iowa

        –Dai Sil born in North Korea

1942   –Gibson family moves to Kay farm, the third of five farms worked by Don's parents, and Don's favorite farm (especially the attic)

1945   –(on August 15) Don turns seven and Korea is liberated from Japan with end of WWII in Asia

1946   –electricity comes to Iowa farms

1948   –town of Tennant population stands at ninety-five

        –Don turns ten and is expected to do "serious farm work"

1956   –Don graduates Tennant High School

        –Don enters Simpson College as freshman, planning to become a minister

        –Don wears I Like Ike campaign button for Eisenhower v. Stevenson presidential race

1957   –Don decides (as a sophomore) not to pursue the ministry

1960   –Don graduates Simpson

        –Don votes in first national election, for JFK

        –Don begins teaching at Andrew High School near Dubuque (government, history, German)

1961   –Don begins teaching at Indianola High School (history, German, social studies)

1962   –Dai Sil comes to United States from Korea for graduate studies in Religion.

1963   –Don travels to Germany as a Fulbright scholar on a two-month program to study German; on day two in Germany, he travels to Berlin to hear JFK's "Ich bin ein Berliner" speech

1964   –Don volunteers as campaign organizer for Warren County Democratic Party

        –Don travels to Mississippi to help register black voters

1965   –Don enters University of Iowa as PhD candidate in history

–Don cofounds Priorities for National Survival (Iowa City antiwar group)

1966   –Don qualifies for a University of Iowa teaching and research fellowship

1968   –Don begins one-year job teaching history and German at Simpson College

–Don becomes coordinator of Iowa state Eugene McCarthy for President campaign

–Don works for Harold Hughes's senate campaign

1969   –through Priorities for National Survival, Don helps plan the Moratorium to End the War in Vietnam march (November)

–Don involved in organizing the Iowa Democratic Coalition

1970   –Don passes comprehensives at University of Iowa "with distinction"

1971   –Don travels to Germany to research the question: Who voted for Hitler and why?

1972   –Don begins teaching history to soldiers at U.S. military bases in Germany

–Don's parents travel to see Europe with Don

1977   –Don starts working at NEH

1978   –Don and Dai Sil meet

1979   –Don and Dai Sil visit Don's family in Tennant

–Don and Dai Sil marry (October 1)

–Don promoted to deputy division director of State Programs at NEH (October 1)

1981   –Don and Dai Sil buy house in Washington DC's Chevy Chase neighborhood

1984   –Don promoted to division director for Public Programs at NEH

1985   –Dai Sil leaves NEH to become director of media programs at New York State Council on the Arts

1986   –Don diagnosed with Crohn's disease

1988   –Dai Sil resigns from NY State Council; becomes freelancer

1989   –Don and Dai Sil buy townhouse in DC Dupont Circle neighborhood

       –Don and Dai Sil take a 10th anniversary trip to Italy

1993   –Don serves as interim chair of NEH (April–August)

1994   –Don's mother dies (December)

1996   –Don diagnosed with endocarditis

1997   –Don retires from NEH

       –Don and Dai Sil buy house in New Paltz, New York

1998   –Don has heart-valve replacement surgery

2000   –town of Tennant population falls to seventy-three

2001   –fire (on December 29) destroys New Paltz house and Don's plans to write a book based on his dissertation research in Germany

2002   –Don and Dai Sil buy an apartment at Castle Village in NYC overlooking Hudson

2004   –Don and Dai Sil take a 25th anniversary trip to Germany and Czechosolvakia

2005   –Dai Sil has surgery for a stomach cancer

2006   –Don's father dies

2009   –Dai Sil promises Don that she will finish their joint memoir

On January 18, 2009 Don passed away.

NOTE ON PHOTOGRAPHS

Dai Sil selected the photos in this book from among the photos that survived the 2001 fire. For some of these she is unsure about where and when they were taken, and what she has put in the captions represents her best guess. She would like to apologize in advance for any inaccurate information provided and asks readers for their understanding.